BOOK THREE - FROM THE DELTA TO DAK TO

D1097590

CALIBER
COMICS

VIETNAM JOURNAL

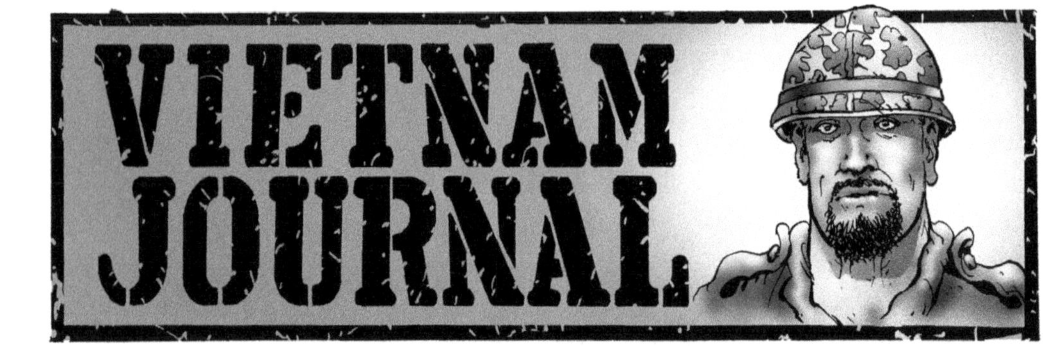

BOOK THREE - FROM THE DELTA TO DAK TO

Written and Illustrated
By
DON LOMAX

Lettered
By
CLEM ROBINS

THIS VOLUME COLLECTS:
ISSUE #9 - "Brown Water Warriors"
ISSUE #10 - "The Path of Reeds"
ISSUE #11 - "Dak To"
ISSUE #12 - "Hill 875"
Short Story - "Dustoff"

Originally published by Apple Comics

VIETNAM JOURNAL

MY BY-LINE READS: SCOTT NEITHAMMER, BUT THE TROOPS CALL ME "JOURNAL."

BROWN WATER WARRIORS

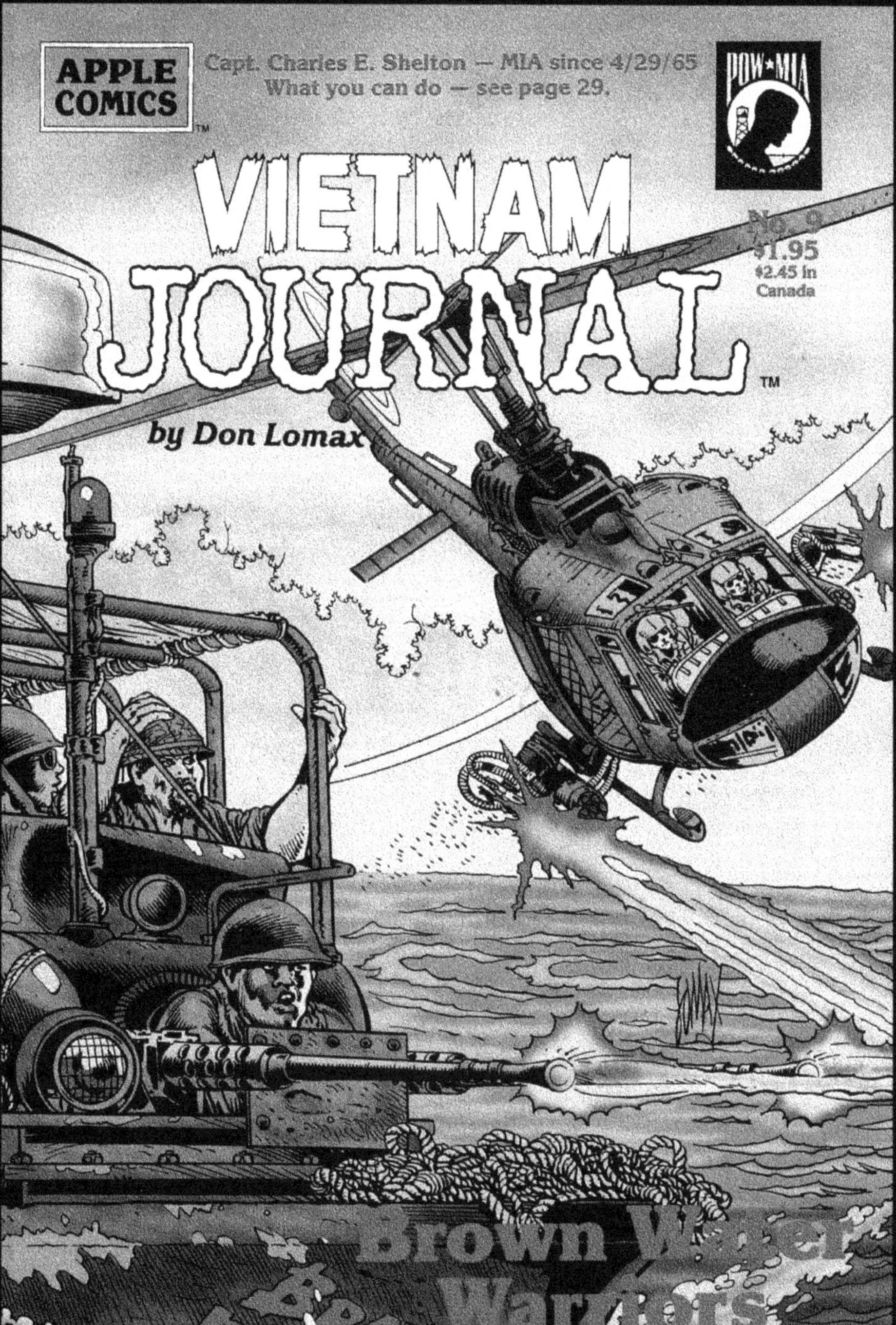
APPLE COMICS
Capt. Charles E. Shelton — MIA since 4/29/65
What you can do — see page 29.
POW★MIA
VIETNAM JOURNAL
No. 9
$1.95
$2.45 in Canada
by Don Lomax
Brown Water Warriors

THE NEW YORK TIMES
Sunday, October 22, 1967 —

Guards Repulse War Protesters At the Pentagon

6 Break Through Line Into Building — Mailer and Dellinger Are Arrested

250 SEIZED IN CLASHES

Spock Tells Demonstrators at Lincoln Memorial That Johnson Is Real 'Enemy'

By JOSEPH A. LOFTUS
Special to the New York Times

WASHINGTON, Oct. 21 — Thousands of demonstrators stormed the Pentagon today after a calm rally and march by some 50,000 persons opposed to the war in Vietnam.

The protesters twice breached the lines of deputy Federal marshals backed by soldiers armed with bayonet-tipped rifles. But they were quickly driven back by the rifle butts of the soldiers and the marshals' nightsticks.

Six demonstrators succeeded in entering a side door at the main Mall entrance of the building but were pushed out immediately by marshalls.

There were no reports of serious injuries but the Pentagon steps were spattered with blood.

Soldiers and marshals arrested at least 250 persons at the Pentagon, including David Dellinger, chairman of the National Mobilization Committee to End the War in Vietnam, which organized the rally and march.

Mailer Arrested

Also arrested were Norman Mailer, the novelist; the Rev. John Boyles, an assistant Episcopal chaplain at Yale University, and Mrs. Dagmar Wilson, a founder of the Women's Strike for Peace organization.

The surging disorderly crowd that milled about the vast Pentagon shouted obscenities and taunted the forces on guard there. Some threw eggs and bottles as darkness fell, built bonfires and waved what they said were burning draft cards.

Several tear gas canisters exploded outside the building at various times. The Defense Department announced that the Army had not used tear gas at any time and charged that the demonstrators had.

Two soliders were reported to have been injured, one by tear gas and one by a missle that struck him in the eye

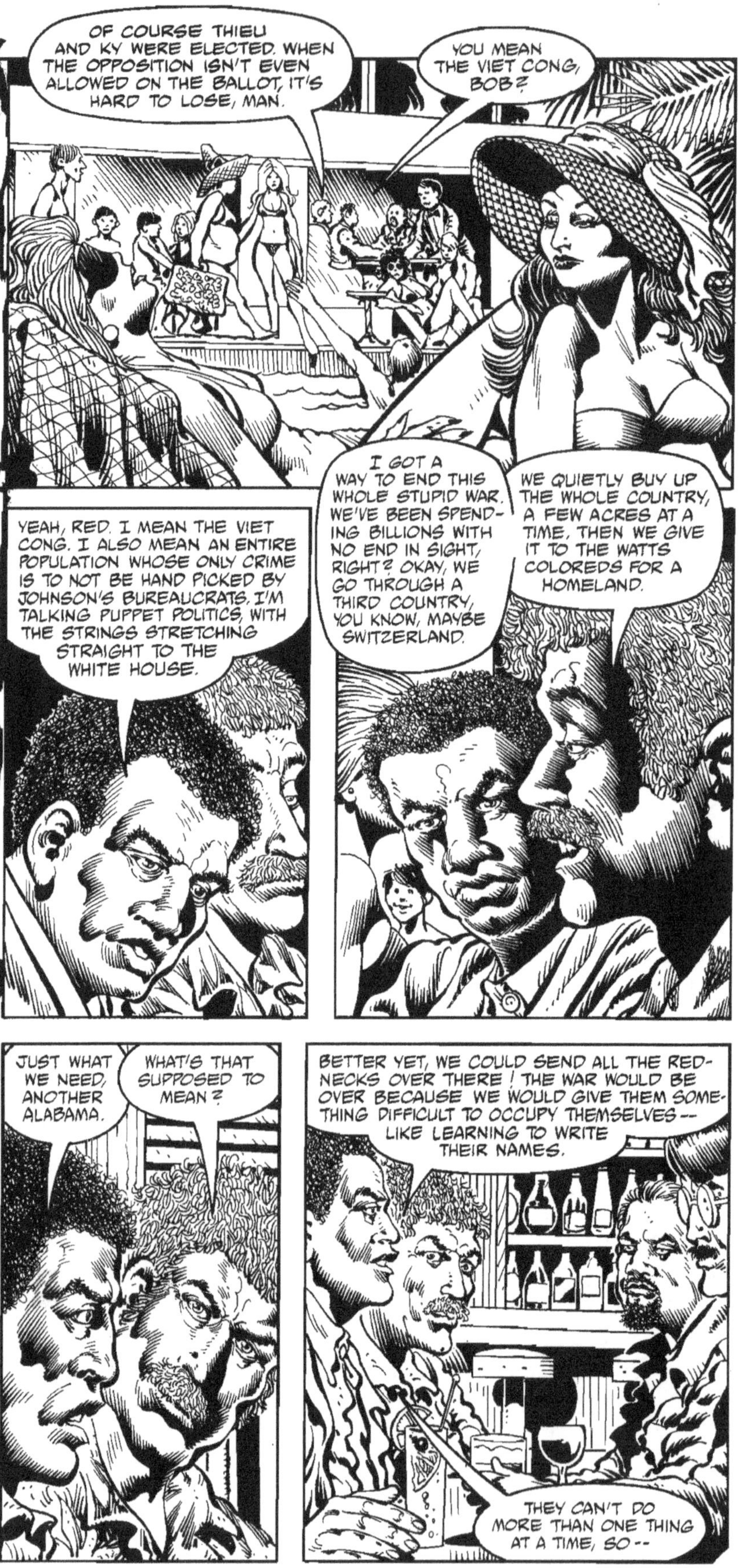
OF COURSE THIEU AND KY WERE ELECTED. WHEN THE OPPOSITION ISN'T EVEN ALLOWED ON THE BALLOT, IT'S HARD TO LOSE, MAN.
YOU MEAN THE VIET CONG, BOB?
YEAH, RED. I MEAN THE VIET CONG. I ALSO MEAN AN ENTIRE POPULATION WHOSE ONLY CRIME IS TO NOT BE HAND PICKED BY JOHNSON'S BUREAUCRATS. I'M TALKING PUPPET POLITICS, WITH THE STRINGS STRETCHING STRAIGHT TO THE WHITE HOUSE.
I GOT A WAY TO END THIS WHOLE STUPID WAR. WE'VE BEEN SPEND-ING BILLIONS WITH NO END IN SIGHT, RIGHT? OKAY, WE GO THROUGH A THIRD COUNTRY, YOU KNOW, MAYBE SWITZERLAND.
WE QUIETLY BUY UP THE WHOLE COUNTRY, A FEW ACRES AT A TIME, THEN WE GIVE IT TO THE WATTS COLOREDS FOR A HOMELAND.
JUST WHAT WE NEED, ANOTHER ALABAMA.
WHAT'S THAT SUPPOSED TO MEAN?
BETTER YET, WE COULD SEND ALL THE RED-NECKS OVER THERE! THE WAR WOULD BE OVER BECAUSE WE WOULD GIVE THEM SOME-THING DIFFICULT TO OCCUPY THEMSELVES -- LIKE LEARNING TO WRITE THEIR NAMES.
THEY CAN'T DO MORE THAN ONE THING AT A TIME, SO --

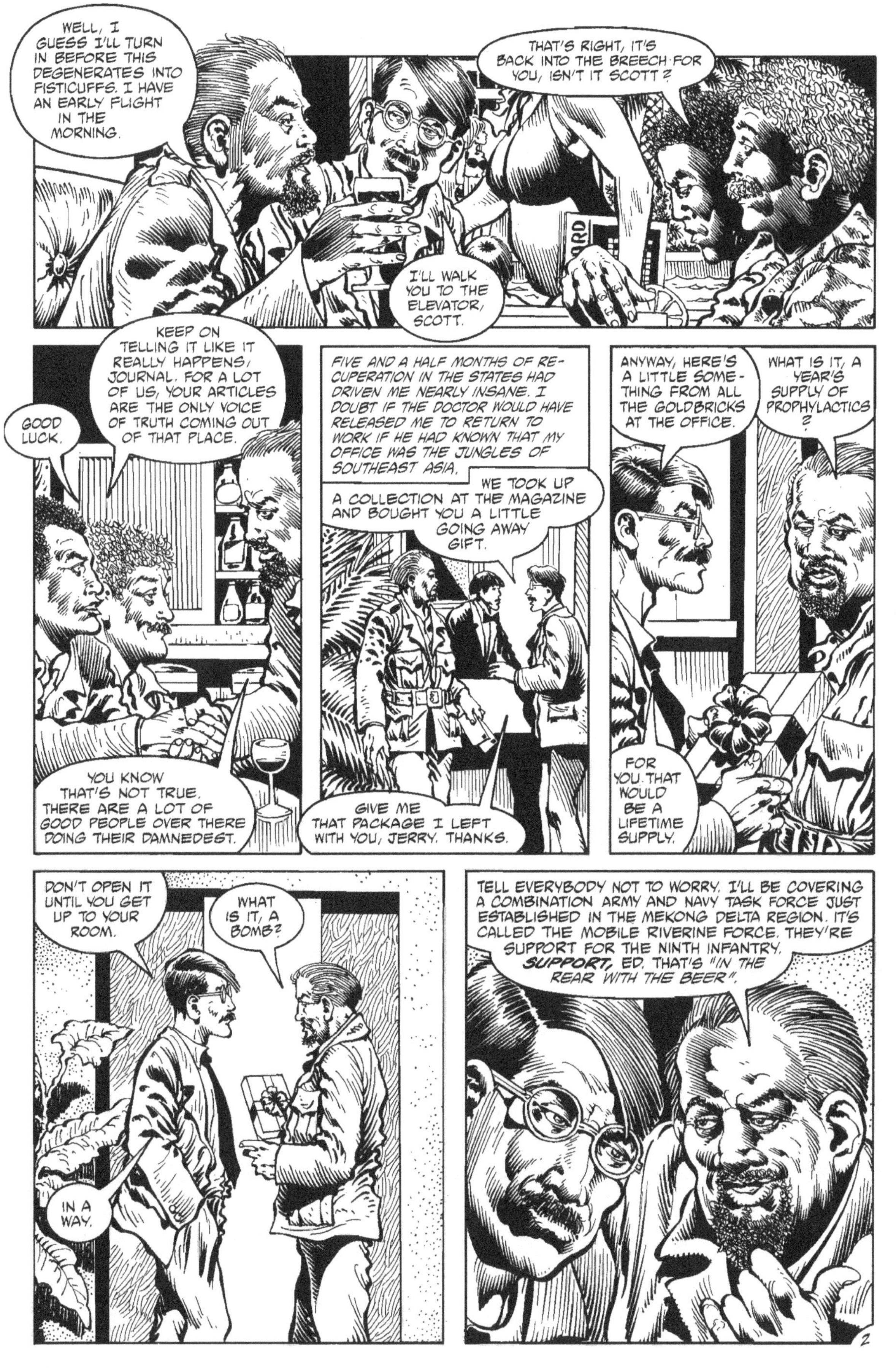
WELL, I GUESS I'LL TURN IN BEFORE THIS DEGENERATES INTO FISTICUFFS. I HAVE AN EARLY FLIGHT IN THE MORNING.
THAT'S RIGHT, IT'S BACK INTO THE BREECH FOR YOU, ISN'T IT SCOTT?
I'LL WALK YOU TO THE ELEVATOR, SCOTT.
GOOD LUCK.
KEEP ON TELLING IT LIKE IT REALLY HAPPENS, JOURNAL. FOR A LOT OF US, YOUR ARTICLES ARE THE ONLY VOICE OF TRUTH COMING OUT OF THAT PLACE.
YOU KNOW THAT'S NOT TRUE. THERE ARE A LOT OF GOOD PEOPLE OVER THERE DOING THEIR DAMNEDEST.
FIVE AND A HALF MONTHS OF RECUPERATION IN THE STATES HAD DRIVEN ME NEARLY INSANE. I DOUBT IF THE DOCTOR WOULD HAVE RELEASED ME TO RETURN TO WORK IF HE HAD KNOWN THAT MY OFFICE WAS THE JUNGLES OF SOUTHEAST ASIA.
WE TOOK UP A COLLECTION AT THE MAGAZINE AND BOUGHT YOU A LITTLE GOING AWAY GIFT.
GIVE ME THAT PACKAGE I LEFT WITH YOU, JERRY. THANKS.
ANYWAY, HERE'S A LITTLE SOMETHING FROM ALL THE GOLDBRICKS AT THE OFFICE.
WHAT IS IT, A YEAR'S SUPPLY OF PROPHYLACTICS?
FOR YOU THAT WOULD BE A LIFETIME SUPPLY.
DON'T OPEN IT UNTIL YOU GET UP TO YOUR ROOM.
WHAT IS IT, A BOMB?
IN A WAY.
TELL EVERYBODY NOT TO WORRY. I'LL BE COVERING A COMBINATION ARMY AND NAVY TASK FORCE JUST ESTABLISHED IN THE MEKONG DELTA REGION. IT'S CALLED THE MOBILE RIVERINE FORCE. THEY'RE SUPPORT FOR THE NINTH INFANTRY. SUPPORT, ED. THAT'S "IN THE REAR WITH THE BEER".

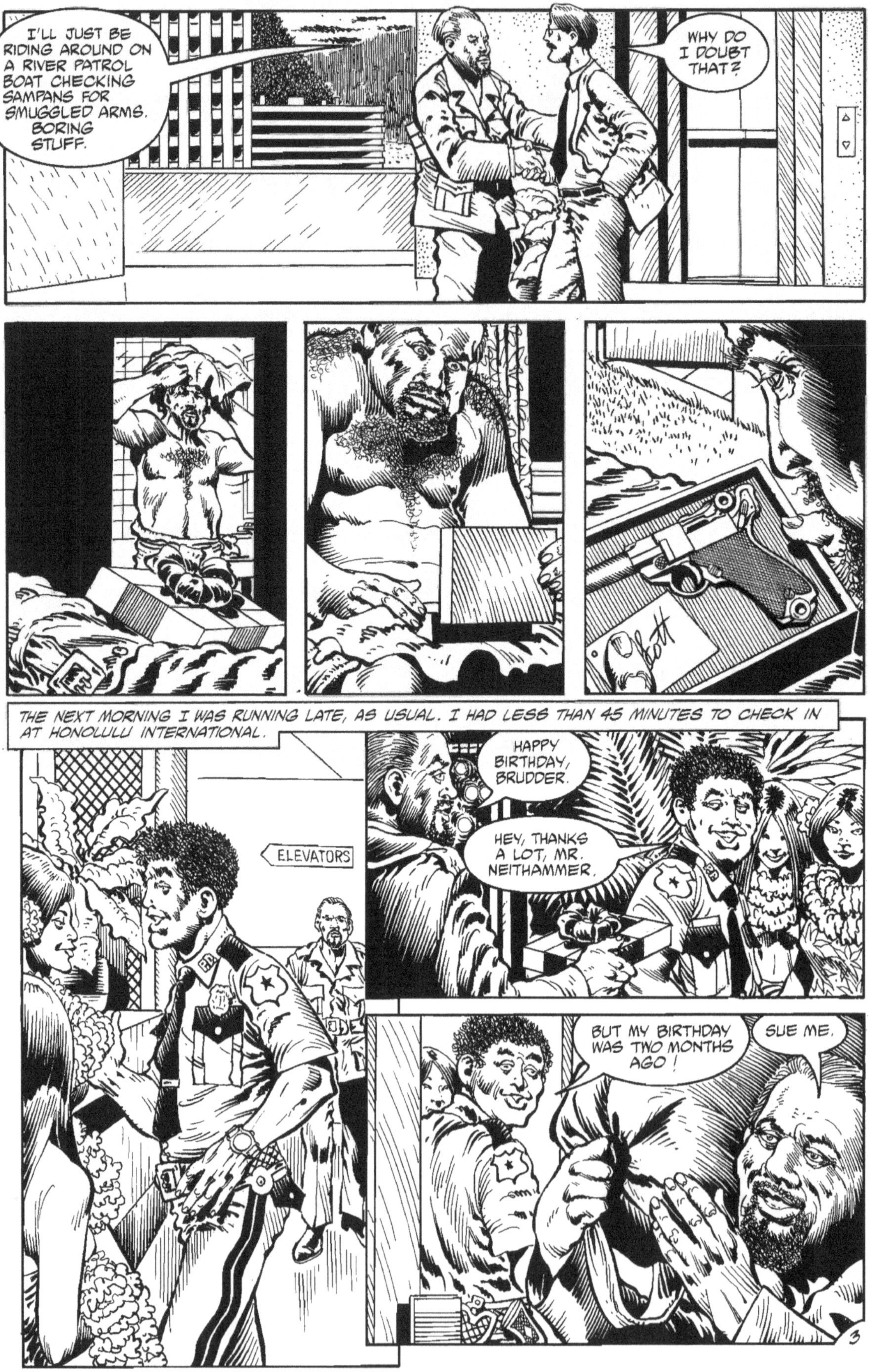
I'LL JUST BE RIDING AROUND ON A RIVER PATROL BOAT CHECKING SAMPANS FOR SMUGGLED ARMS. BORING STUFF.
WHY DO I DOUBT THAT?
THE NEXT MORNING I WAS RUNNING LATE, AS USUAL. I HAD LESS THAN 45 MINUTES TO CHECK IN AT HONOLULU INTERNATIONAL.
ELEVATORS
HAPPY BIRTHDAY, BRUDDER.
HEY, THANKS A LOT, MR. NEITHAMMER.
BUT MY BIRTHDAY WAS TWO MONTHS AGO!
SUE ME.

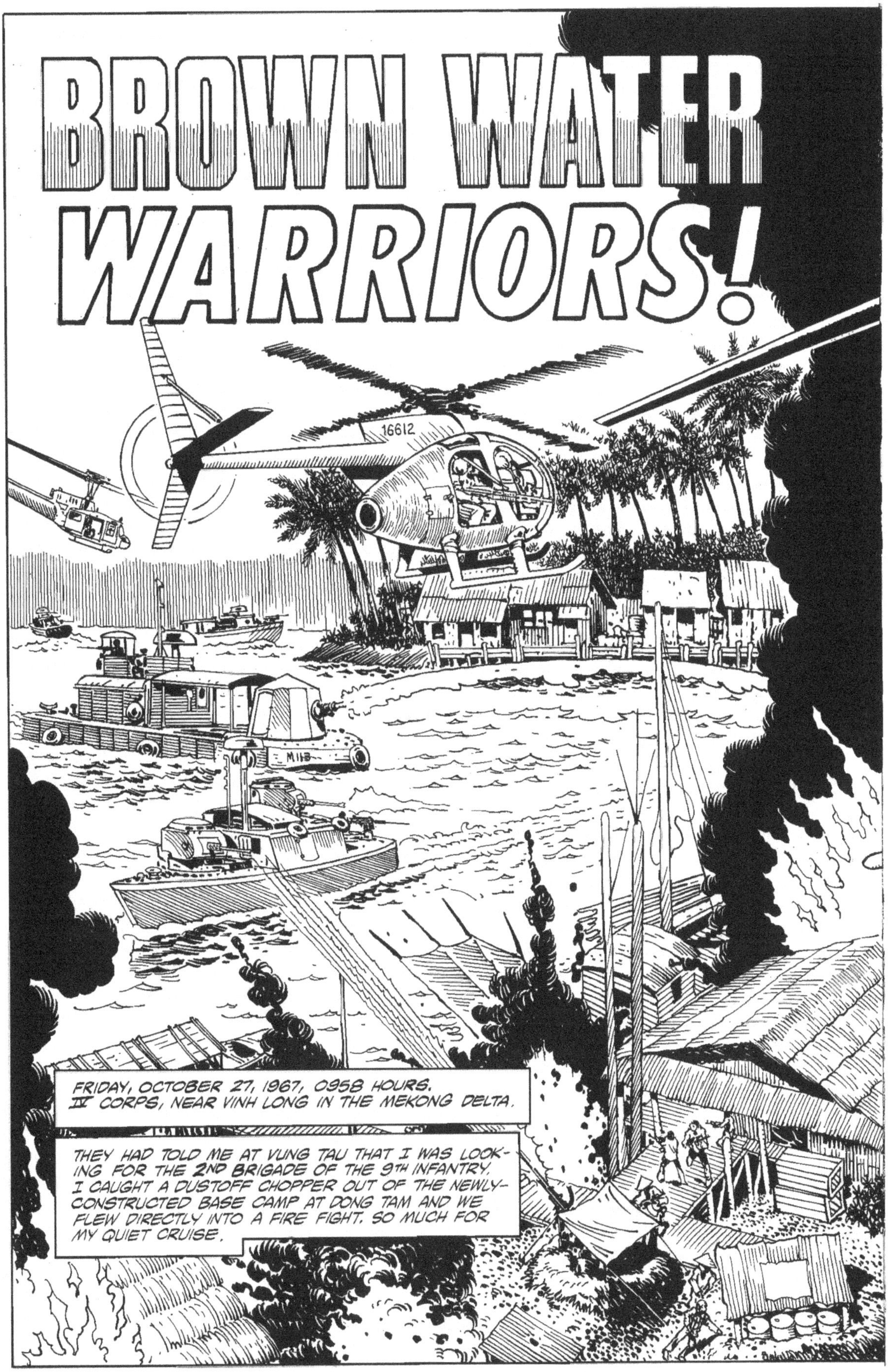
BROWN WATER WARRIORS!
16612
M113
FRIDAY, OCTOBER 27, 1967, 0958 HOURS. IV CORPS, NEAR VINH LONG IN THE MEKONG DELTA.
THEY HAD TOLD ME AT VUNG TAU THAT I WAS LOOKING FOR THE 2ND BRIGADE OF THE 9TH INFANTRY. I CAUGHT A DUSTOFF CHOPPER OUT OF THE NEWLY-CONSTRUCTED BASE CAMP AT DONG TAM AND WE FLEW DIRECTLY INTO A FIRE FIGHT. SO MUCH FOR MY QUIET CRUISE.

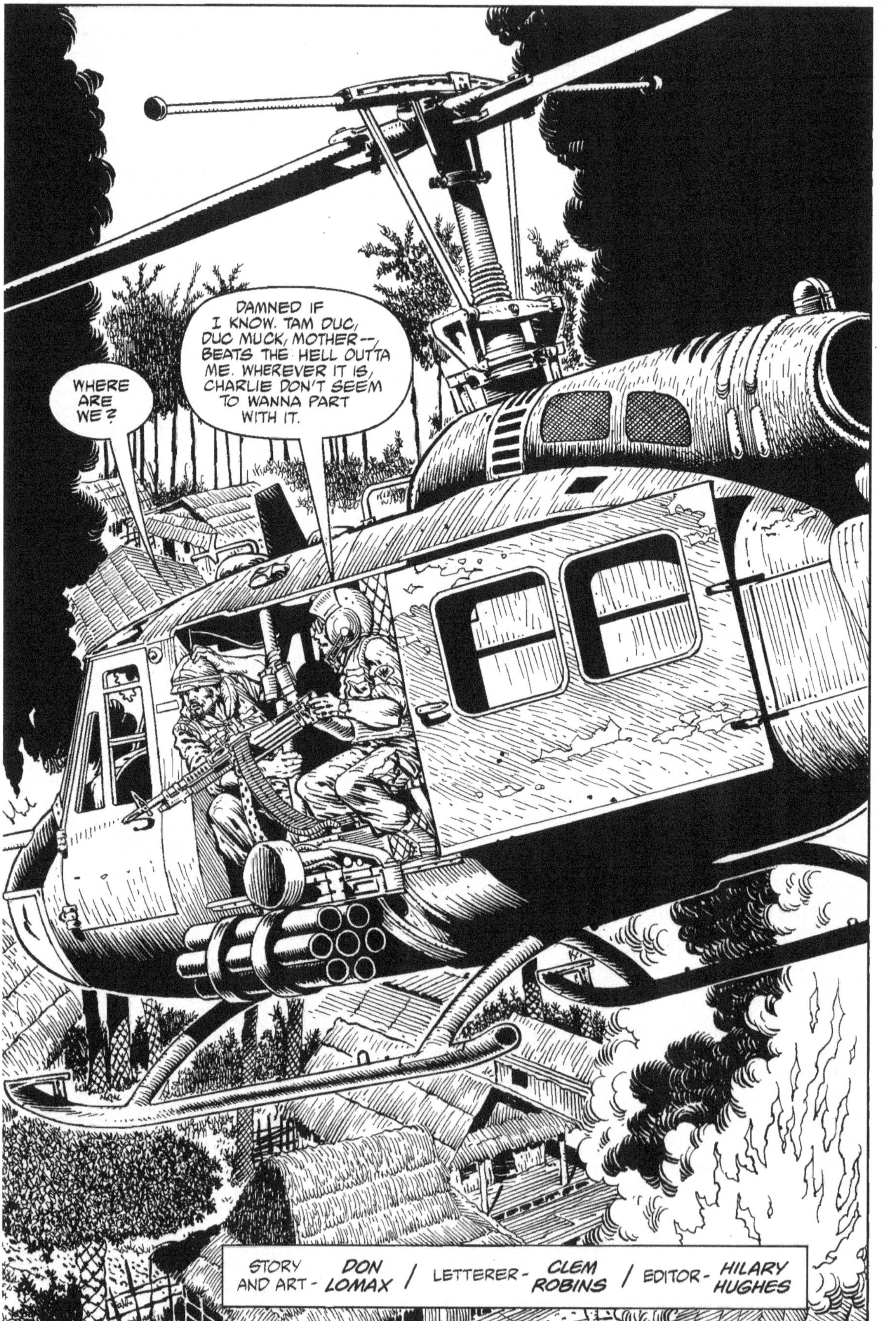
WHERE ARE WE?
DAMNED IF I KNOW. TAM DUC, DUC MUCK, MOTHER--, BEATS THE HELL OUTTA ME. WHEREVER IT IS, CHARLIE DON'T SEEM TO WANNA PART WITH IT.
STORY AND ART - DON LOMAX / LETTERER - CLEM ROBINS / EDITOR - HILARY HUGHES

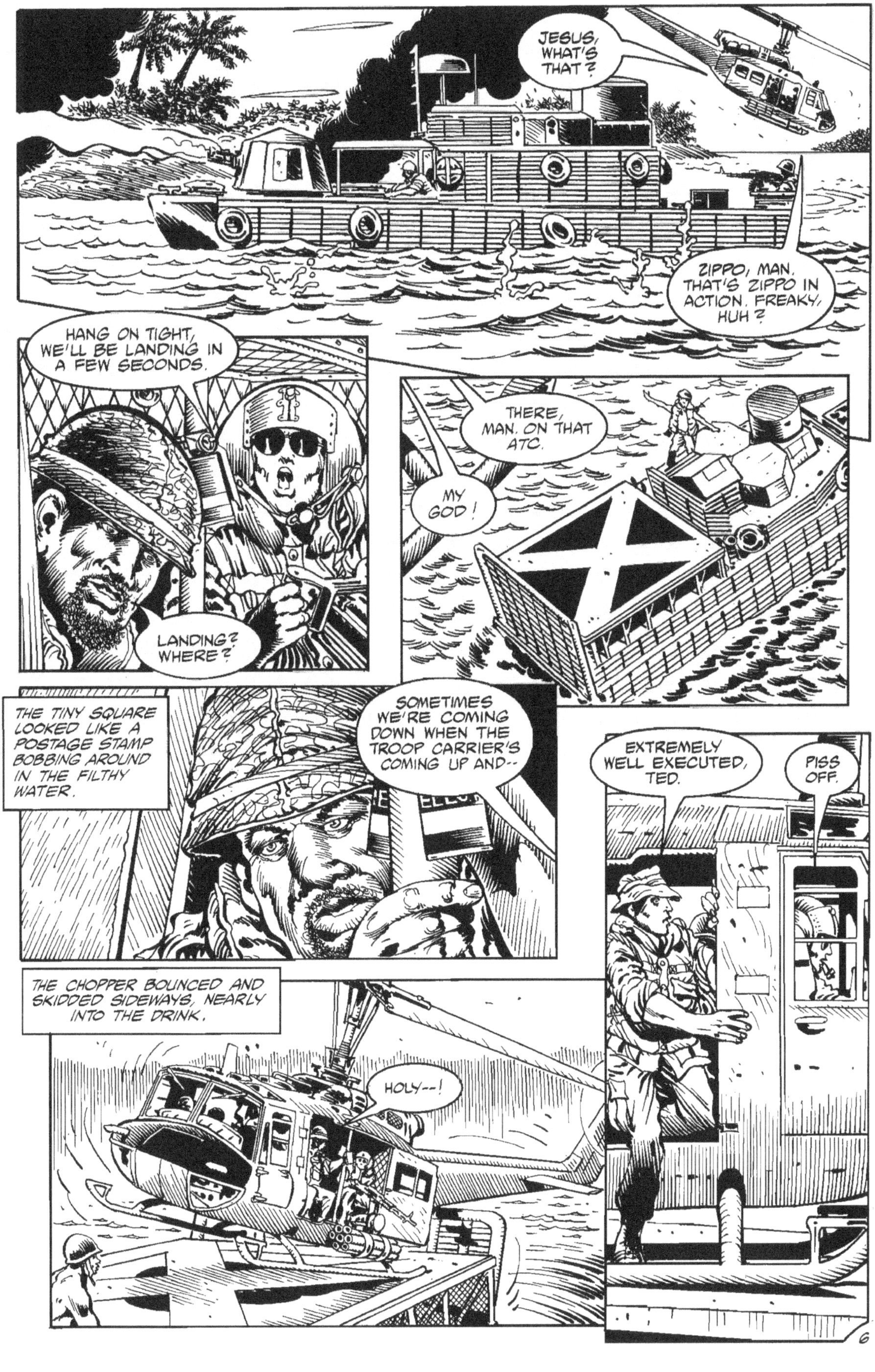

JESUS, WHAT'S THAT?
ZIPPO, MAN. THAT'S ZIPPO IN ACTION. FREAKY, HUH?
HANG ON TIGHT, WE'LL BE LANDING IN A FEW SECONDS.
LANDING? WHERE?
THERE, MAN. ON THAT ATC.
MY GOD!
THE TINY SQUARE LOOKED LIKE A POSTAGE STAMP BOBBING AROUND IN THE FILTHY WATER.
SOMETIMES WE'RE COMING DOWN WHEN THE TROOP CARRIER'S COMING UP AND--
THE CHOPPER BOUNCED AND SKIDDED SIDEWAYS, NEARLY INTO THE DRINK.
HOLY--!
EXTREMELY WELL EXECUTED, TED.
PISS OFF.

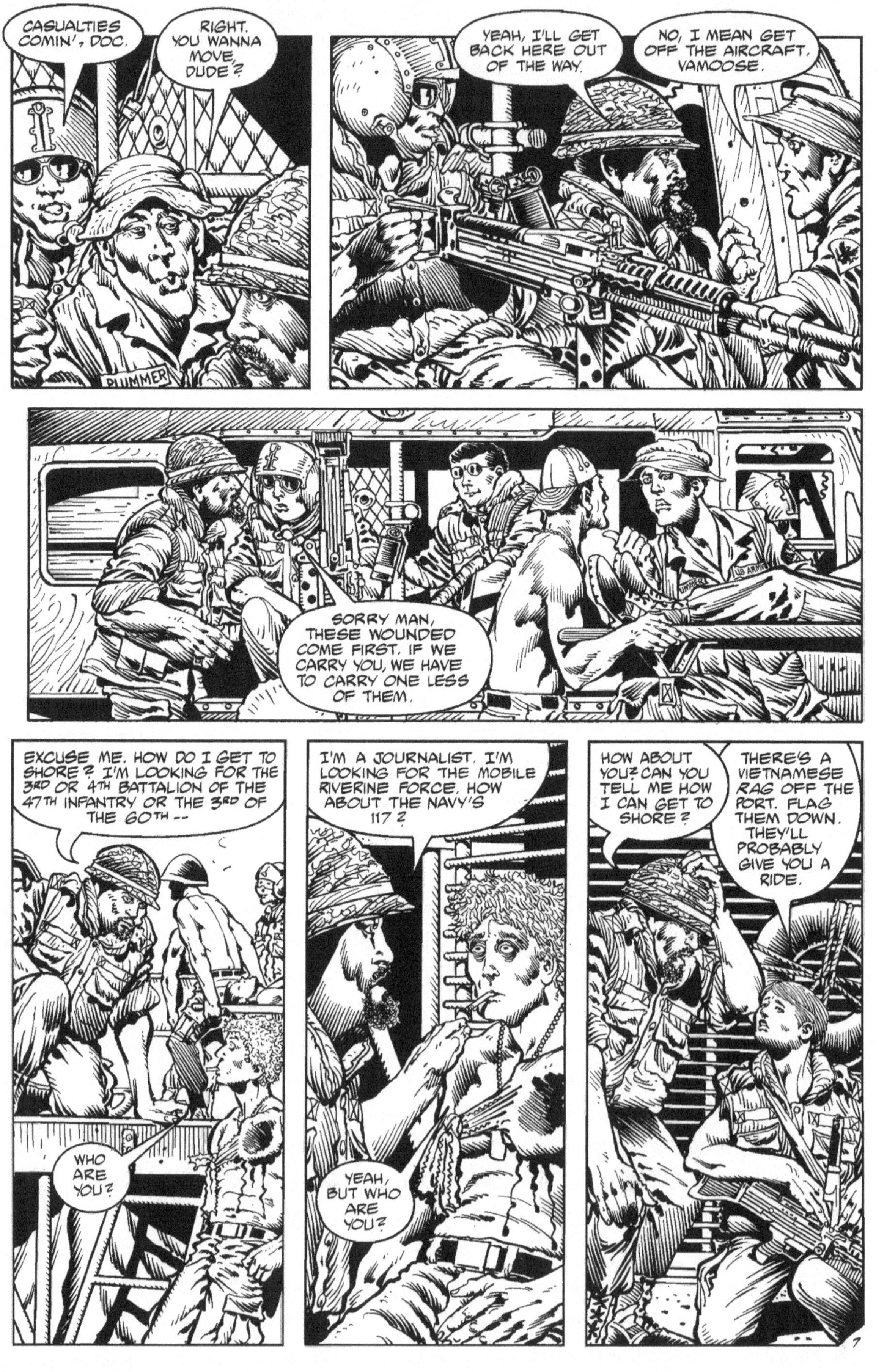
CASUALTIES COMIN', DOC.
RIGHT. YOU WANNA MOVE, DUDE?
PLUMMER
YEAH, I'LL GET BACK HERE OUT OF THE WAY.
NO, I MEAN GET OFF THE AIRCRAFT. VAMOOSE.
SORRY MAN, THESE WOUNDED COME FIRST. IF WE CARRY YOU, WE HAVE TO CARRY ONE LESS OF THEM.
EXCUSE ME. HOW DO I GET TO SHORE? I'M LOOKING FOR THE 3RD OR 4TH BATTALION OF THE 47TH INFANTRY OR THE 3RD OF THE 60TH --
WHO ARE YOU?
I'M A JOURNALIST. I'M LOOKING FOR THE MOBILE RIVERINE FORCE. HOW ABOUT THE NAVY'S 117?
YEAH, BUT WHO ARE YOU?
HOW ABOUT YOU? CAN YOU TELL ME HOW I CAN GET TO SHORE?
THERE'S A VIETNAMESE *RAG* OFF THE PORT. FLAG THEM DOWN. THEY'LL PROBABLY GIVE YOU A RIDE.

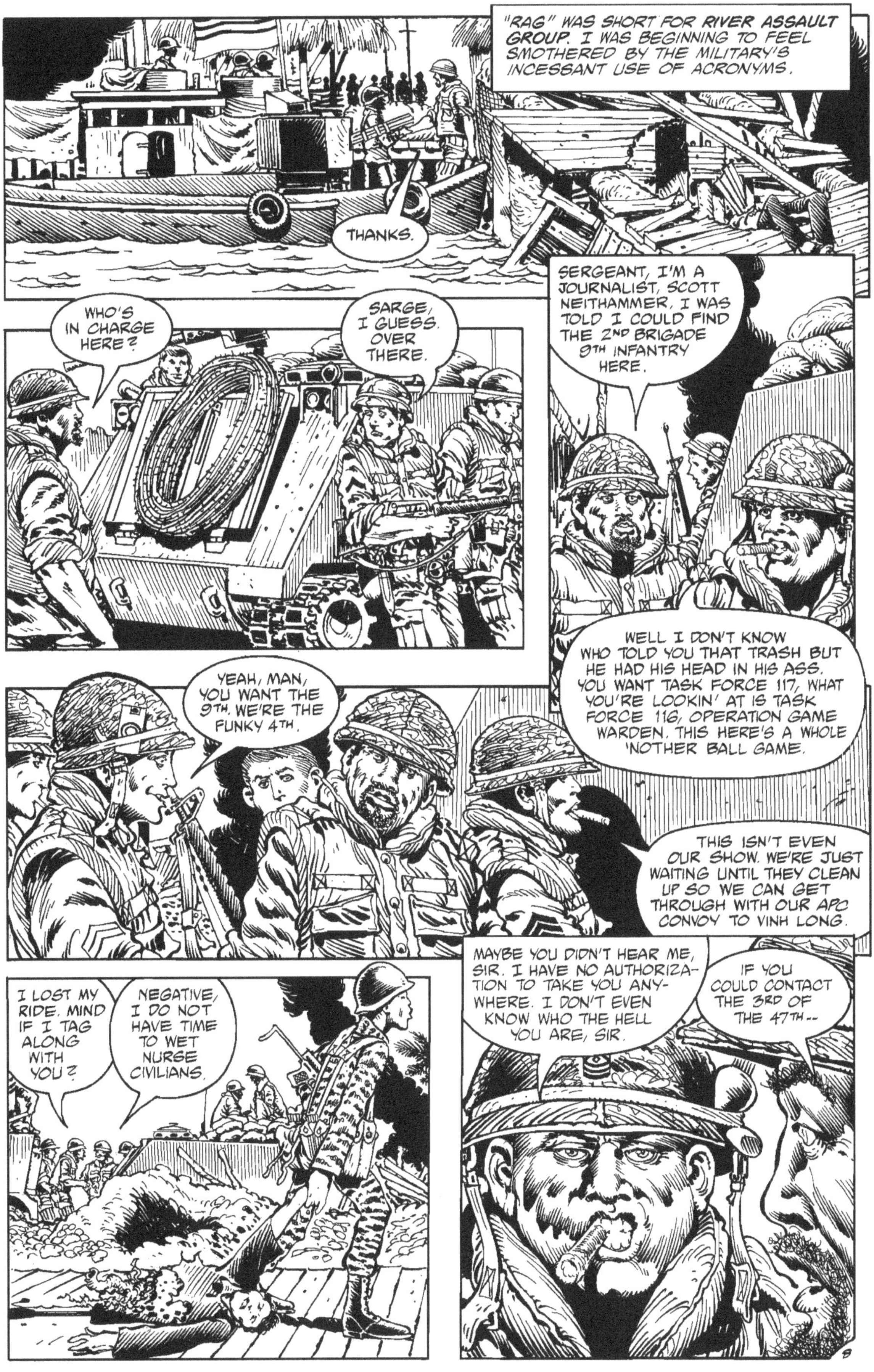
"RAG" WAS SHORT FOR RIVER ASSAULT GROUP. I WAS BEGINNING TO FEEL SMOTHERED BY THE MILITARY'S INCESSANT USE OF ACRONYMS.
THANKS.
WHO'S IN CHARGE HERE?
SARGE, I GUESS. OVER THERE.
SERGEANT, I'M A JOURNALIST, SCOTT NEITHAMMER. I WAS TOLD I COULD FIND THE 2ND BRIGADE 9TH INFANTRY HERE.
WELL I DON'T KNOW WHO TOLD YOU THAT TRASH BUT HE HAD HIS HEAD IN HIS ASS. YOU WANT TASK FORCE 117, WHAT YOU'RE LOOKIN' AT IS TASK FORCE 116, OPERATION GAME WARDEN. THIS HERE'S A WHOLE 'NOTHER BALL GAME.
YEAH, MAN, YOU WANT THE 9TH. WE'RE THE FUNKY 4TH.
THIS ISN'T EVEN OUR SHOW. WE'RE JUST WAITING UNTIL THEY CLEAN UP SO WE CAN GET THROUGH WITH OUR APC CONVOY TO VINH LONG.
I LOST MY RIDE. MIND IF I TAG ALONG WITH YOU?
NEGATIVE, I DO NOT HAVE TIME TO WET NURSE CIVILIANS.
MAYBE YOU DIDN'T HEAR ME, SIR. I HAVE NO AUTHORIZATION TO TAKE YOU ANYWHERE. I DON'T EVEN KNOW WHO THE HELL YOU ARE, SIR.
IF YOU COULD CONTACT THE 3RD OF THE 47TH --

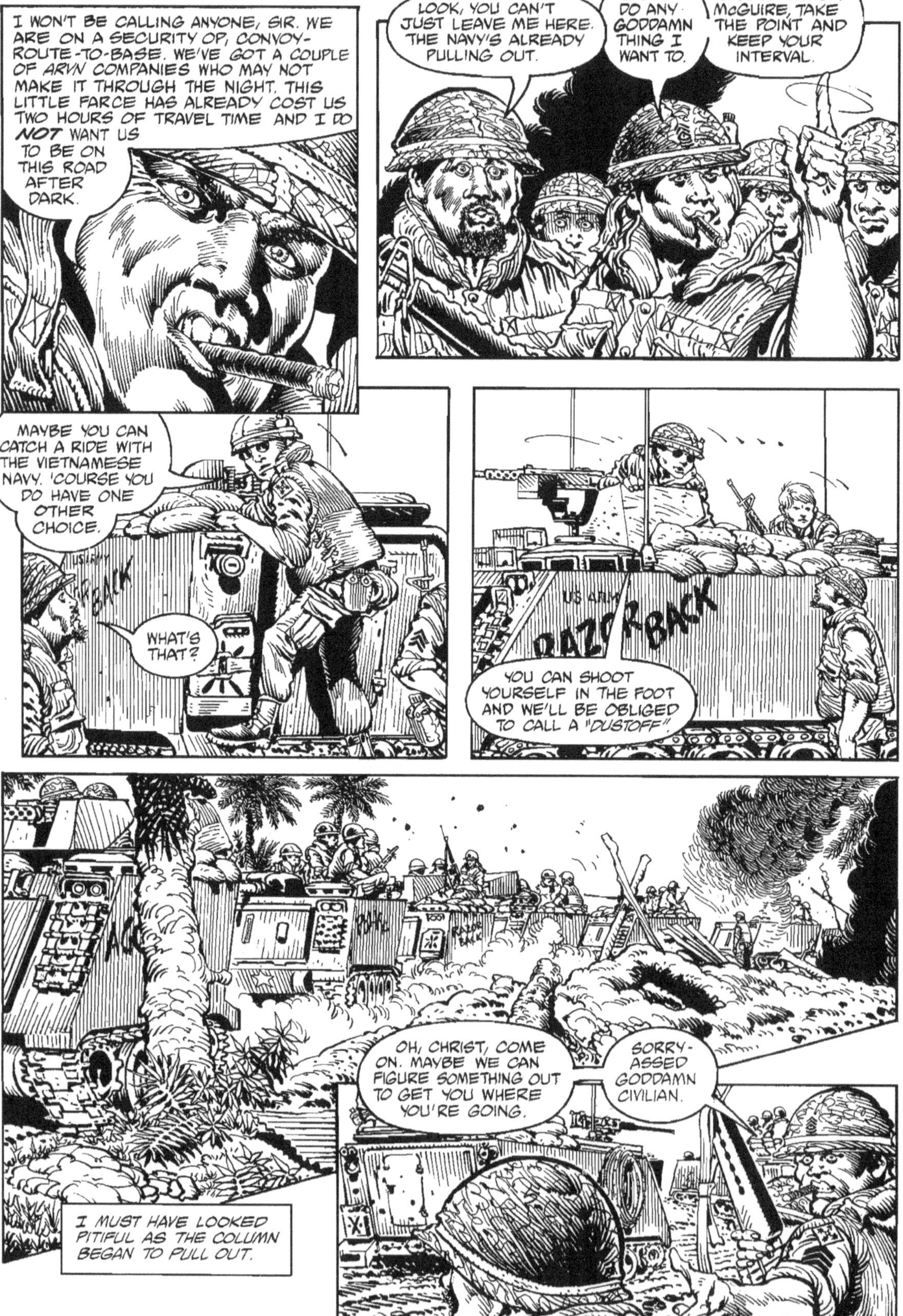

I WON'T BE CALLING ANYONE, SIR. WE ARE ON A SECURITY OP, CONVOY-ROUTE-TO-BASE. WE'VE GOT A COUPLE OF ARVN COMPANIES WHO MAY NOT MAKE IT THROUGH THE NIGHT. THIS LITTLE FARCE HAS ALREADY COST US TWO HOURS OF TRAVEL TIME AND I DO *NOT* WANT US TO BE ON THIS ROAD AFTER DARK.
LOOK, YOU CAN'T JUST LEAVE ME HERE. THE NAVY'S ALREADY PULLING OUT.
I CAN DO ANY GODDAMN THING I WANT TO.
CRANK 'EM UP, McGUIRE, TAKE THE POINT AND KEEP YOUR INTERVAL.
MAYBE YOU CAN CATCH A RIDE WITH THE VIETNAMESE NAVY. 'COURSE YOU DO HAVE ONE OTHER CHOICE.
WHAT'S THAT?
YOU CAN SHOOT YOURSELF IN THE FOOT AND WE'LL BE OBLIGED TO CALL A "DUSTOFF".
I MUST HAVE LOOKED PITIFUL AS THE COLUMN BEGAN TO PULL OUT.
OH, CHRIST, COME ON. MAYBE WE CAN FIGURE SOMETHING OUT TO GET YOU WHERE YOU'RE GOING.
SORRY-ASSED GODDAMN CIVILIAN.

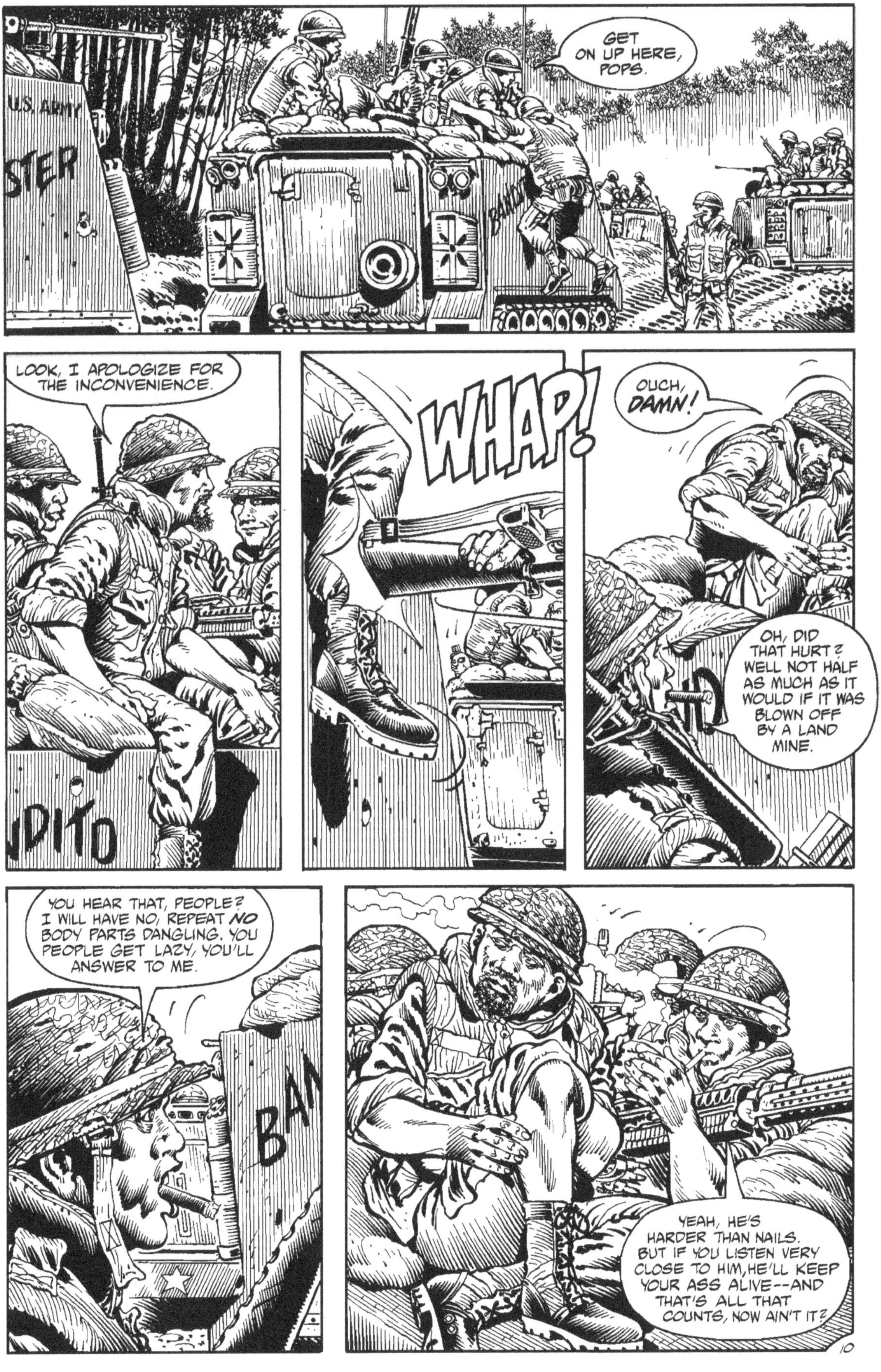
GET ON UP HERE, POPS.
U.S. ARMY
LOOK, I APOLOGIZE FOR THE INCONVENIENCE.
WHAP!
OUCH, DAMN!
OH, DID THAT HURT? WELL NOT HALF AS MUCH AS IT WOULD IF IT WAS BLOWN OFF BY A LAND MINE.
YOU HEAR THAT, PEOPLE? I WILL HAVE NO, REPEAT NO BODY PARTS DANGLING. YOU PEOPLE GET LAZY, YOU'LL ANSWER TO ME.
YEAH, HE'S HARDER THAN NAILS. BUT IF YOU LISTEN VERY CLOSE TO HIM, HE'LL KEEP YOUR ASS ALIVE--AND THAT'S ALL THAT COUNTS, NOW AIN'T IT?

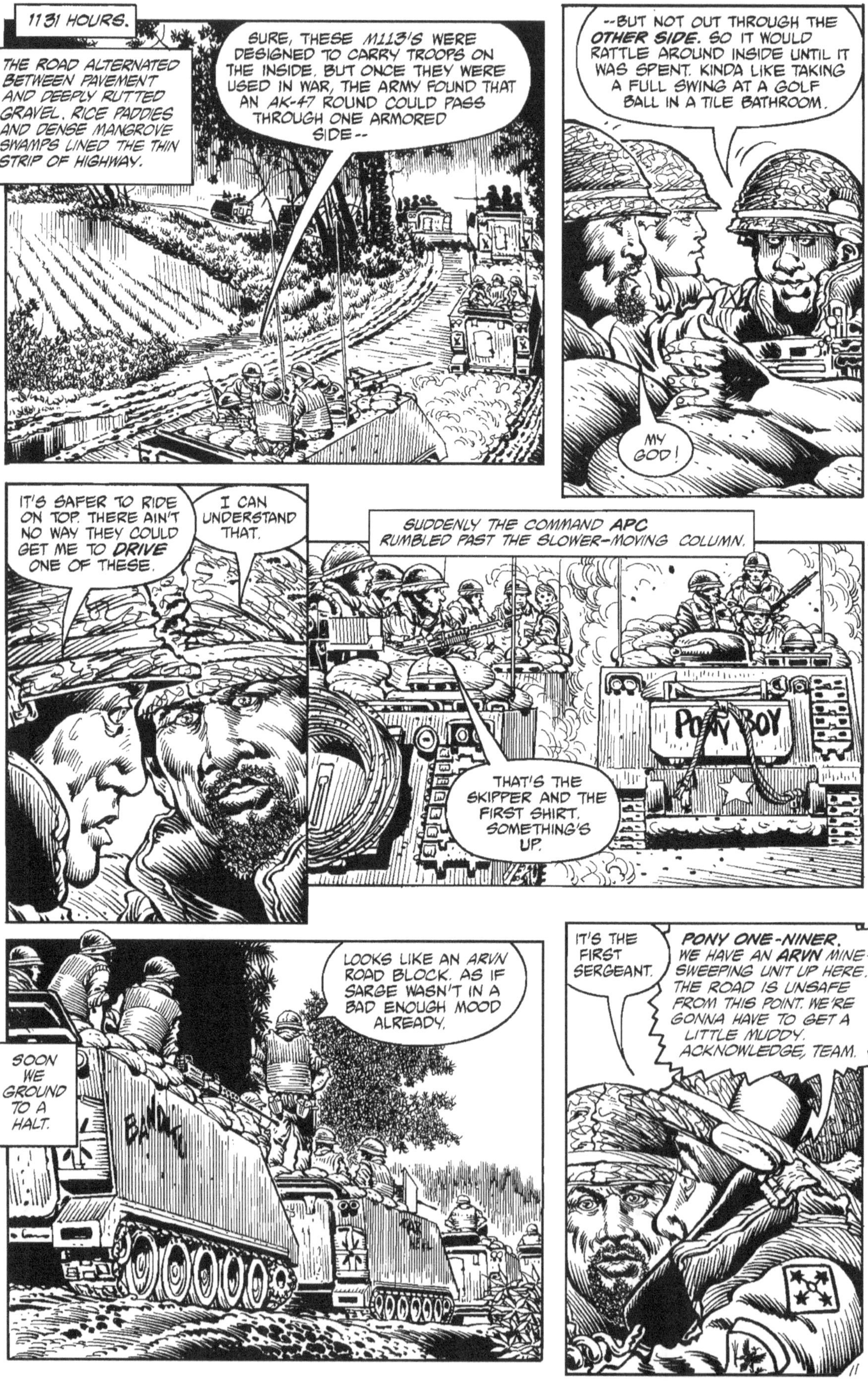

1131 HOURS.
THE ROAD ALTERNATED BETWEEN PAVEMENT AND DEEPLY RUTTED GRAVEL. RICE PADDIES AND DENSE MANGROVE SWAMPS LINED THE THIN STRIP OF HIGHWAY.
SURE, THESE M113'S WERE DESIGNED TO CARRY TROOPS ON THE INSIDE. BUT ONCE THEY WERE USED IN WAR, THE ARMY FOUND THAT AN AK-47 ROUND COULD PASS THROUGH ONE ARMORED SIDE--
--BUT NOT OUT THROUGH THE OTHER SIDE. SO IT WOULD RATTLE AROUND INSIDE UNTIL IT WAS SPENT. KINDA LIKE TAKING A FULL SWING AT A GOLF BALL IN A TILE BATHROOM.
MY GOD!
IT'S SAFER TO RIDE ON TOP. THERE AIN'T NO WAY THEY COULD GET ME TO DRIVE ONE OF THESE.
I CAN UNDERSTAND THAT.
SUDDENLY THE COMMAND APC RUMBLED PAST THE SLOWER-MOVING COLUMN.
PONY BOY
THAT'S THE SKIPPER AND THE FIRST SHIRT. SOMETHING'S UP.
SOON WE GROUND TO A HALT.
LOOKS LIKE AN ARVN ROAD BLOCK. AS IF SARGE WASN'T IN A BAD ENOUGH MOOD ALREADY.
IT'S THE FIRST SERGEANT.
PONY ONE-NINER. WE HAVE AN ARVN MINE-SWEEPING UNIT UP HERE. THE ROAD IS UNSAFE FROM THIS POINT. WE'RE GONNA HAVE TO GET A LITTLE MUDDY. ACKNOWLEDGE, TEAM.

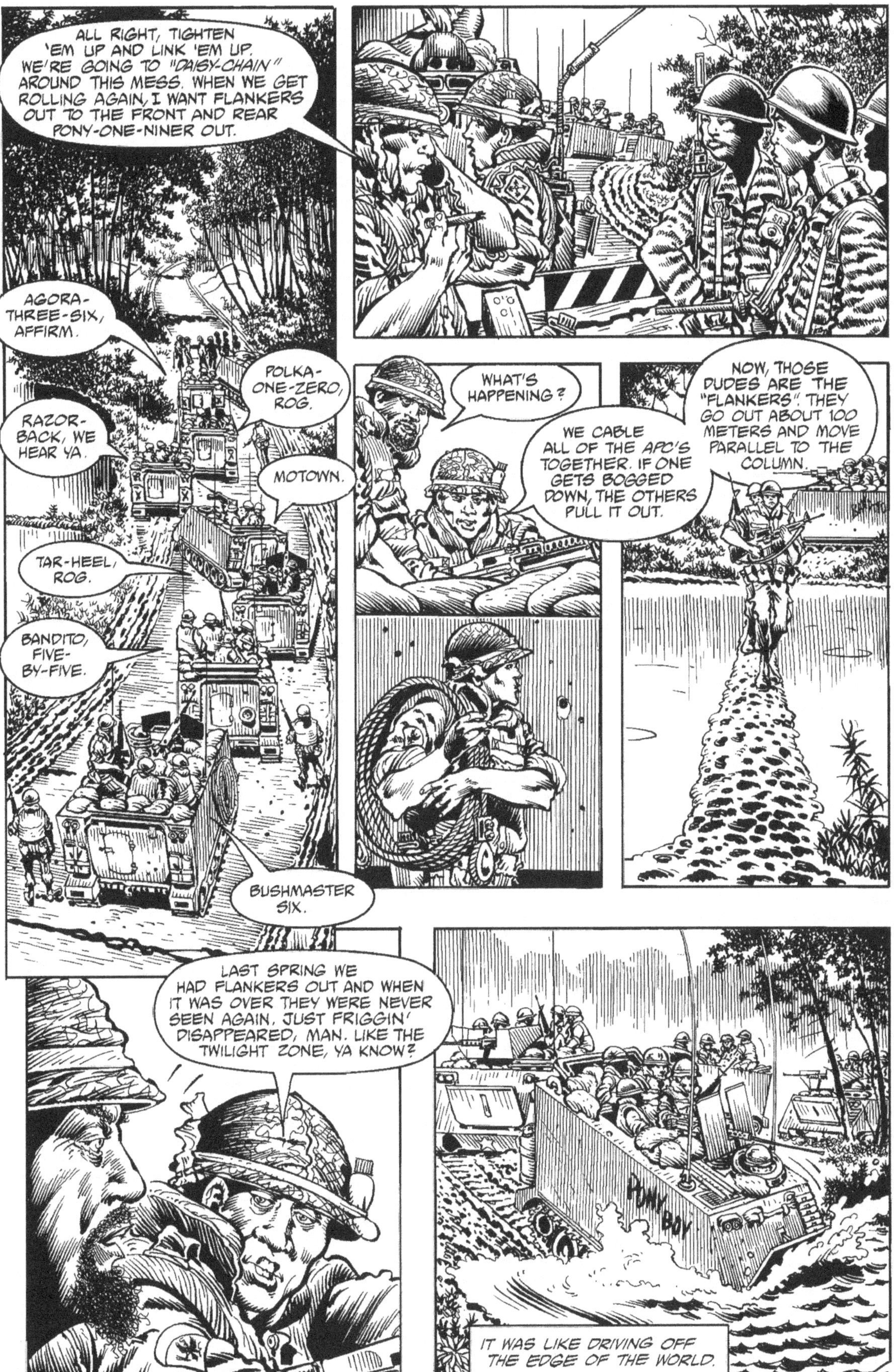

ALL RIGHT, TIGHTEN 'EM UP AND LINK 'EM UP. WE'RE GOING TO "DAISY-CHAIN" AROUND THIS MESS. WHEN WE GET ROLLING AGAIN, I WANT FLANKERS OUT TO THE FRONT AND REAR PONY-ONE-NINER OUT.
AGORA-THREE-SIX, AFFIRM.
POLKA-ONE-ZERO, ROG.
RAZOR-BACK, WE HEAR YA.
MOTOWN.
TAR-HEEL, ROG.
BANDITO, FIVE-BY-FIVE.
BUSHMASTER SIX.
WHAT'S HAPPENING?
WE CABLE ALL OF THE APC'S TOGETHER. IF ONE GETS BOGGED DOWN, THE OTHERS PULL IT OUT.
NOW, THOSE DUDES ARE THE "FLANKERS." THEY GO OUT ABOUT 100 METERS AND MOVE PARALLEL TO THE COLUMN.
LAST SPRING WE HAD FLANKERS OUT AND WHEN IT WAS OVER THEY WERE NEVER SEEN AGAIN. JUST FRIGGIN' DISAPPEARED, MAN. LIKE THE TWILIGHT ZONE, YA KNOW?
PONY BOY
IT WAS LIKE DRIVING OFF THE EDGE OF THE WORLD.

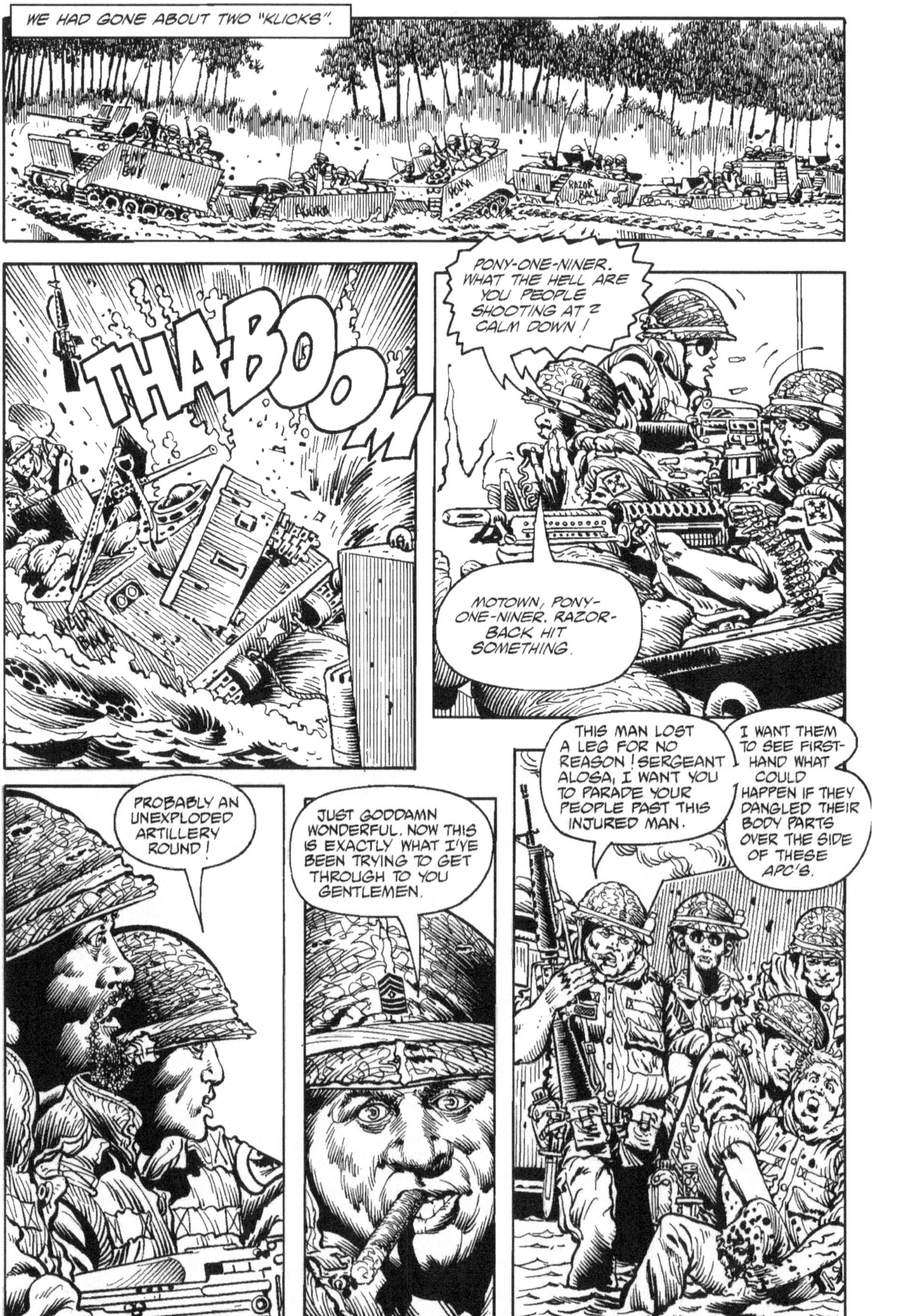

WE HAD GONE ABOUT TWO "KLICKS".
RAZOR BACK
THABOOM
PONY-ONE-NINER. WHAT THE HELL ARE YOU PEOPLE SHOOTING AT? CALM DOWN!
MOTOWN, PONY-ONE-NINER. RAZOR-BACK HIT SOMETHING.
PROBABLY AN UNEXPLODED ARTILLERY ROUND!
JUST GODDAMN WONDERFUL. NOW THIS IS EXACTLY WHAT I'VE BEEN TRYING TO GET THROUGH TO YOU GENTLEMEN.
THIS MAN LOST A LEG FOR NO REASON! SERGEANT ALOSA, I WANT YOU TO PARADE YOUR PEOPLE PAST THIS INJURED MAN.
I WANT THEM TO SEE FIRST-HAND WHAT COULD HAPPEN IF THEY DANGLED THEIR BODY PARTS OVER THE SIDE OF THESE APC'S.

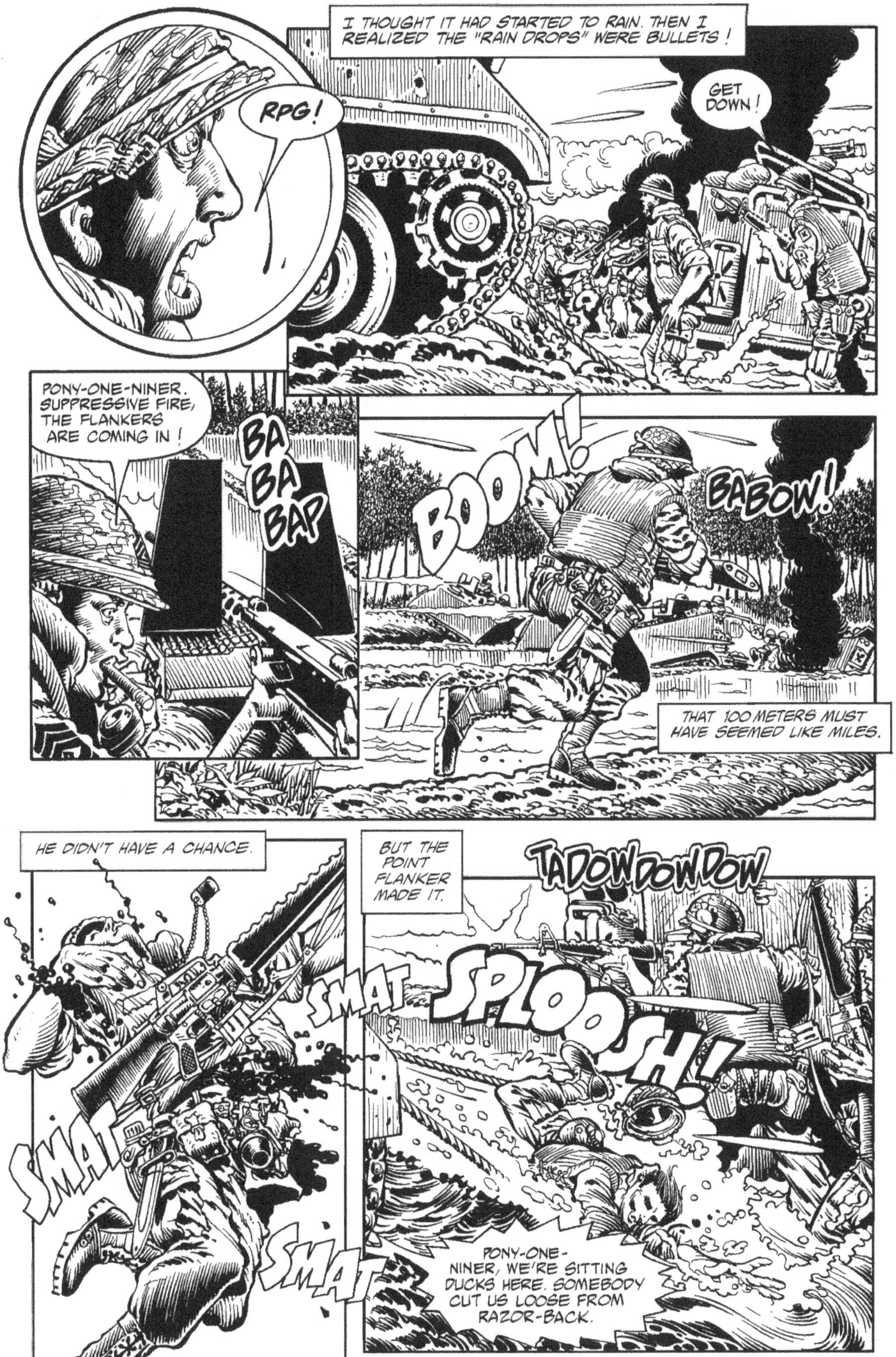
I THOUGHT IT HAD STARTED TO RAIN. THEN I REALIZED THE "RAIN DROPS" WERE BULLETS !
RPG!
GET DOWN !
PONY-ONE-NINER. SUPPRESSIVE FIRE, THE FLANKERS ARE COMING IN !
BA BA BAP
BOOM!
BABOW!
THAT 100 METERS MUST HAVE SEEMED LIKE MILES.
HE DIDN'T HAVE A CHANCE.
SMAT
SMAT
SMAT
BUT THE POINT FLANKER MADE IT.
TADOWDOWDOW
SPLOOSH!
PONY-ONE-NINER, WE'RE SITTING DUCKS HERE. SOMEBODY CUT US LOOSE FROM RAZOR-BACK.

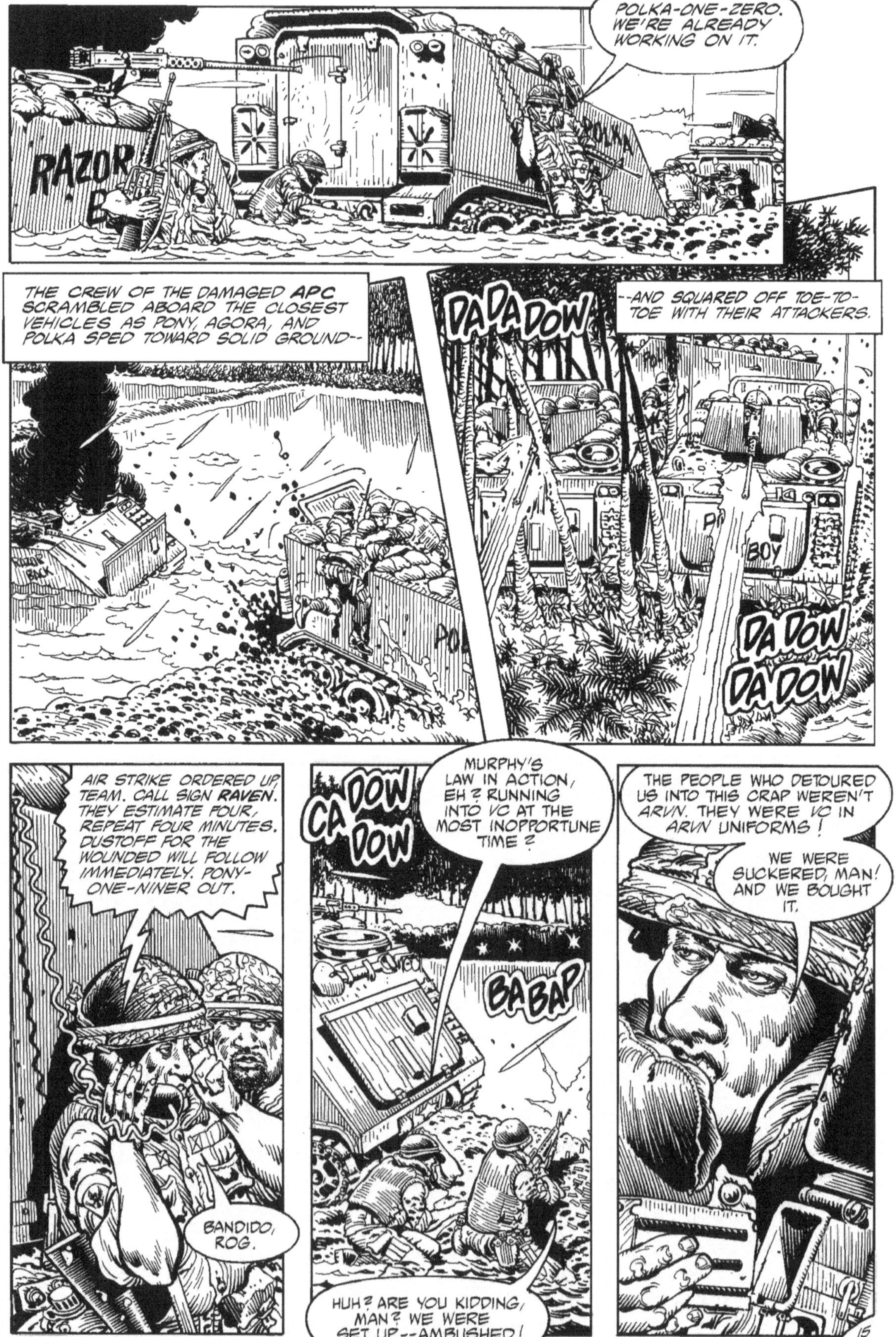
POLKA-ONE-ZERO. WE'RE ALREADY WORKING ON IT.
RAZOR B
POLKA
THE CREW OF THE DAMAGED APC SCRAMBLED ABOARD THE CLOSEST VEHICLES AS PONY, AGORA, AND POLKA SPED TOWARD SOLID GROUND--
DADADOW
--AND SQUARED OFF TOE-TO-TOE WITH THEIR ATTACKERS.
BOY
DADOW DADOW
AIR STRIKE ORDERED UP TEAM. CALL SIGN RAVEN. THEY ESTIMATE FOUR, REPEAT FOUR MINUTES. DUSTOFF FOR THE WOUNDED WILL FOLLOW IMMEDIATELY. PONY-ONE-NINER OUT.
BANDIDO, ROG.
CADOW DOW
MURPHY'S LAW IN ACTION, EH? RUNNING INTO VC AT THE MOST INOPPORTUNE TIME?
BABAP
HUH? ARE YOU KIDDING, MAN? WE WERE SET UP--AMBUSHED!
THE PEOPLE WHO DETOURED US INTO THIS CRAP WEREN'T ARVN. THEY WERE VC IN ARVN UNIFORMS!
WE WERE SUCKERED, MAN! AND WE BOUGHT IT.

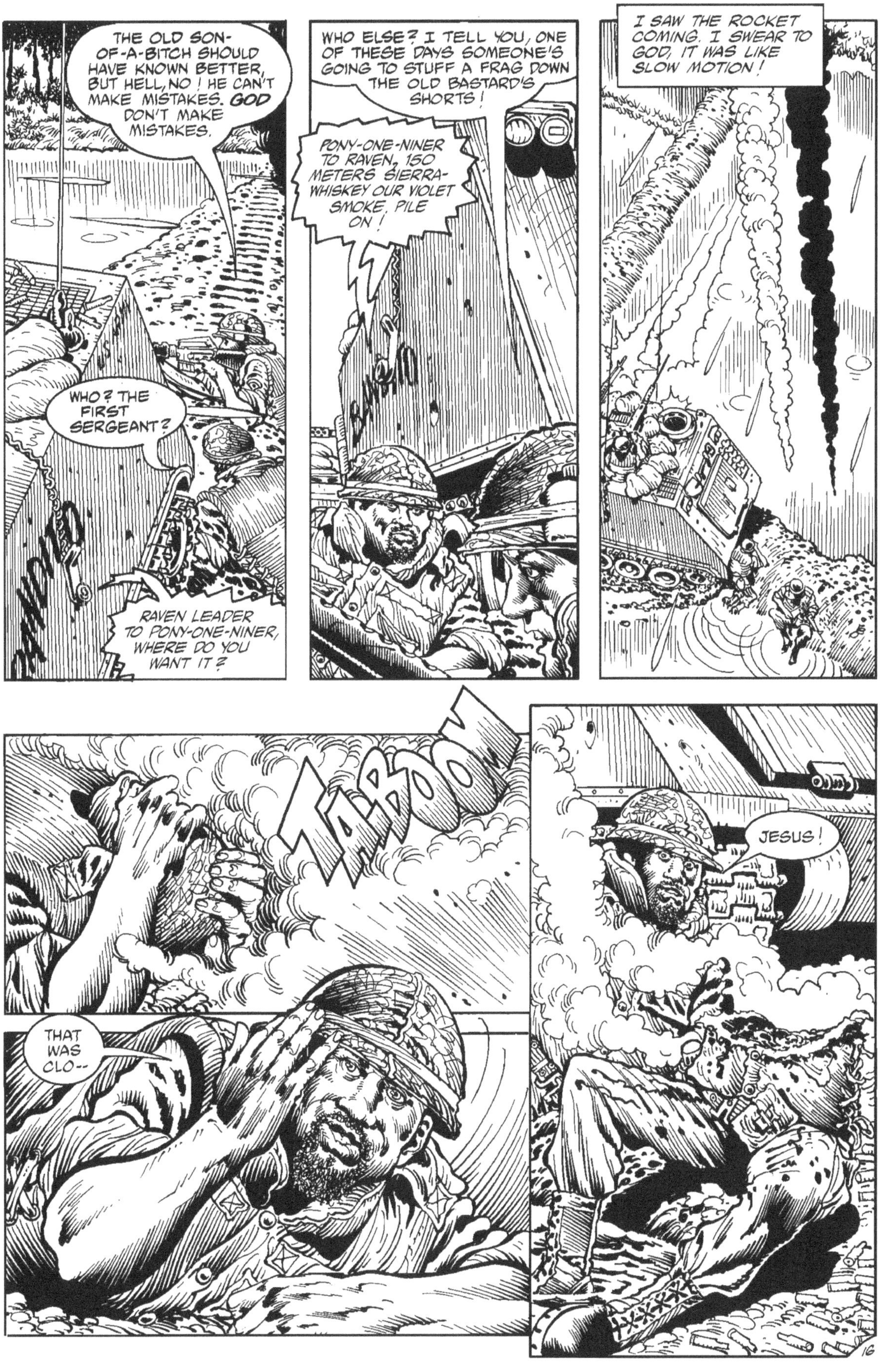
THE OLD SON-OF-A-BITCH SHOULD HAVE KNOWN BETTER, BUT HELL, NO ! HE CAN'T MAKE MISTAKES. GOD DON'T MAKE MISTAKES.
WHO? THE FIRST SERGEANT?
RAVEN LEADER TO PONY-ONE-NINER, WHERE DO YOU WANT IT?
WHO ELSE? I TELL YOU, ONE OF THESE DAYS SOMEONE'S GOING TO STUFF A FRAG DOWN THE OLD BASTARD'S SHORTS!
PONY-ONE-NINER TO RAVEN. 150 METERS SIERRA-WHISKEY OUR VIOLET SMOKE. PILE ON!
I SAW THE ROCKET COMING. I SWEAR TO GOD, IT WAS LIKE SLOW MOTION!
TABOOM
THAT WAS CLO--
JESUS!

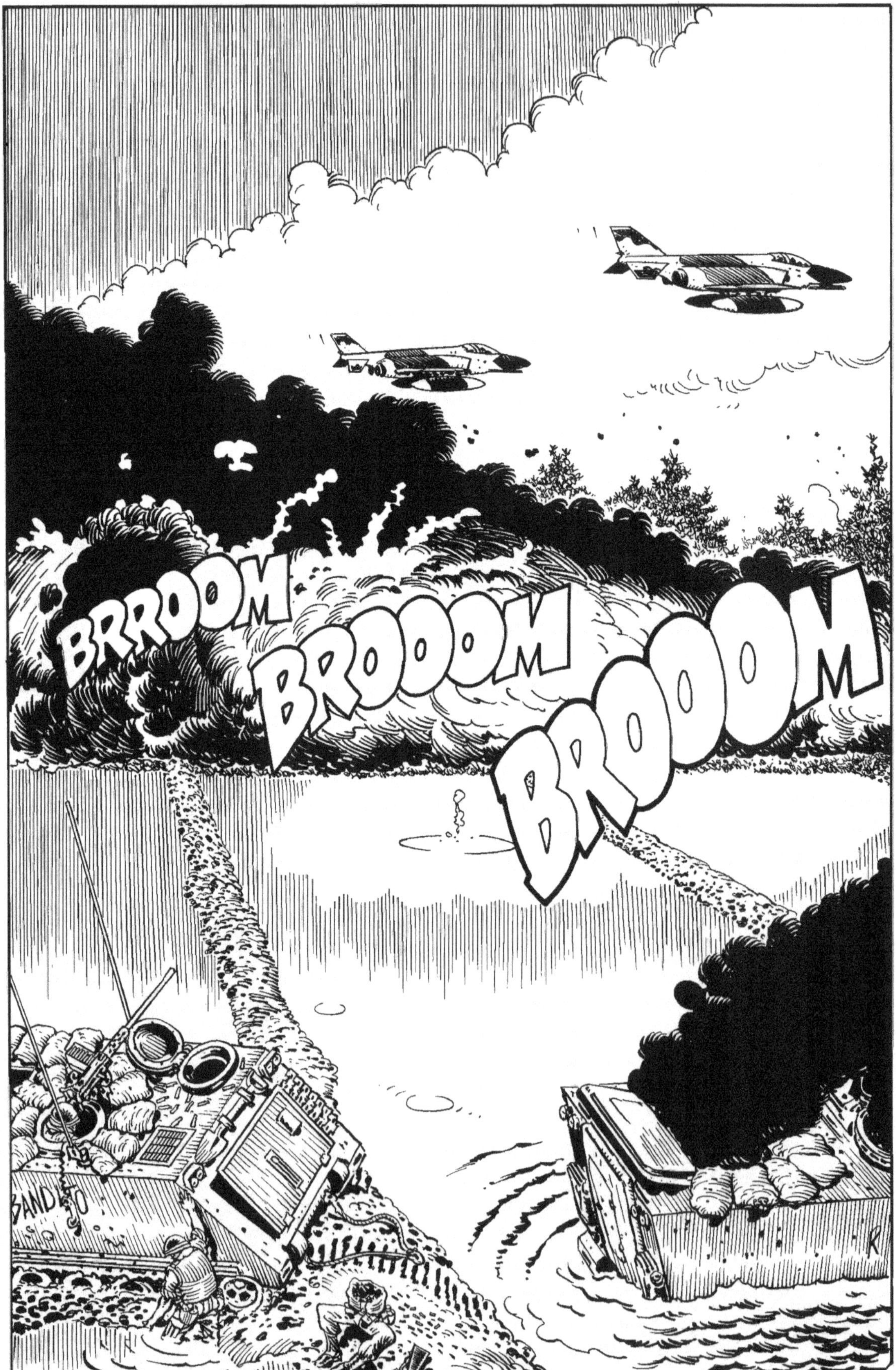
BRROOM
BROOOM
BROOOM

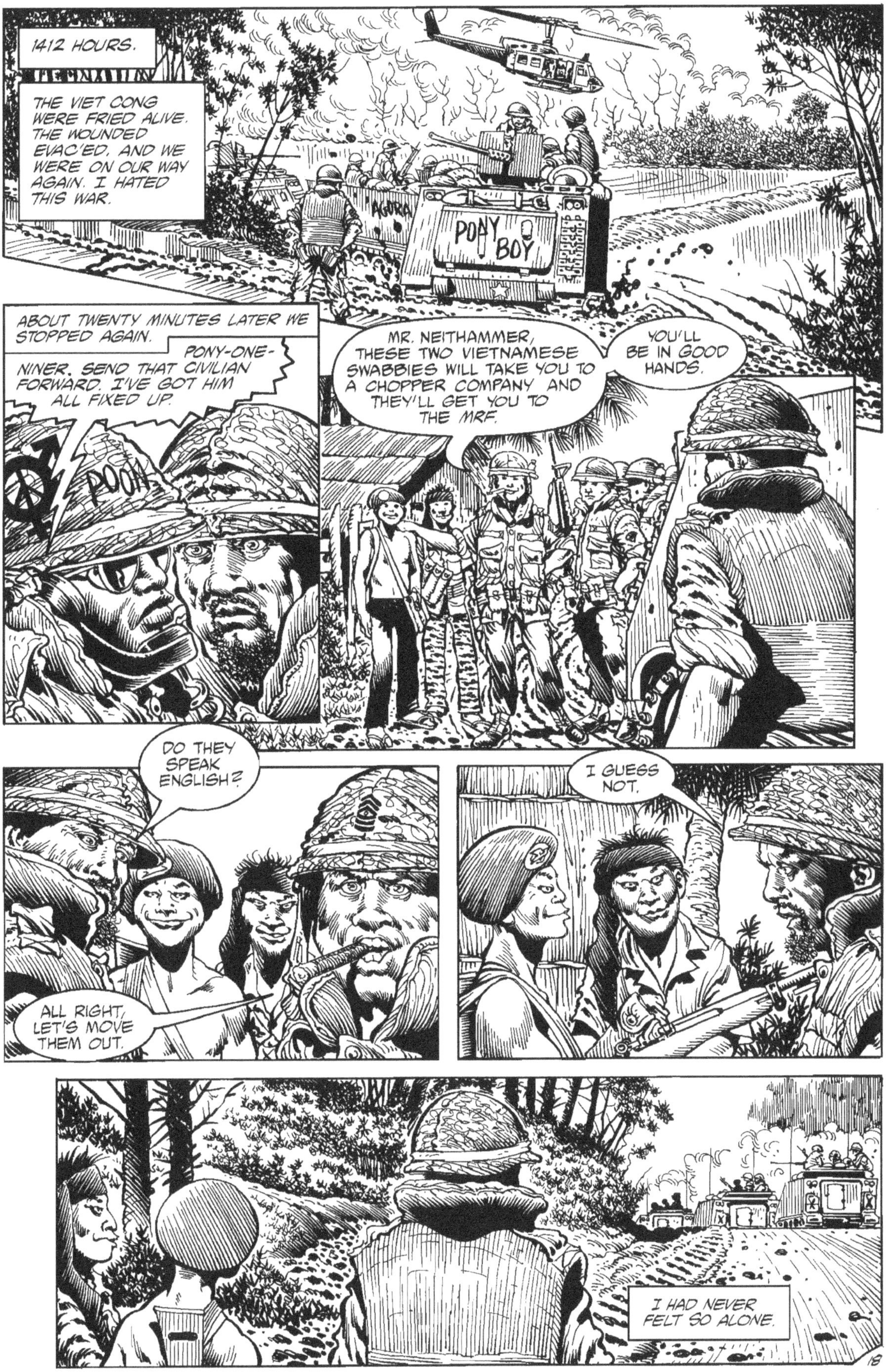
1412 HOURS.
THE VIET CONG WERE FRIED ALIVE. THE WOUNDED EVAC'ED. AND WE WERE ON OUR WAY AGAIN. I HATED THIS WAR.
PONY BOY
ABOUT TWENTY MINUTES LATER WE STOPPED AGAIN.
PONY-ONE-NINER. SEND THAT CIVILIAN FORWARD. I'VE GOT HIM ALL FIXED UP.
POON
MR. NEITHAMMER, THESE TWO VIETNAMESE SWABBIES WILL TAKE YOU TO A CHOPPER COMPANY AND THEY'LL GET YOU TO THE MRF.
YOU'LL BE IN GOOD HANDS.
DO THEY SPEAK ENGLISH?
ALL RIGHT, LET'S MOVE THEM OUT.
I GUESS NOT.
I HAD NEVER FELT SO ALONE.

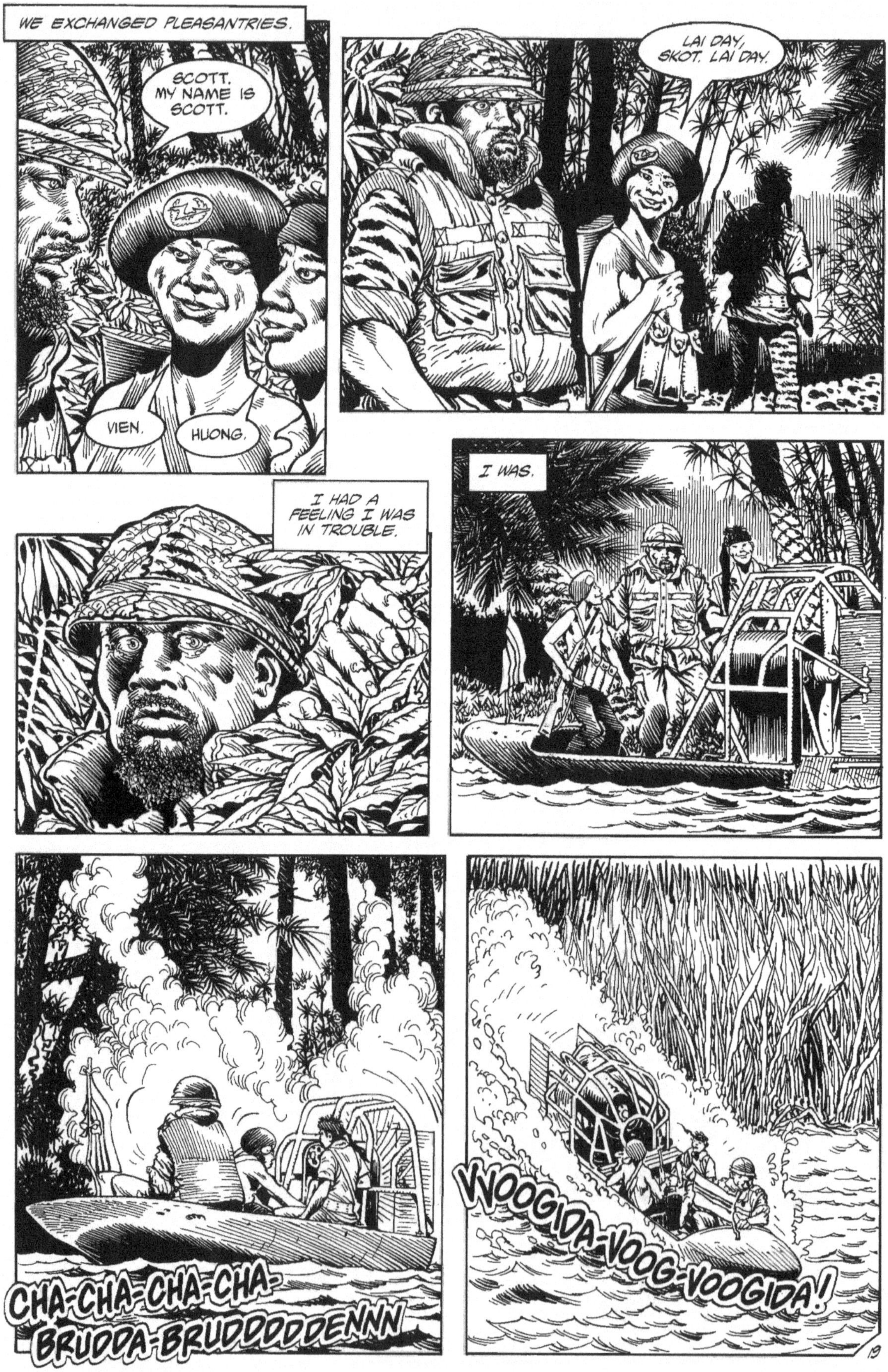
WE EXCHANGED PLEASANTRIES.
SCOTT. MY NAME IS SCOTT.
VIEN.
HUONG.
LAI DAY, SKOT. LAI DAY.
I HAD A FEELING I WAS IN TROUBLE.
I WAS.
CHA-CHA-CHA-CHA-BRUDDA-BRUDDDDDENNN
VVOOGIDA-VOOG-VOOGIDA!

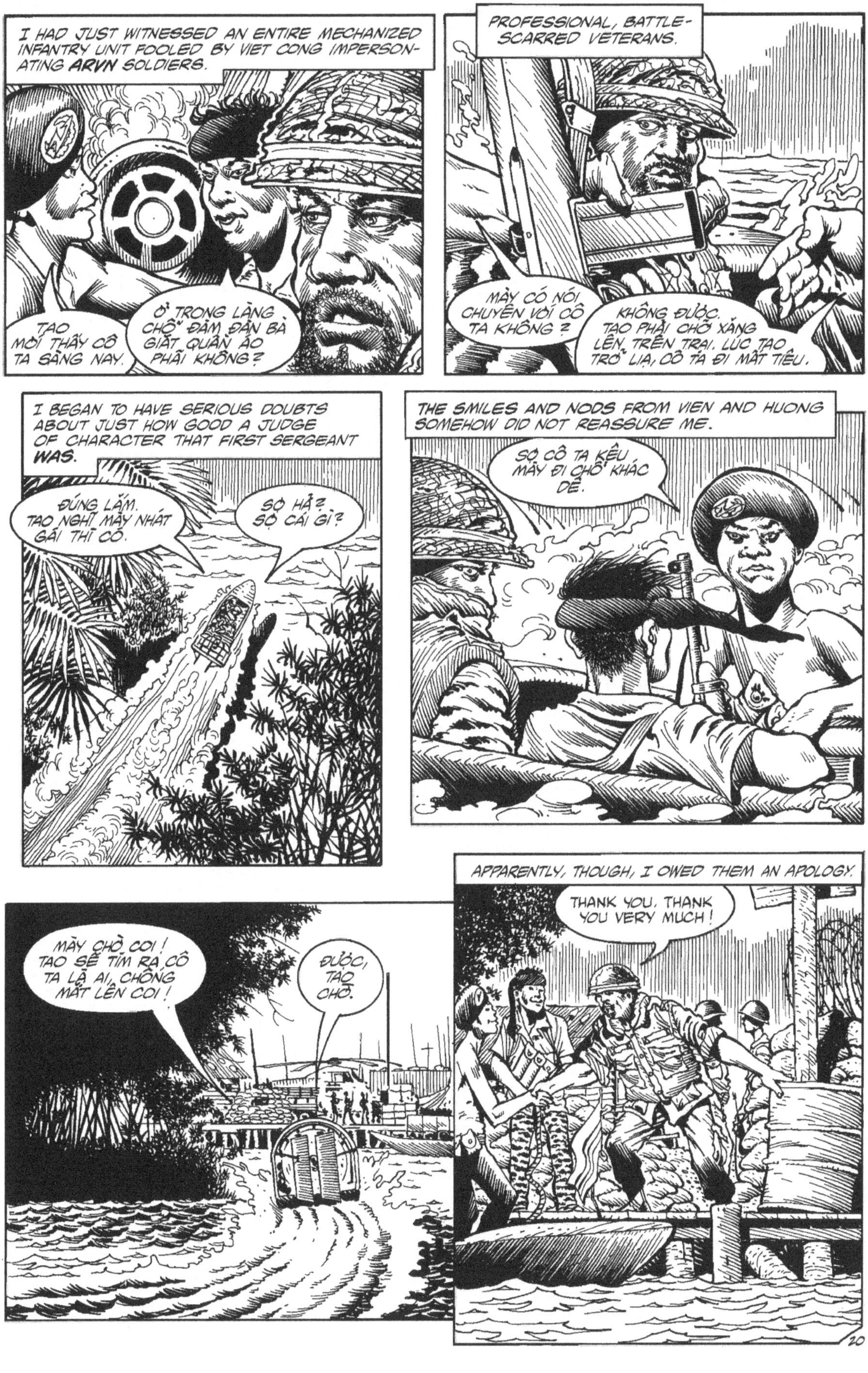

I HAD JUST WITNESSED AN ENTIRE MECHANIZED INFANTRY UNIT FOOLED BY VIET CONG IMPERSONATING ARVN SOLDIERS.
TAO MỚI THẤY CÔ TA SÀNG NAY.
Ở TRONG LÀNG CHỖ ĐÀM ĐÀN BÀ GIẶT QUẦN ÁO PHẢI KHÔNG?
PROFESSIONAL, BATTLE-SCARRED VETERANS.
MÀY CÓ NÓI CHUYỆN VỚI CÔ TA KHÔNG?
KHÔNG ĐƯỢC. TAO PHẢI CHỞ XĂNG LÊN TRÊN TRẠI. LÚC TAO TRỞ LẠI, CÔ TA ĐI MẤT TIÊU.
I BEGAN TO HAVE SERIOUS DOUBTS ABOUT JUST HOW GOOD A JUDGE OF CHARACTER THAT FIRST SERGEANT WAS.
ĐÚNG LẮM. TAO NGHĨ MÀY NHÁT GÁI THÌ CÓ.
SỢ HẢ? SỢ CÁI GÌ?
THE SMILES AND NODS FROM VIEN AND HUONG SOMEHOW DID NOT REASSURE ME.
SỢ CÔ TA KÊU MÀY ĐI CHỖ KHÁC ĐÊ.
MÀY CHỜ COI! TAO SẼ TÌM RA CÔ TA LÀ AI, CHỐNG MẮT LÊN COI!
ĐƯỢC, TAO CHỜ.
APPARENTLY, THOUGH, I OWED THEM AN APOLOGY.
THANK YOU. THANK YOU VERY MUCH!

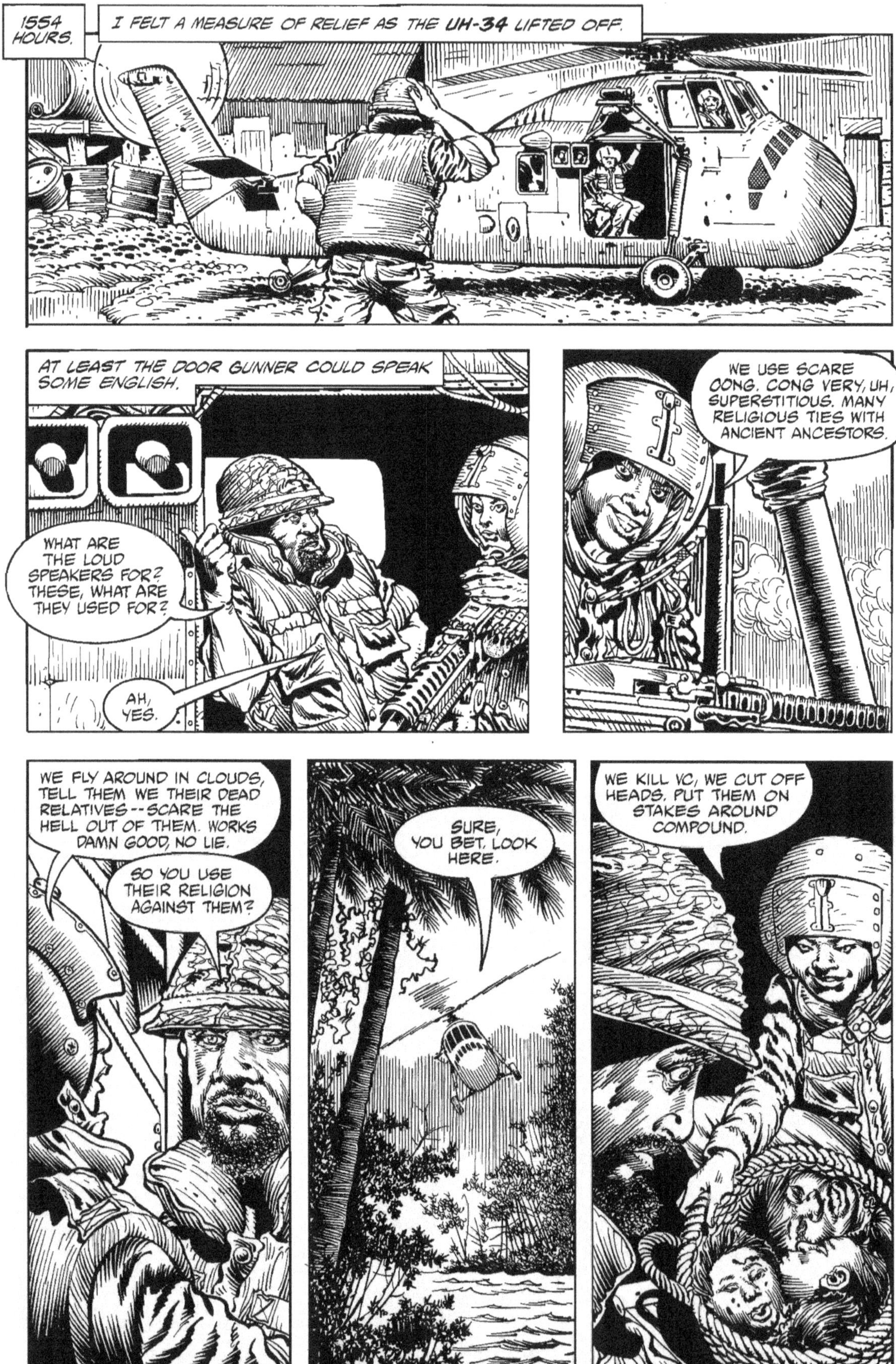
1554 HOURS.
I FELT A MEASURE OF RELIEF AS THE UH-34 LIFTED OFF.
AT LEAST THE DOOR GUNNER COULD SPEAK SOME ENGLISH.
WHAT ARE THE LOUD SPEAKERS FOR? THESE, WHAT ARE THEY USED FOR?
AH, YES.
WE USE SCARE CONG. CONG VERY, UH, SUPERSTITIOUS. MANY RELIGIOUS TIES WITH ANCIENT ANCESTORS.
WE FLY AROUND IN CLOUDS, TELL THEM WE THEIR DEAD RELATIVES--SCARE THE HELL OUT OF THEM. WORKS DAMN GOOD, NO LIE.
SO YOU USE THEIR RELIGION AGAINST THEM?
SURE, YOU BET. LOOK HERE.
WE KILL VC, WE CUT OFF HEADS. PUT THEM ON STAKES AROUND COMPOUND.

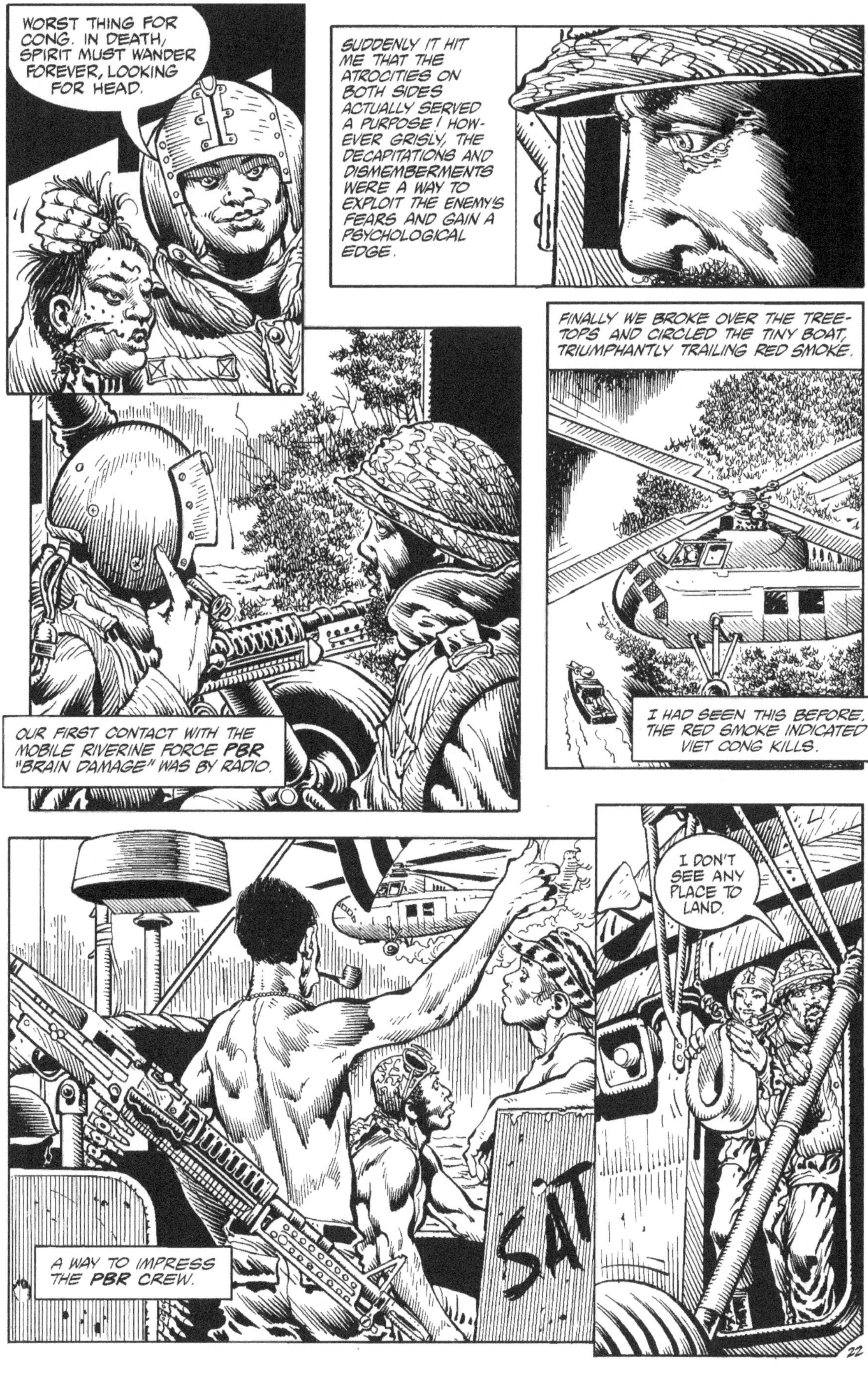

WORST THING FOR CONG. IN DEATH, SPIRIT MUST WANDER FOREVER, LOOKING FOR HEAD.
SUDDENLY IT HIT ME THAT THE ATROCITIES ON BOTH SIDES ACTUALLY SERVED A PURPOSE! HOW-EVER GRISLY, THE DECAPITATIONS AND DISMEMBERMENTS WERE A WAY TO EXPLOIT THE ENEMY'S FEARS AND GAIN A PSYCHOLOGICAL EDGE.
OUR FIRST CONTACT WITH THE MOBILE RIVERINE FORCE PBR "BRAIN DAMAGE" WAS BY RADIO.
FINALLY WE BROKE OVER THE TREE-TOPS AND CIRCLED THE TINY BOAT, TRIUMPHANTLY TRAILING RED SMOKE.
I HAD SEEN THIS BEFORE. THE RED SMOKE INDICATED VIET CONG KILLS.
A WAY TO IMPRESS THE PBR CREW.
SAT
I DON'T SEE ANY PLACE TO LAND.

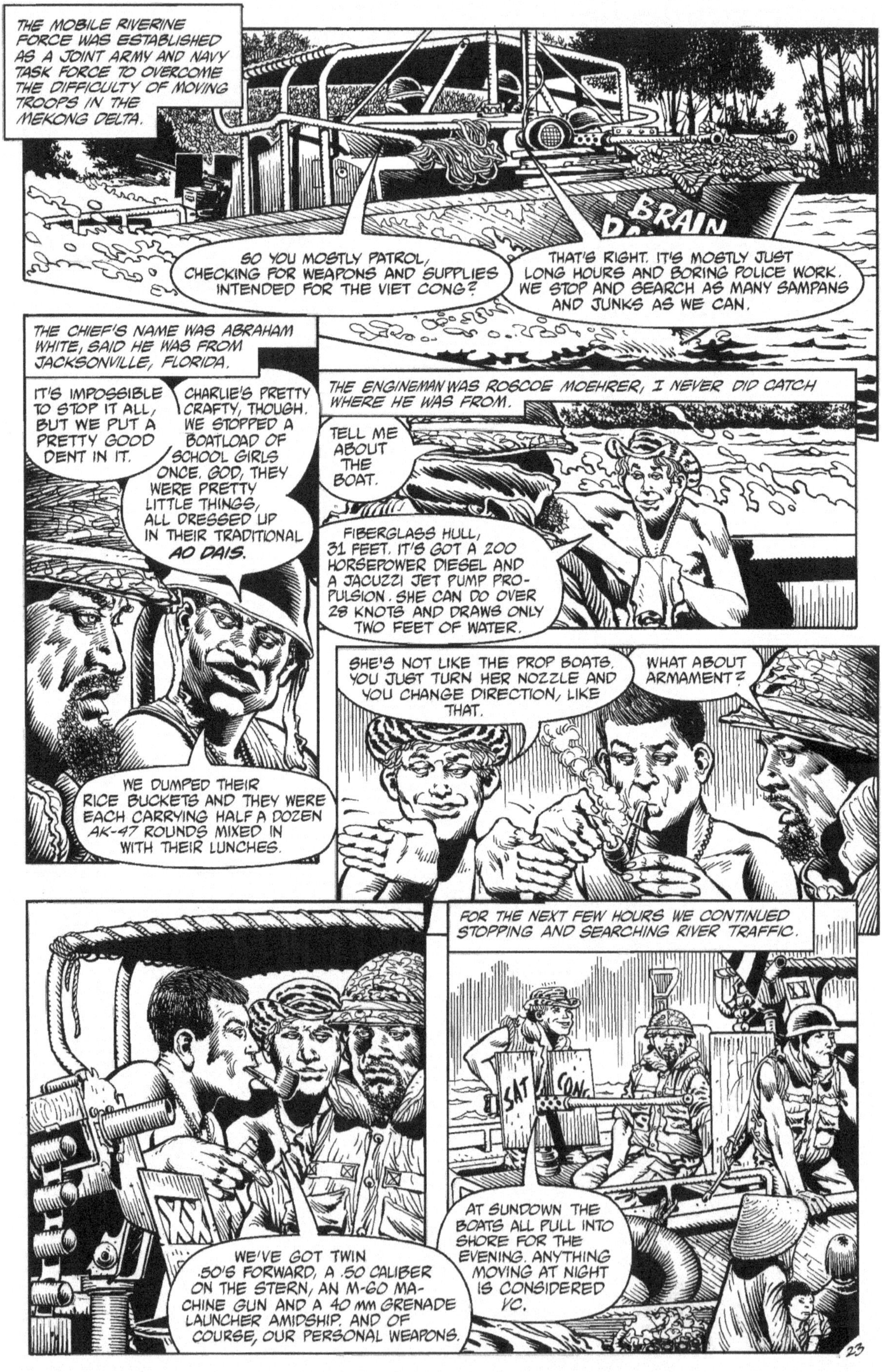

THE MOBILE RIVERINE FORCE WAS ESTABLISHED AS A JOINT ARMY AND NAVY TASK FORCE TO OVERCOME THE DIFFICULTY OF MOVING TROOPS IN THE MEKONG DELTA.
BRAIN
SO YOU MOSTLY PATROL, CHECKING FOR WEAPONS AND SUPPLIES INTENDED FOR THE VIET CONG?
THAT'S RIGHT. IT'S MOSTLY JUST LONG HOURS AND BORING POLICE WORK. WE STOP AND SEARCH AS MANY SAMPANS AND JUNKS AS WE CAN.
THE CHIEF'S NAME WAS ABRAHAM WHITE, SAID HE WAS FROM JACKSONVILLE, FLORIDA.
IT'S IMPOSSIBLE TO STOP IT ALL, BUT WE PUT A PRETTY GOOD DENT IN IT.
CHARLIE'S PRETTY CRAFTY, THOUGH. WE STOPPED A BOATLOAD OF SCHOOL GIRLS ONCE. GOD, THEY WERE PRETTY LITTLE THINGS, ALL DRESSED UP IN THEIR TRADITIONAL AO DAIS.
WE DUMPED THEIR RICE BUCKETS AND THEY WERE EACH CARRYING HALF A DOZEN AK-47 ROUNDS MIXED IN WITH THEIR LUNCHES.
THE ENGINEMAN WAS ROSCOE MOEHRER, I NEVER DID CATCH WHERE HE WAS FROM.
TELL ME ABOUT THE BOAT.
FIBERGLASS HULL, 31 FEET. IT'S GOT A 200 HORSEPOWER DIESEL AND A JACUZZI JET PUMP PROPULSION. SHE CAN DO OVER 28 KNOTS AND DRAWS ONLY TWO FEET OF WATER.
SHE'S NOT LIKE THE PROP BOATS. YOU JUST TURN HER NOZZLE AND YOU CHANGE DIRECTION, LIKE THAT.
WHAT ABOUT ARMAMENT?
WE'VE GOT TWIN .50'S FORWARD, A .50 CALIBER ON THE STERN, AN M-60 MACHINE GUN AND A 40 MM GRENADE LAUNCHER AMIDSHIP. AND OF COURSE, OUR PERSONAL WEAPONS.
FOR THE NEXT FEW HOURS WE CONTINUED STOPPING AND SEARCHING RIVER TRAFFIC.
AT SUNDOWN THE BOATS ALL PULL INTO SHORE FOR THE EVENING. ANYTHING MOVING AT NIGHT IS CONSIDERED VC.

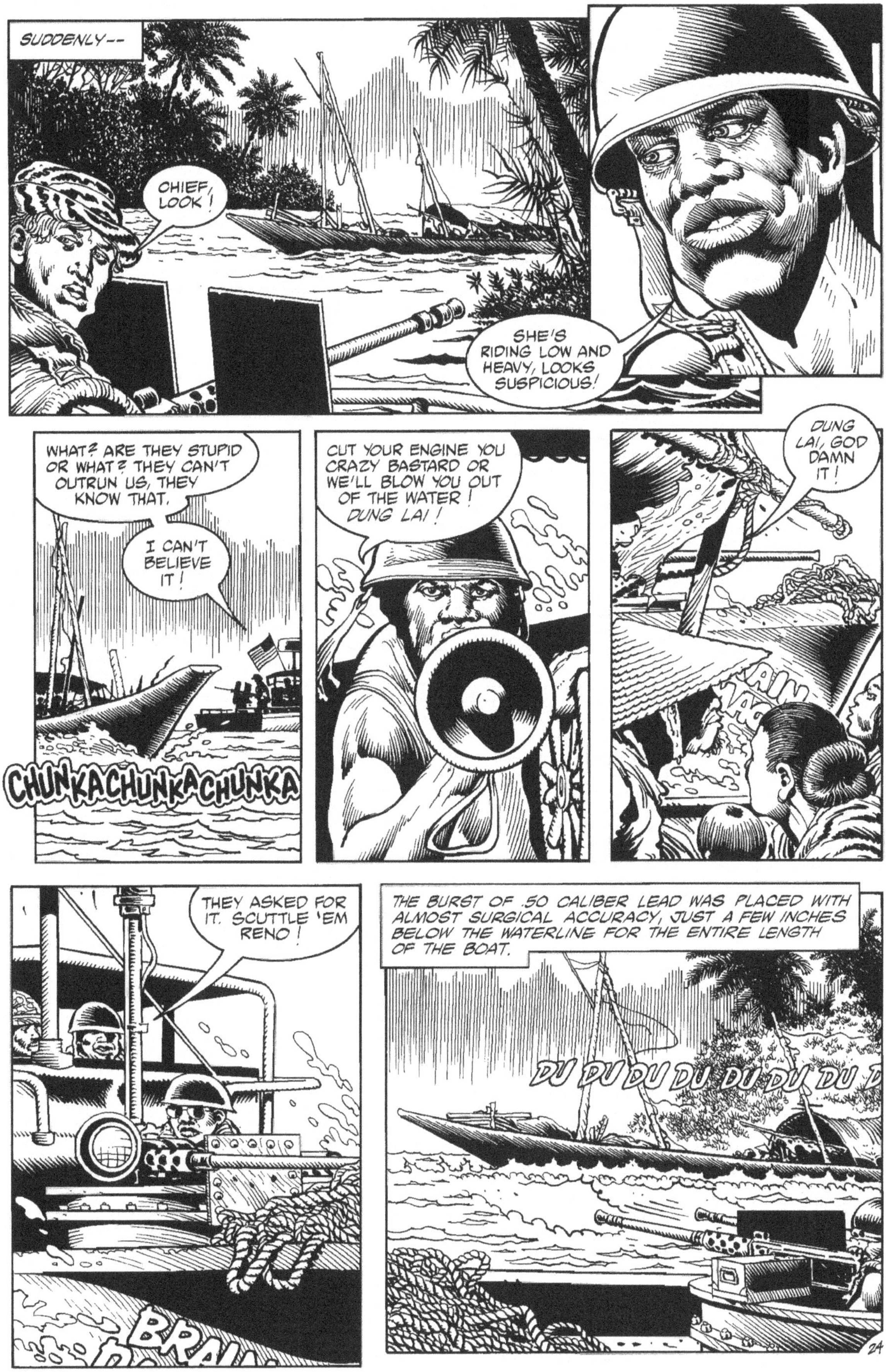
SUDDENLY--
CHIEF, LOOK!
SHE'S RIDING LOW AND HEAVY, LOOKS SUSPICIOUS!
WHAT? ARE THEY STUPID OR WHAT? THEY CAN'T OUTRUN US, THEY KNOW THAT.
I CAN'T BELIEVE IT!
CHUNKACHUNKACHUNKA
CUT YOUR ENGINE YOU CRAZY BASTARD OR WE'LL BLOW YOU OUT OF THE WATER! DUNG LAI!
DUNG LAI, GOD DAMN IT!
THEY ASKED FOR IT. SCUTTLE 'EM RENO!
THE BURST OF .50 CALIBER LEAD WAS PLACED WITH ALMOST SURGICAL ACCURACY, JUST A FEW INCHES BELOW THE WATERLINE FOR THE ENTIRE LENGTH OF THE BOAT.
DU DU DU DU DU DU DU D

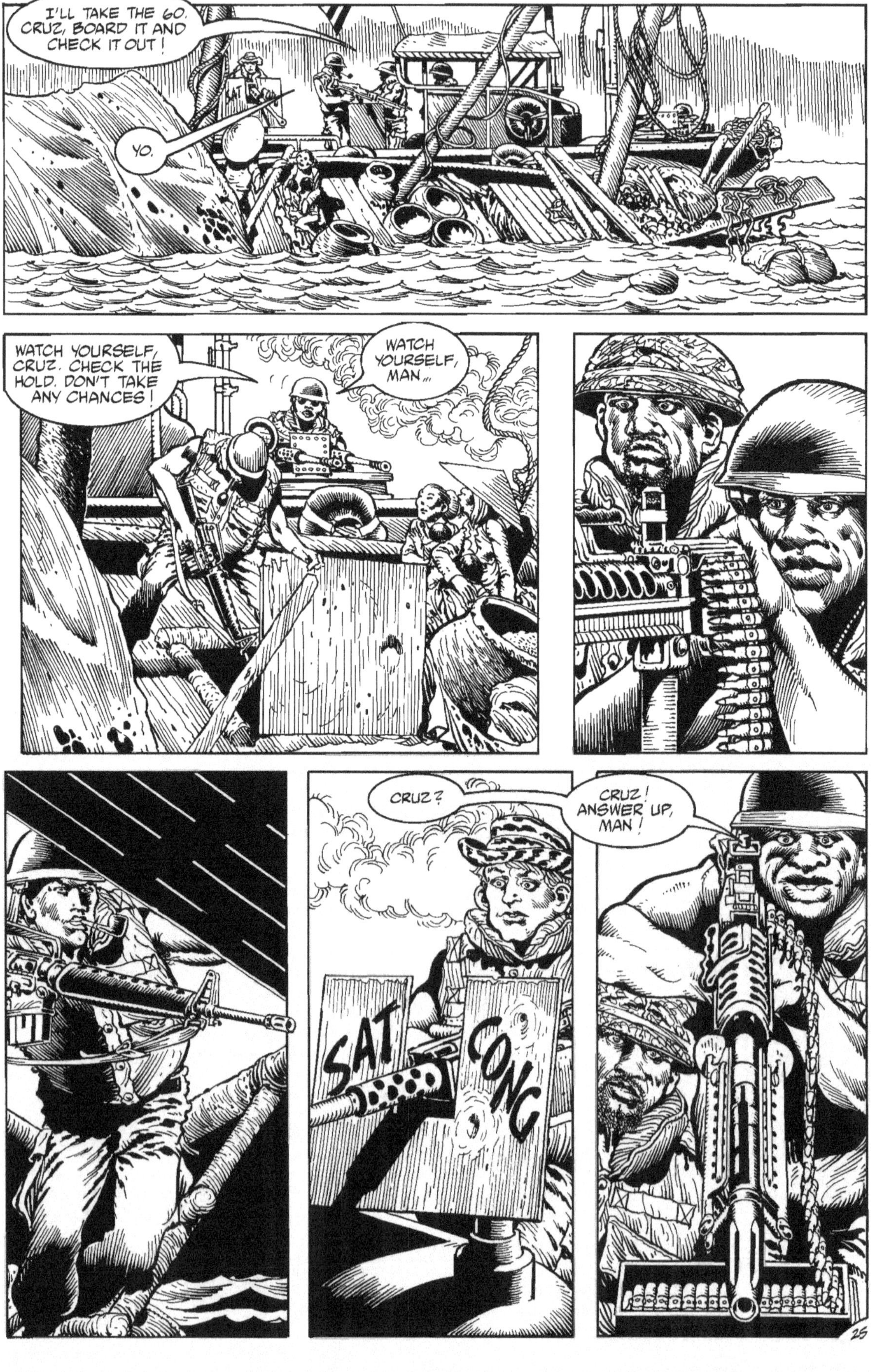
I'LL TAKE THE 60. CRUZ, BOARD IT AND CHECK IT OUT!
YO.
SAT
WATCH YOURSELF, CRUZ. CHECK THE HOLD. DON'T TAKE ANY CHANCES!
WATCH YOURSELF, MAN...
CRUZ?
CRUZ! ANSWER UP, MAN!
SAT
CONG

CHIEF?
I'LL CHECK ON
HIM, CHIEF.

STAY
PUT.

CRUZ!
WHERE THE HELL
ARE YOU?

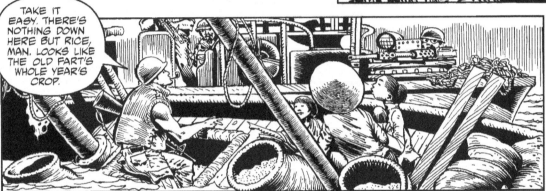

TAKE IT
EASY. THERE'S
NOTHING DOWN
HERE BUT RICE,
MAN. LOOKS LIKE
THE OLD FART'S
WHOLE YEAR'S
CROP.

GET
THEM ON
BOARD.

COME ON, LET'S
GO. MOVE IT.

I'LL TAKE
THEM. HAND
THEM TO ME.

MOVE! GO
ON MOVE
IT!

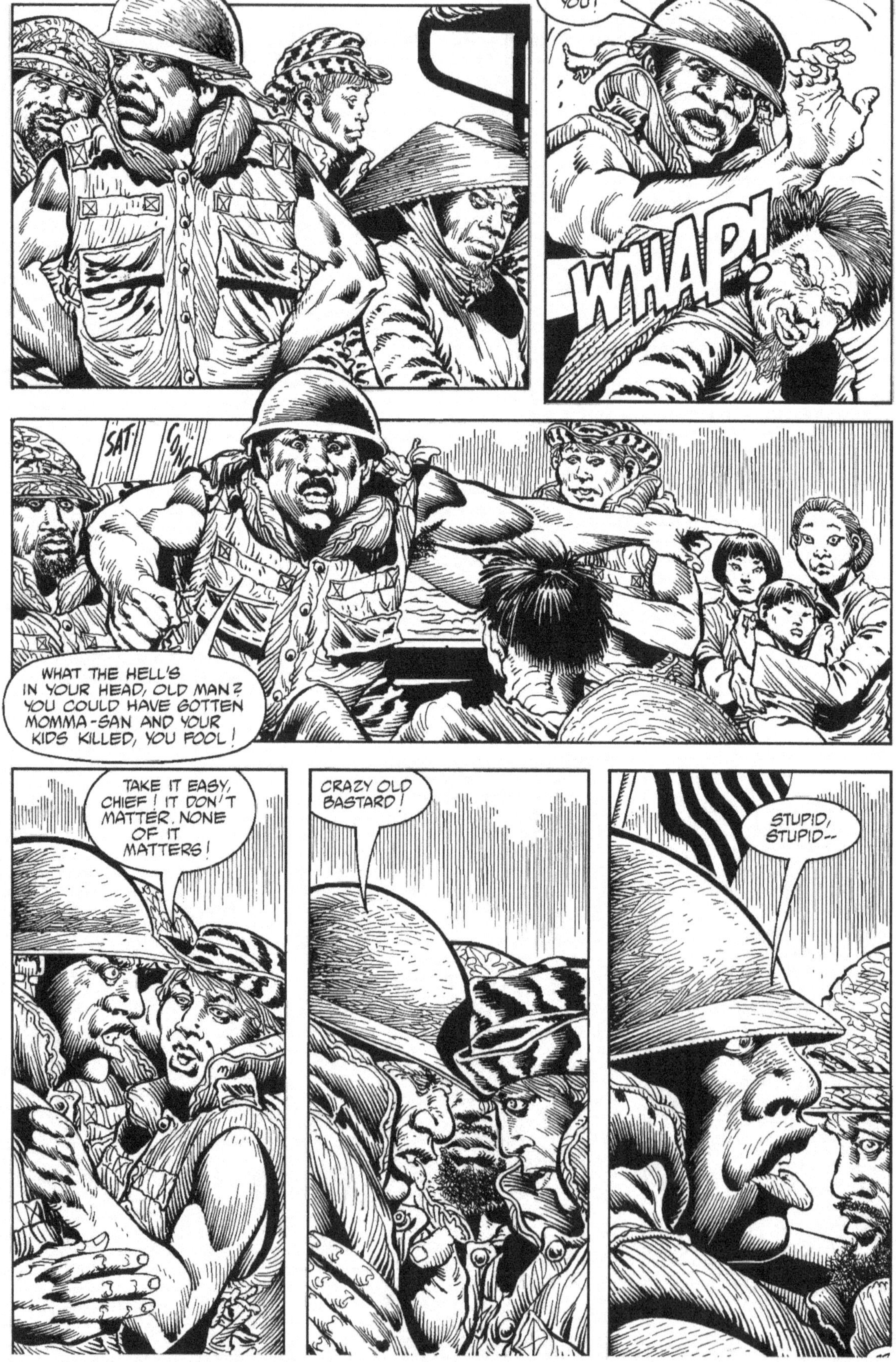
DAMN YOU!
WHAP!
SAT
CONG
WHAT THE HELL'S IN YOUR HEAD, OLD MAN? YOU COULD HAVE GOTTEN MOMMA-SAN AND YOUR KIDS KILLED, YOU FOOL!
TAKE IT EASY, CHIEF! IT DON'T MATTER. NONE OF IT MATTERS!
CRAZY OLD BASTARD!
STUPID, STUPID--

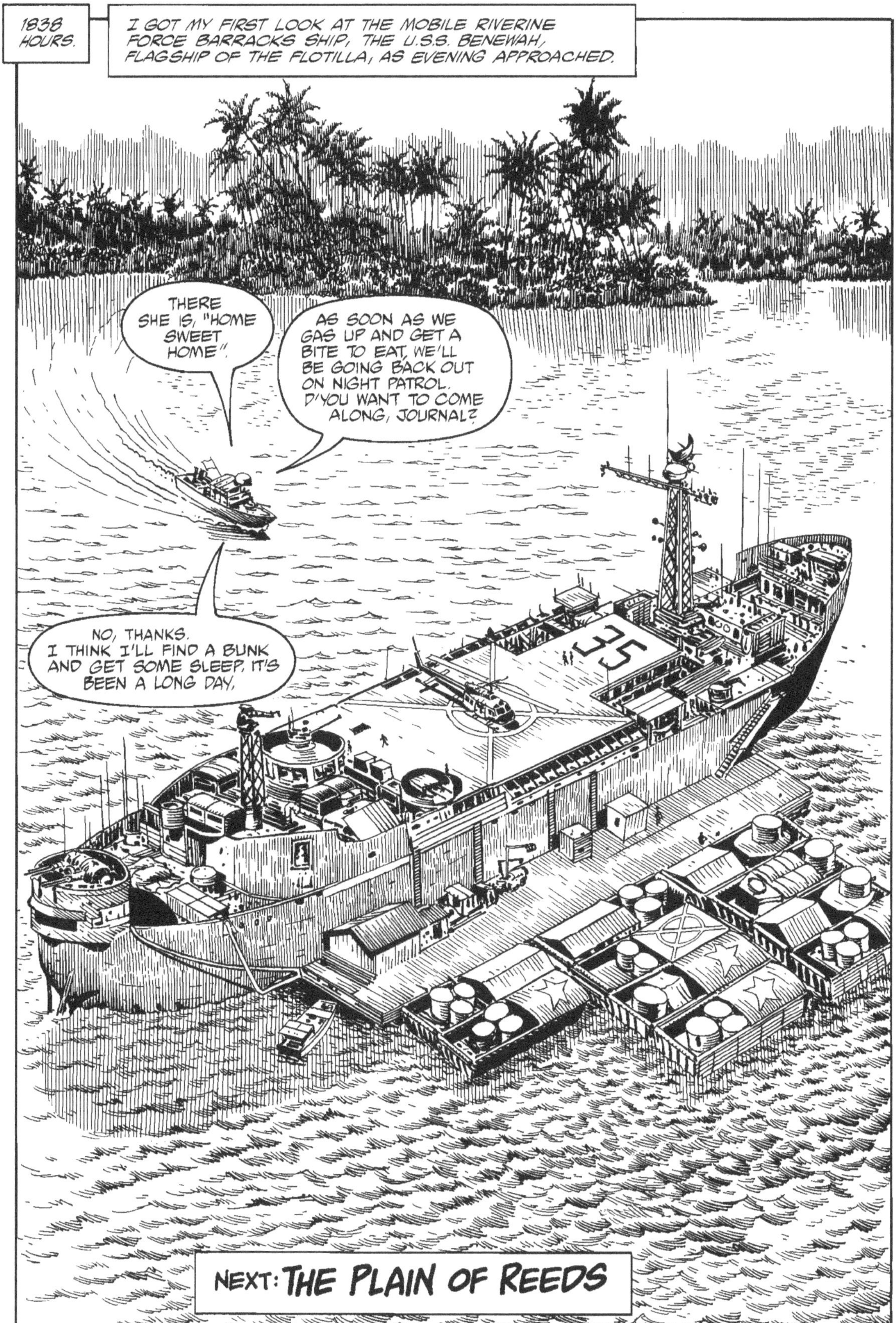

1838 HOURS.
I GOT MY FIRST LOOK AT THE MOBILE RIVERINE FORCE BARRACKS SHIP, THE U.S.S. BENEWAH, FLAGSHIP OF THE FLOTILLA, AS EVENING APPROACHED.
THERE SHE IS, "HOME SWEET HOME".
AS SOON AS WE GAS UP AND GET A BITE TO EAT, WE'LL BE GOING BACK OUT ON NIGHT PATROL. D'YOU WANT TO COME ALONG, JOURNAL?
NO, THANKS. I THINK I'LL FIND A BUNK AND GET SOME SLEEP. IT'S BEEN A LONG DAY.
35
NEXT: THE PLAIN OF REEDS

Missing American™

Capt. Charles E. Shelton, USAF
'Iron Man' beat his captors to death with his chain!

When the U.S. ended its involvement in the Vietnam War, many questions remained unanswered. But the most agonizing questions were those asked by the families of some 2,400 Americans listed as "Missing in Action."

The following is the information we have on just one of those missing Americans.

The saga of US Air Force Captain Charles Ervin Shelton, of Owensboro, Kentucky, is one of the most amazing POW tales we have ever heard — he is also the only man still officially listed by the Pentagon as a Prisoner of War.

On April 29, 1965, his 33rd birthday, Capt. Shelton left Udorn AFB, Thailand, in an RF-101 "Voodoo" aircraft for a reconnaissance mission over Laos. He wore a "sanitized" flight suit, devoid of rank, patches, or other insignia. He was armed with only a .45 automatic.

At 11:59 a.m., over the Laotian province of Sam Neua, Capt. Shelton's plane was shot down and he ejected. He waved to his wingman from the ground and radioed to an F-105 pilot that he was in good condition. He waited two hours on a hilltop for rescue. One source said adverse weather aborted a helicopter rescue, but another says rescue orders never came.

He evaded the Pathet Lao for three days, but intelligence reported him surrounded by two platoons. He surrendered without a shot.

The Laotians took his boots to prevent him from running away. He refused to cooperate, went limp, and had to be carried to a POW camp. He was imprisoned in a cave or caves, south of Ban Nakay Neua, in Houa Pan Province, Laos. Intelligence sources say he was held there with another POW, David Hrdlicka.

Because of his repeated attempts at escape, Charles was kept in shackles at all times and chained to the walls of the cave at night.

On June 10, 1968, according to the CIA, Charles was brought into a North Vietnamese Army office for interrogation. But when the NVA soldiers tried to chain him to a desk, he somehow managed to overturn the desk and beat three of his captors to death with his chain.

On another occasion that year, in retaliation for his attempts to escape, Charles was put into a shallow grave which was then covered with bars and rigged with hand grenades. Sentries poked him with bayonets to keep him awake.

Early in 1971, perhaps even earlier, in "Operation Duck Soup," Charles Shelton and David Hrdlicka were rescued by a combined team of CIA, Special Forces, and Hmong fighters. (The Hmong were native tribesmen fighting on the US side and paid by the CIA.)

After being rescued, the two were debriefed while on the run to Thailand. But about ten days later they were recaptured, although the details are not known.

According to the Air Force, Charles has survived hard labor, excruciating torture, malaria, and pneumonia. He has escaped several times and has been shot twice, once in each leg, to discourage further escape attempts.

Charles Shelton has achieved a kind of legendary status among communist interroga-

tors from around the world who have taken turns trying to break him. His name is known among terrorists who have trained in Vietnam, Cuba, the USSR, and East Germany.

Charles' eldest son, Father Charles Shelton, Jr., a Catholic priest, says he knows "exactly" where his father is today. "He is being held in a maximum security prison, on an island similar to Alcatraz, called Ho Thac Bai. It is located about 40 miles northwest of Hanoi."

Charles's wife, Marian, has doggedly compiled his story. But more, in June, 1973, after the US was officially out of the war and the North had said it had returned all POWs, she tried to find Charles herself. Entering Laos illegally, she pleaded with various Pathet Lao, Viet Cong, and North Vietnamese officials. They told her nothing, suggesting he had perhaps been eaten by a tiger. She returned home.

Since his capture, Charles's parents have died. His five children are grown and he now has two grandchildren. His wife lives in California. "Whether my husband is alive or dead, I don't know," Marian Shelton says. "I do know that there are prisoners of war over there and I'm told almost daily that Charles is alive."

"Since I am Catholic, I was taught that we were all put here on Earth by God for a purpose. So, if Charles is gone, then he has served his purpose here on Earth.

"I'm very worried about the future and the honor of this country. I believe that all of our men who fought for this country should be brought home with honor. For, as President Reagan once said, 'A country that forgets its fighting men is a country that, in itself, will be forgotten.'"

THE PATH OF REEDS

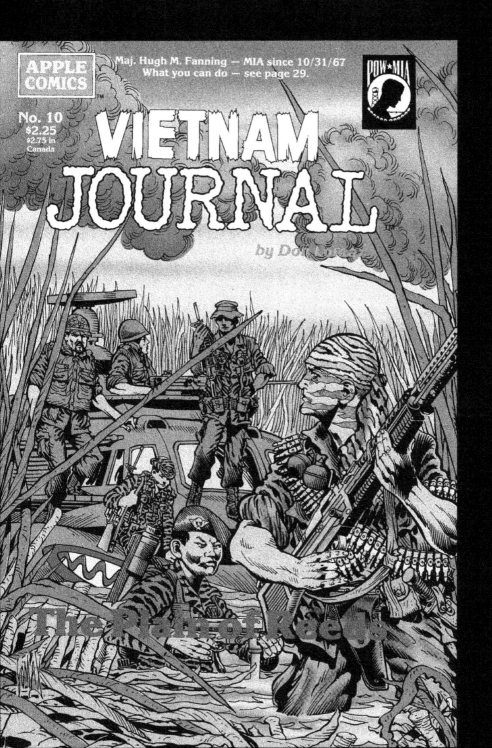

APPLE
COMICS

Maj. Hugh M. Fanning — MIA since 10/31/67
What you can do — see page 29.

POW★MIA

No. 10
$2.25
$2.75 in
Canada

VIETNAM
JOURNAL

by Don Lomax

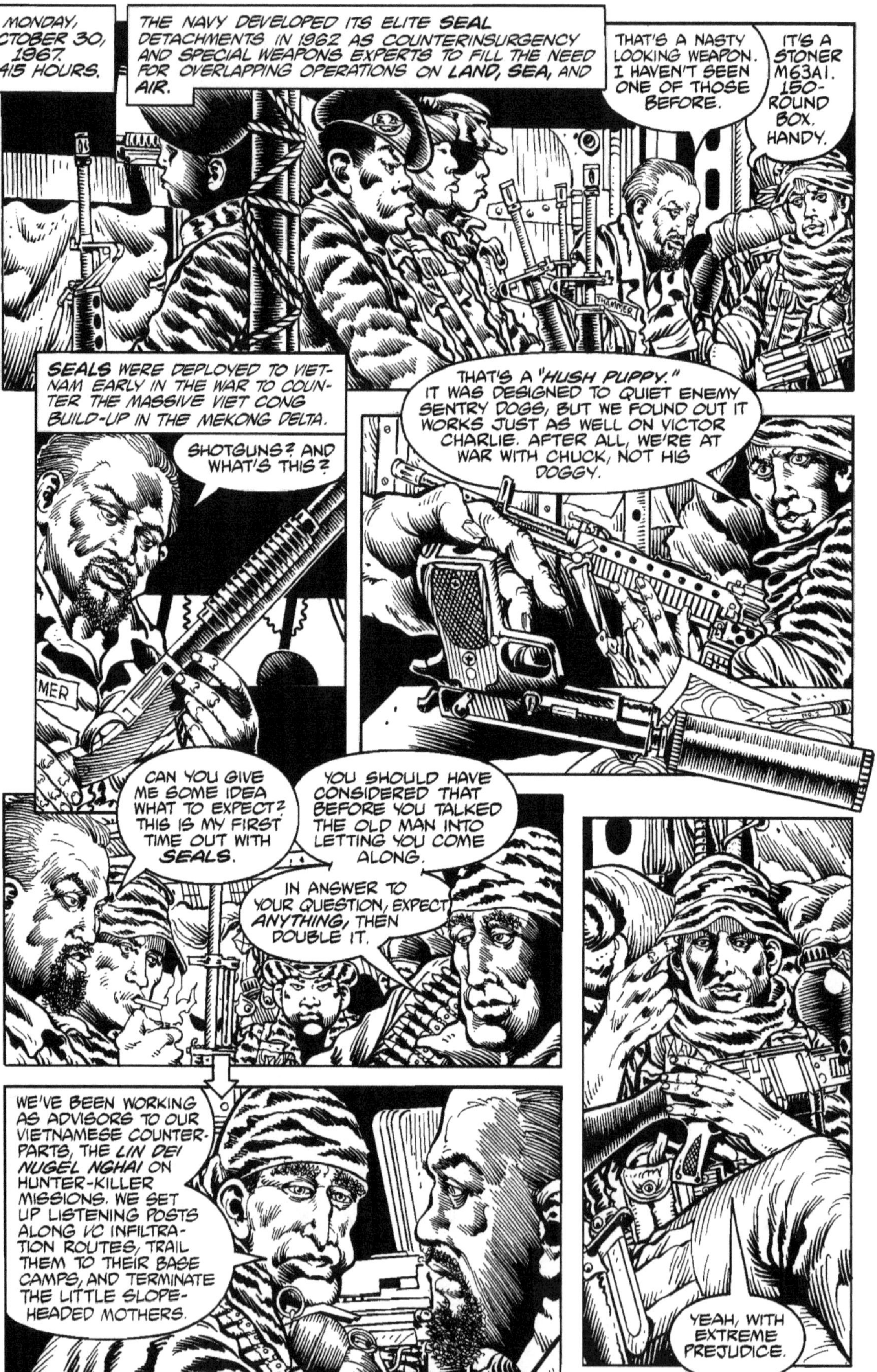
MONDAY, OCTOBER 30, 1967. 0415 HOURS.
THE NAVY DEVELOPED ITS ELITE SEAL DETACHMENTS IN 1962 AS COUNTERINSURGENCY AND SPECIAL WEAPONS EXPERTS TO FILL THE NEED FOR OVERLAPPING OPERATIONS ON LAND, SEA, AND AIR.
THAT'S A NASTY LOOKING WEAPON. I HAVEN'T SEEN ONE OF THOSE BEFORE.
IT'S A STONER M63A1. 150-ROUND BOX. HANDY.
SEALS WERE DEPLOYED TO VIETNAM EARLY IN THE WAR TO COUNTER THE MASSIVE VIET CONG BUILD-UP IN THE MEKONG DELTA.
SHOTGUNS? AND WHAT'S THIS?
THAT'S A "HUSH PUPPY." IT WAS DESIGNED TO QUIET ENEMY SENTRY DOGS, BUT WE FOUND OUT IT WORKS JUST AS WELL ON VICTOR CHARLIE. AFTER ALL, WE'RE AT WAR WITH CHUCK, NOT HIS DOGGY.
CAN YOU GIVE ME SOME IDEA WHAT TO EXPECT? THIS IS MY FIRST TIME OUT WITH SEALS.
YOU SHOULD HAVE CONSIDERED THAT BEFORE YOU TALKED THE OLD MAN INTO LETTING YOU COME ALONG.
IN ANSWER TO YOUR QUESTION, EXPECT ANYTHING, THEN DOUBLE IT.
WE'VE BEEN WORKING AS ADVISORS TO OUR VIETNAMESE COUNTERPARTS, THE LIN DEI NUGEL NGHAI ON HUNTER-KILLER MISSIONS. WE SET UP LISTENING POSTS ALONG VC INFILTRATION ROUTES, TRAIL THEM TO THEIR BASE CAMPS, AND TERMINATE THE LITTLE SLOPE-HEADED MOTHERS.
YEAH, WITH EXTREME PREJUDICE.

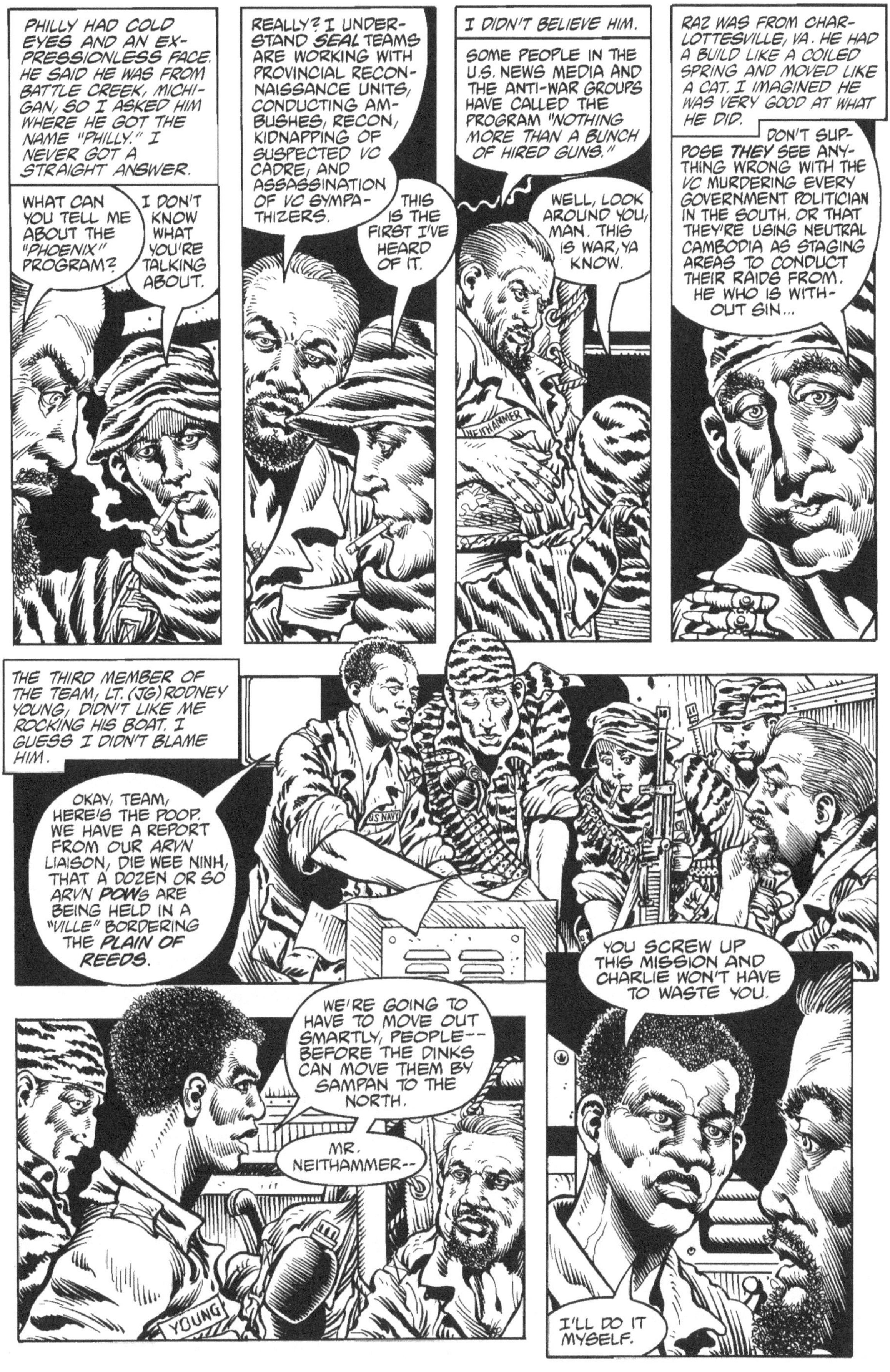

PHILLY HAD COLD EYES AND AN EXPRESSIONLESS FACE. HE SAID HE WAS FROM BATTLE CREEK, MICHIGAN, SO I ASKED HIM WHERE HE GOT THE NAME "PHILLY." I NEVER GOT A STRAIGHT ANSWER.
WHAT CAN YOU TELL ME ABOUT THE "PHOENIX" PROGRAM?
I DON'T KNOW WHAT YOU'RE TALKING ABOUT.
REALLY? I UNDERSTAND SEAL TEAMS ARE WORKING WITH PROVINCIAL RECONNAISSANCE UNITS, CONDUCTING AMBUSHES, RECON, KIDNAPPING OF SUSPECTED VC CADRE, AND ASSASSINATION OF VC SYMPATHIZERS.
THIS IS THE FIRST I'VE HEARD OF IT.
I DIDN'T BELIEVE HIM.
SOME PEOPLE IN THE U.S. NEWS MEDIA AND THE ANTI-WAR GROUPS HAVE CALLED THE PROGRAM "NOTHING MORE THAN A BUNCH OF HIRED GUNS."
WELL, LOOK AROUND YOU, MAN. THIS IS WAR, YA KNOW.
RAZ WAS FROM CHARLOTTESVILLE, VA. HE HAD A BUILD LIKE A COILED SPRING AND MOVED LIKE A CAT. I IMAGINED HE WAS VERY GOOD AT WHAT HE DID.
DON'T SUPPOSE THEY SEE ANYTHING WRONG WITH THE VC MURDERING EVERY GOVERNMENT POLITICIAN IN THE SOUTH. OR THAT THEY'RE USING NEUTRAL CAMBODIA AS STAGING AREAS TO CONDUCT THEIR RAIDS FROM. HE WHO IS WITHOUT SIN...
NEITHAMMER
THE THIRD MEMBER OF THE TEAM, LT. (JG) RODNEY YOUNG, DIDN'T LIKE ME ROCKING HIS BOAT. I GUESS I DIDN'T BLAME HIM.
OKAY, TEAM, HERE'S THE POOP. WE HAVE A REPORT FROM OUR ARVN LIAISON, DIE WEE NINH, THAT A DOZEN OR SO ARVN POWs ARE BEING HELD IN A "VILLE" BORDERING THE PLAIN OF REEDS.
US NAVY
WE'RE GOING TO HAVE TO MOVE OUT SMARTLY, PEOPLE-- BEFORE THE DINKS CAN MOVE THEM BY SAMPAN TO THE NORTH.
MR. NEITHAMMER--
YOUNG
YOU SCREW UP THIS MISSION AND CHARLIE WON'T HAVE TO WASTE YOU.
I'LL DO IT MYSELF.

VIETNAM JOURNAL™

the PLAIN OF REEDS

STORY AND ART DON LOMAX
LETTERER CLEM ROBINS
EDITOR HILARY HUGHES

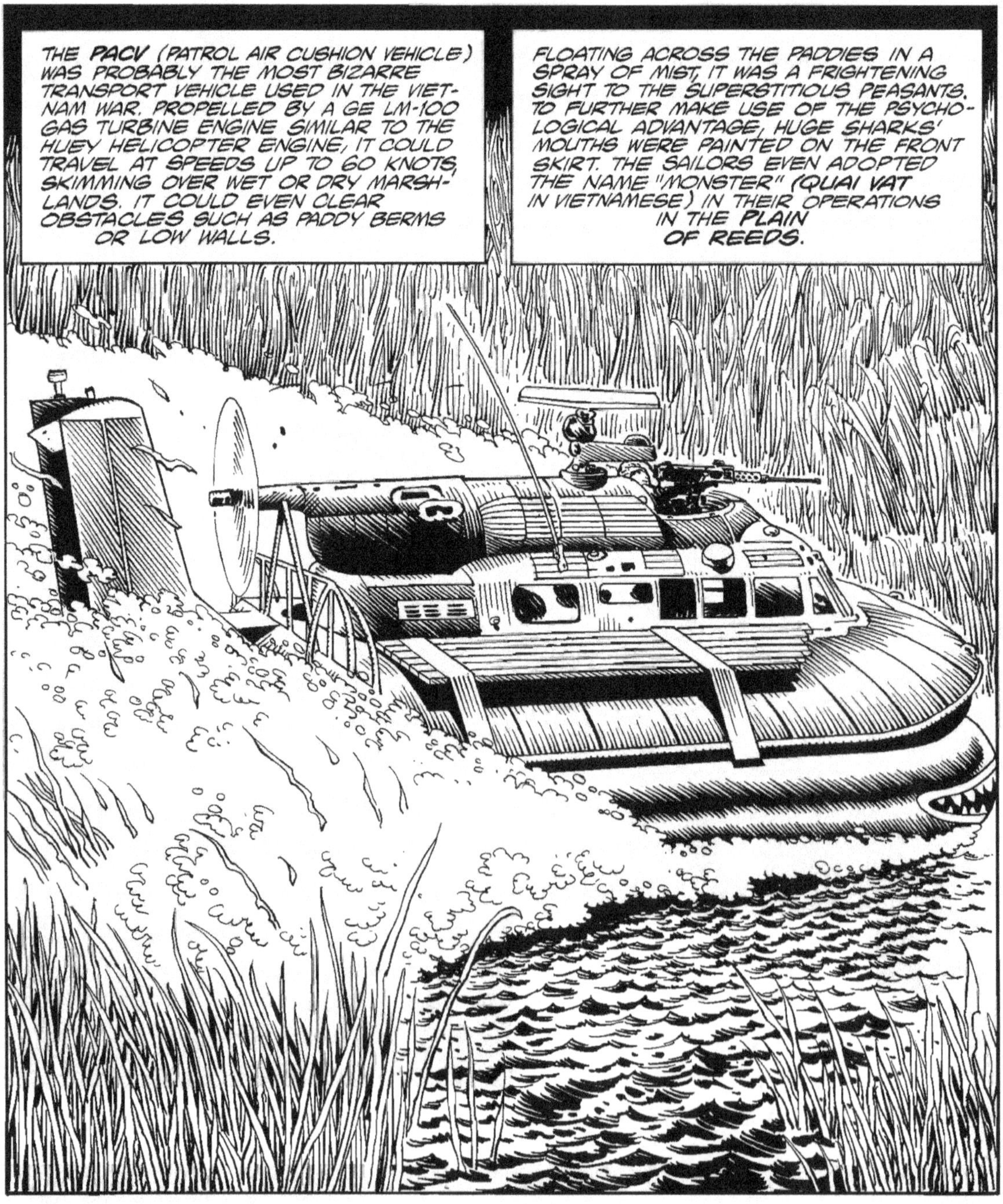
THE PACV (PATROL AIR CUSHION VEHICLE) WAS PROBABLY THE MOST BIZARRE TRANSPORT VEHICLE USED IN THE VIETNAM WAR. PROPELLED BY A GE LM-100 GAS TURBINE ENGINE SIMILAR TO THE HUEY HELICOPTER ENGINE, IT COULD TRAVEL AT SPEEDS UP TO 60 KNOTS, SKIMMING OVER WET OR DRY MARSHLANDS. IT COULD EVEN CLEAR OBSTACLES SUCH AS PADDY BERMS OR LOW WALLS.
FLOATING ACROSS THE PADDIES IN A SPRAY OF MIST, IT WAS A FRIGHTENING SIGHT TO THE SUPERSTITIOUS PEASANTS. TO FURTHER MAKE USE OF THE PSYCHOLOGICAL ADVANTAGE, HUGE SHARKS' MOUTHS WERE PAINTED ON THE FRONT SKIRT. THE SAILORS EVEN ADOPTED THE NAME "MONSTER" (QUAI VAT IN VIETNAMESE) IN THEIR OPERATIONS IN THE PLAIN OF REEDS.

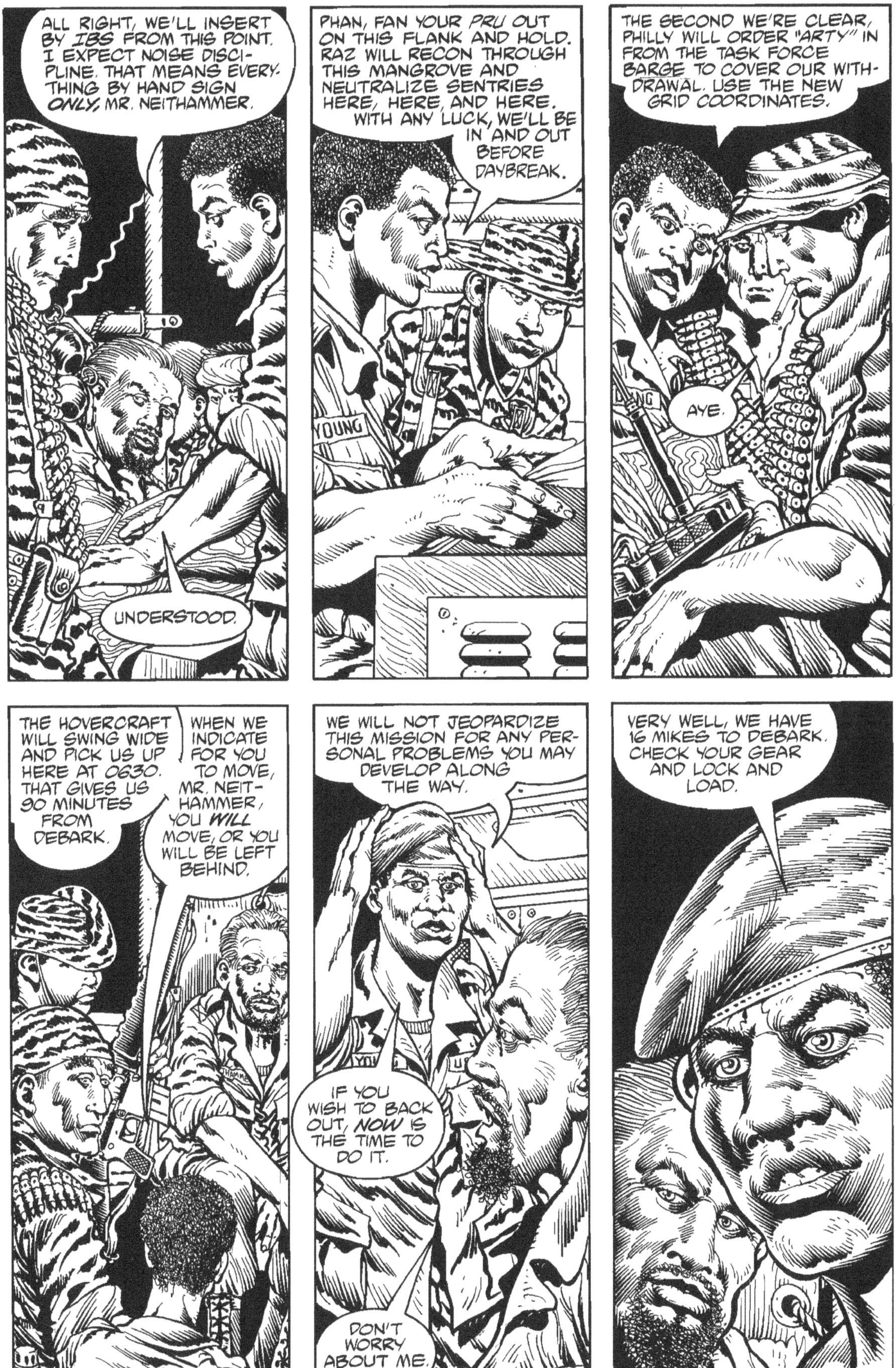
ALL RIGHT, WE'LL INSERT BY IBS FROM THIS POINT. I EXPECT NOISE DISCIPLINE. THAT MEANS EVERYTHING BY HAND SIGN ONLY, MR. NEITHAMMER.
UNDERSTOOD.
PHAN, FAN YOUR PRU OUT ON THIS FLANK AND HOLD. RAZ WILL RECON THROUGH THIS MANGROVE AND NEUTRALIZE SENTRIES HERE, HERE, AND HERE.
WITH ANY LUCK, WE'LL BE IN AND OUT BEFORE DAYBREAK.
YOUNG
THE SECOND WE'RE CLEAR, PHILLY WILL ORDER "ARTY" IN FROM THE TASK FORCE BARGE TO COVER OUR WITHDRAWAL. USE THE NEW GRID COORDINATES.
AYE.
THE HOVERCRAFT WILL SWING WIDE AND PICK US UP HERE AT 0630. THAT GIVES US 90 MINUTES FROM DEBARK.
WHEN WE INDICATE FOR YOU TO MOVE, MR. NEITHAMMER, YOU WILL MOVE, OR YOU WILL BE LEFT BEHIND.
WE WILL NOT JEOPARDIZE THIS MISSION FOR ANY PERSONAL PROBLEMS YOU MAY DEVELOP ALONG THE WAY.
IF YOU WISH TO BACK OUT, NOW IS THE TIME TO DO IT.
DON'T WORRY ABOUT ME.
VERY WELL, WE HAVE 16 MIKES TO DEBARK. CHECK YOUR GEAR AND LOCK AND LOAD.

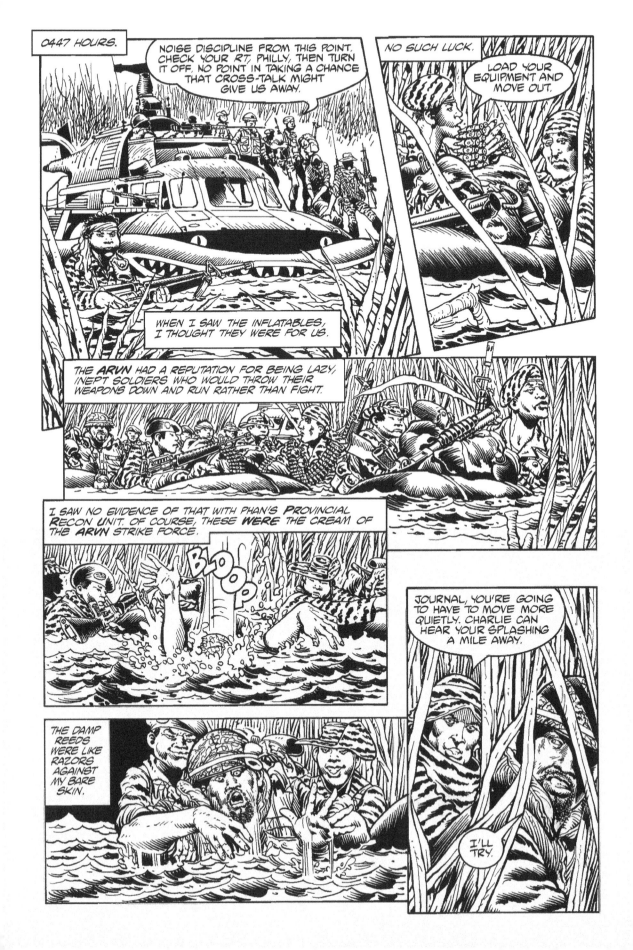

0447 HOURS.

NOISE DISCIPLINE FROM THIS POINT. CHECK YOUR *RT*, PHILLY, THEN TURN IT OFF. NO POINT IN TAKING A CHANCE THAT CROSS-TALK MIGHT GIVE US AWAY.

NO SUCH LUCK.

LOAD YOUR EQUIPMENT AND MOVE OUT.

WHEN I SAW THE INFLATABLES, I THOUGHT THEY WERE FOR US.

THE *ARVN* HAD A REPUTATION FOR BEING LAZY, INEPT SOLDIERS WHO WOULD THROW THEIR WEAPONS DOWN AND RUN RATHER THAN FIGHT.

I SAW NO EVIDENCE OF THAT WITH PHAN'S *PROVINCIAL RECON UNIT.* OF COURSE, THESE *WERE* THE CREAM OF THE *ARVN* STRIKE FORCE.

BLOOP

JOURNAL, YOU'RE GOING TO HAVE TO MOVE MORE QUIETLY. CHARLIE CAN HEAR YOUR SPLASHING A MILE AWAY.

THE DAMP REEDS WERE LIKE RAZORS AGAINST MY BARE SKIN.

I'LL TRY.

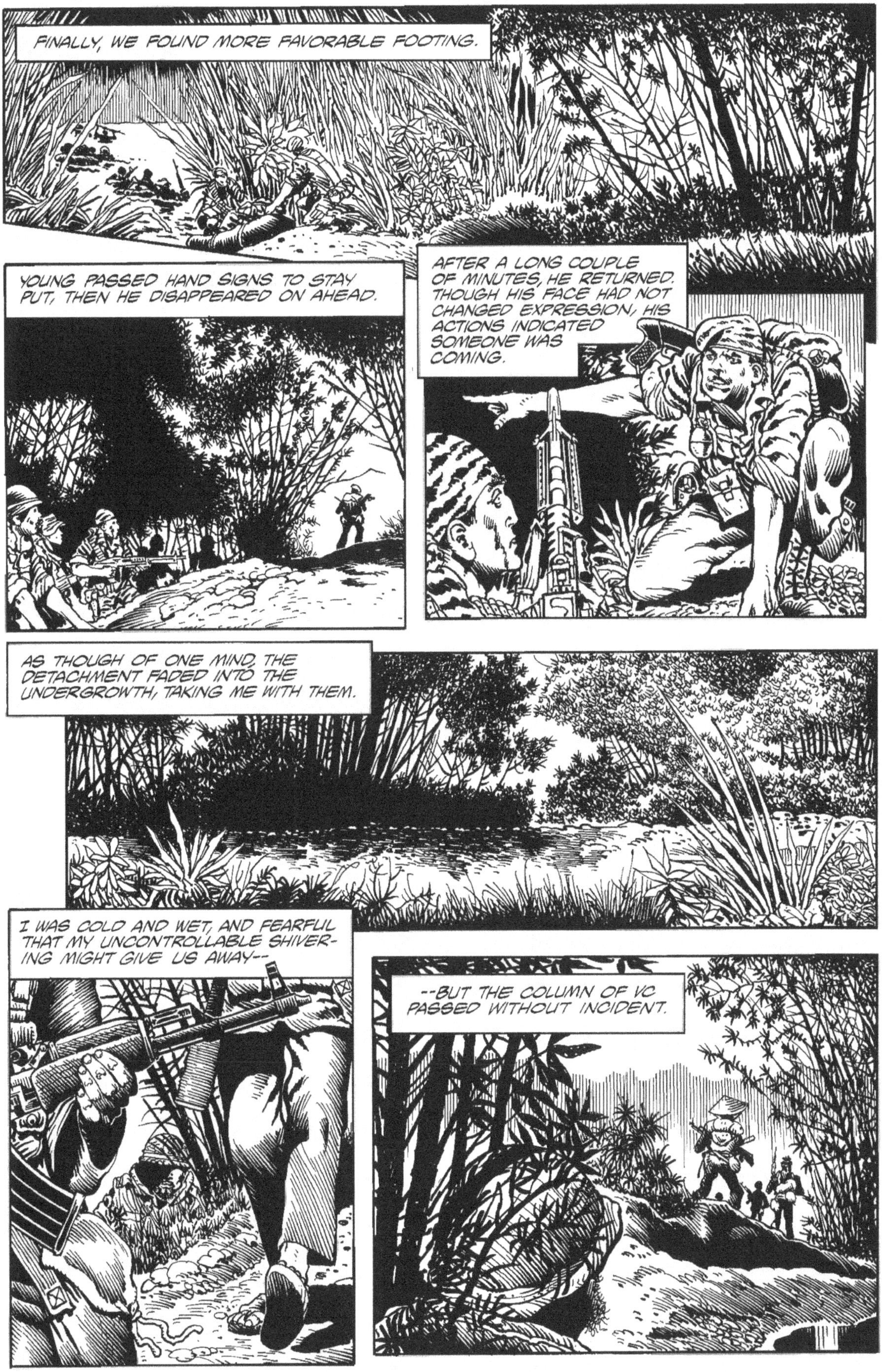
FINALLY, WE FOUND MORE FAVORABLE FOOTING.
YOUNG PASSED HAND SIGNS TO STAY PUT, THEN HE DISAPPEARED ON AHEAD.
AFTER A LONG COUPLE OF MINUTES, HE RETURNED. THOUGH HIS FACE HAD NOT CHANGED EXPRESSION, HIS ACTIONS INDICATED SOMEONE WAS COMING.
AS THOUGH OF ONE MIND, THE DETACHMENT FADED INTO THE UNDERGROWTH, TAKING ME WITH THEM.
I WAS COLD AND WET, AND FEARFUL THAT MY UNCONTROLLABLE SHIVERING MIGHT GIVE US AWAY--
--BUT THE COLUMN OF VC PASSED WITHOUT INCIDENT.

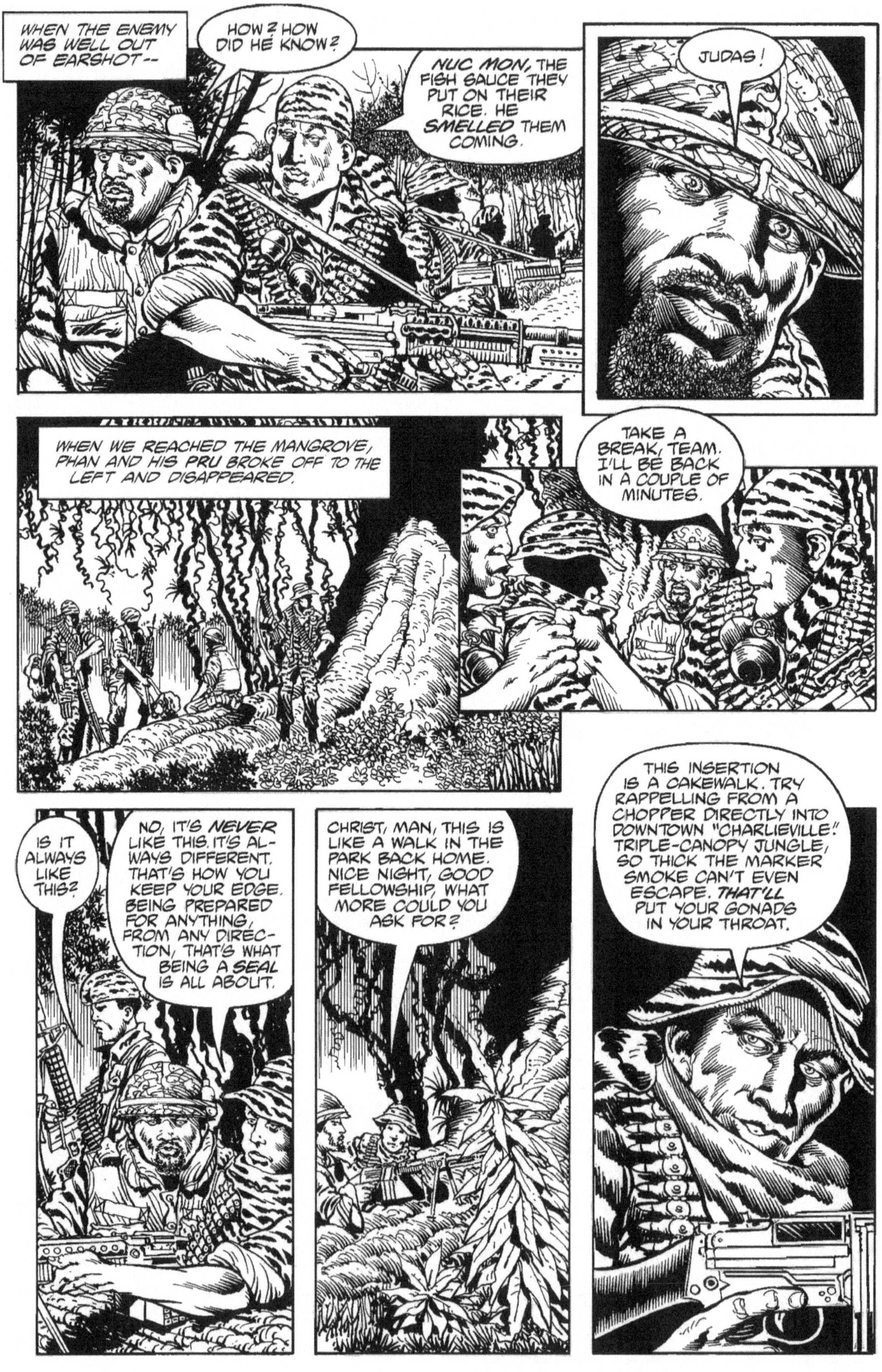
WHEN THE ENEMY WAS WELL OUT OF EARSHOT--
HOW? HOW DID HE KNOW?
NUC MON, THE FISH SAUCE THEY PUT ON THEIR RICE. HE SMELLED THEM COMING.
JUDAS!
WHEN WE REACHED THE MANGROVE, PHAN AND HIS PRU BROKE OFF TO THE LEFT AND DISAPPEARED.
TAKE A BREAK, TEAM. I'LL BE BACK IN A COUPLE OF MINUTES.
IS IT ALWAYS LIKE THIS?
NO, IT'S NEVER LIKE THIS. IT'S ALWAYS DIFFERENT. THAT'S HOW YOU KEEP YOUR EDGE. BEING PREPARED FOR ANYTHING, FROM ANY DIRECTION, THAT'S WHAT BEING A SEAL IS ALL ABOUT.
CHRIST, MAN, THIS IS LIKE A WALK IN THE PARK BACK HOME. NICE NIGHT, GOOD FELLOWSHIP, WHAT MORE COULD YOU ASK FOR?
THIS INSERTION IS A CAKEWALK. TRY RAPPELLING FROM A CHOPPER DIRECTLY INTO DOWNTOWN "CHARLIEVILLE." TRIPLE-CANOPY JUNGLE, SO THICK THE MARKER SMOKE CAN'T EVEN ESCAPE. THAT'LL PUT YOUR GONADS IN YOUR THROAT.

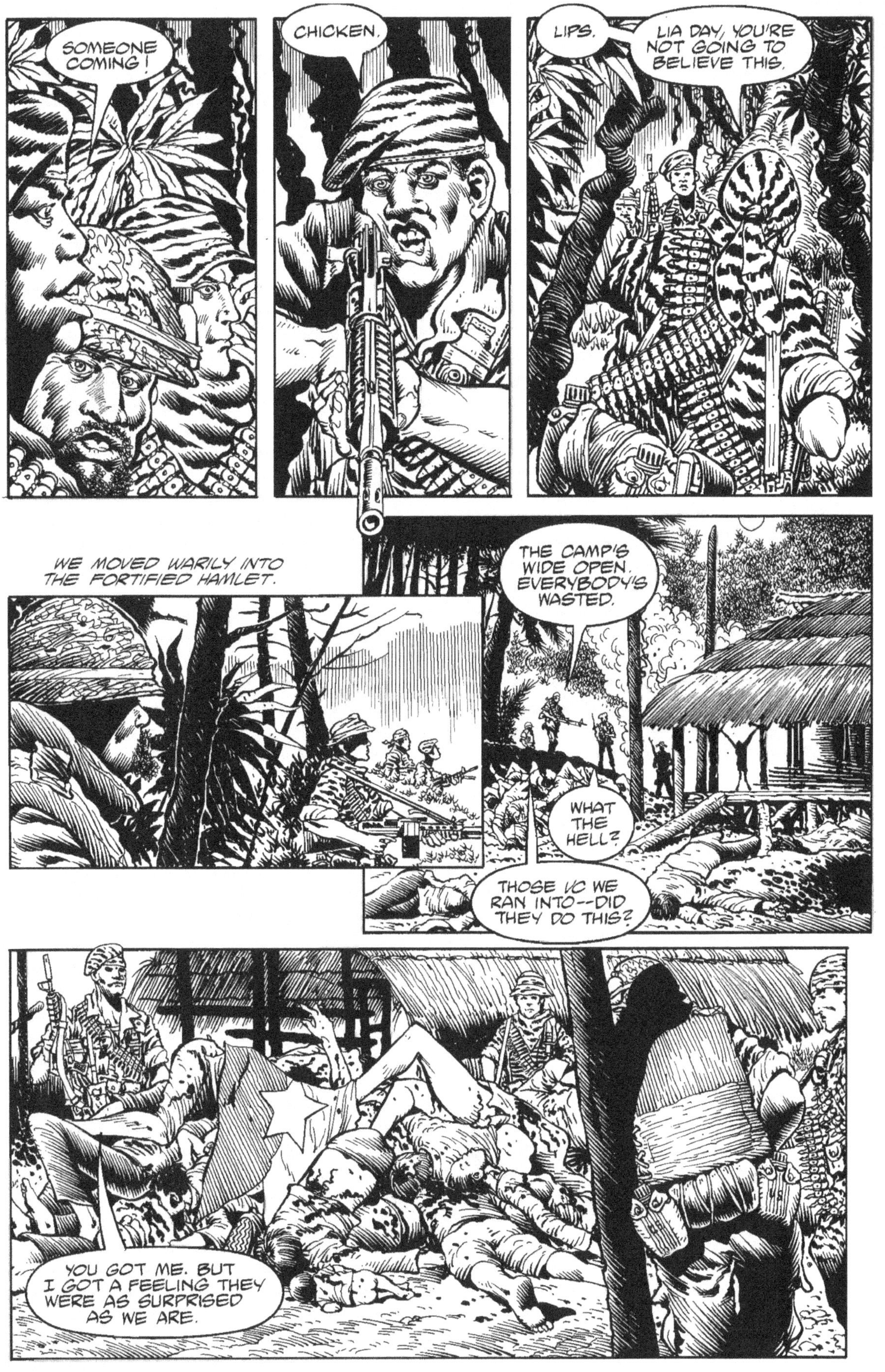
SOMEONE COMING!
CHICKEN.
LIPS.
LIA DAY, YOU'RE NOT GOING TO BELIEVE THIS.
WE MOVED WARILY INTO THE FORTIFIED HAMLET.
THE CAMP'S WIDE OPEN. EVERYBODY'S WASTED.
WHAT THE HELL?
THOSE VC WE RAN INTO--DID THEY DO THIS?
YOU GOT ME. BUT I GOT A FEELING THEY WERE AS SURPRISED AS WE ARE.

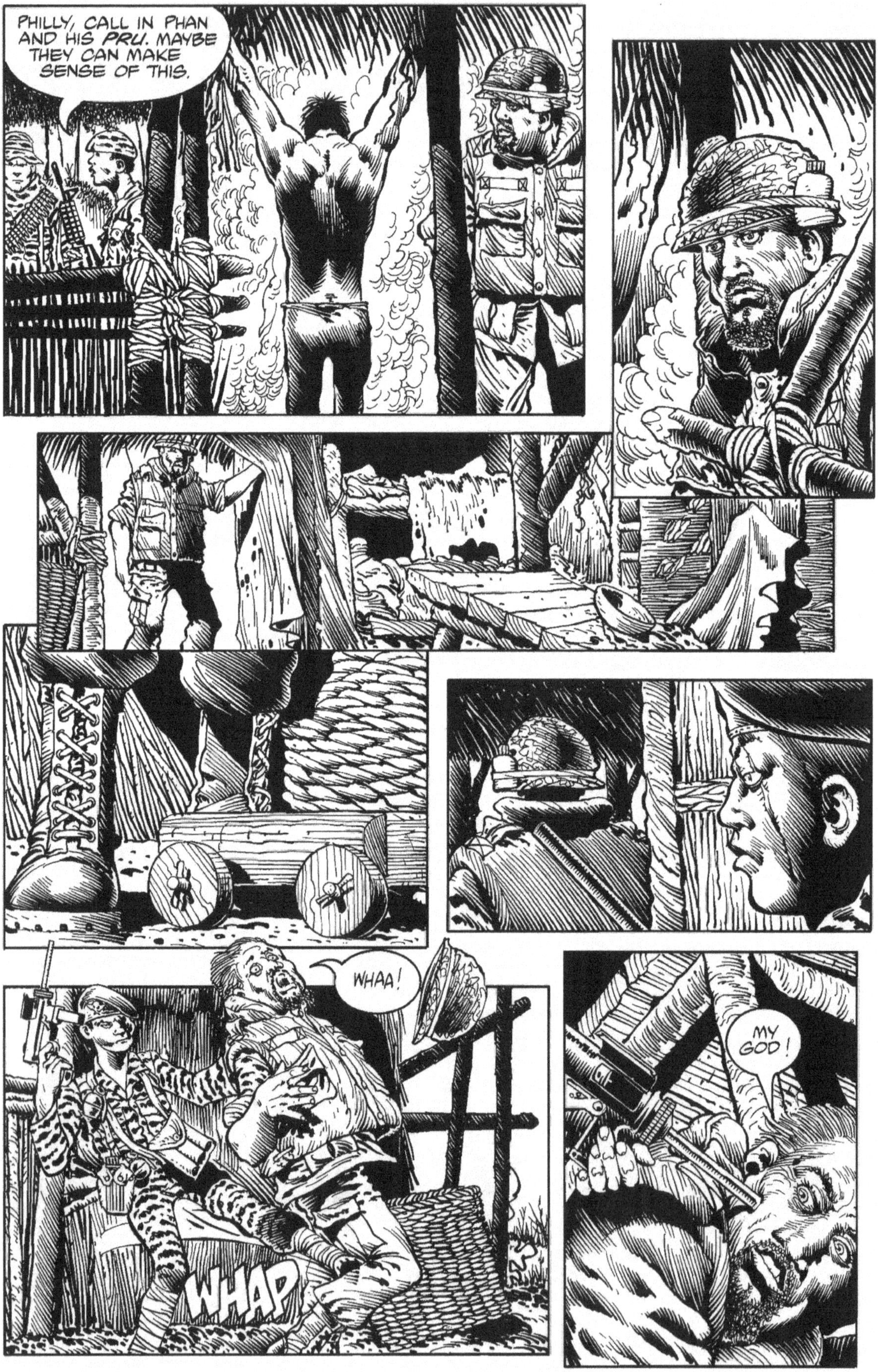
PHILLY, CALL IN PHAN AND HIS PRU. MAYBE THEY CAN MAKE SENSE OF THIS.
WHAA!
WHAP
MY GOD!

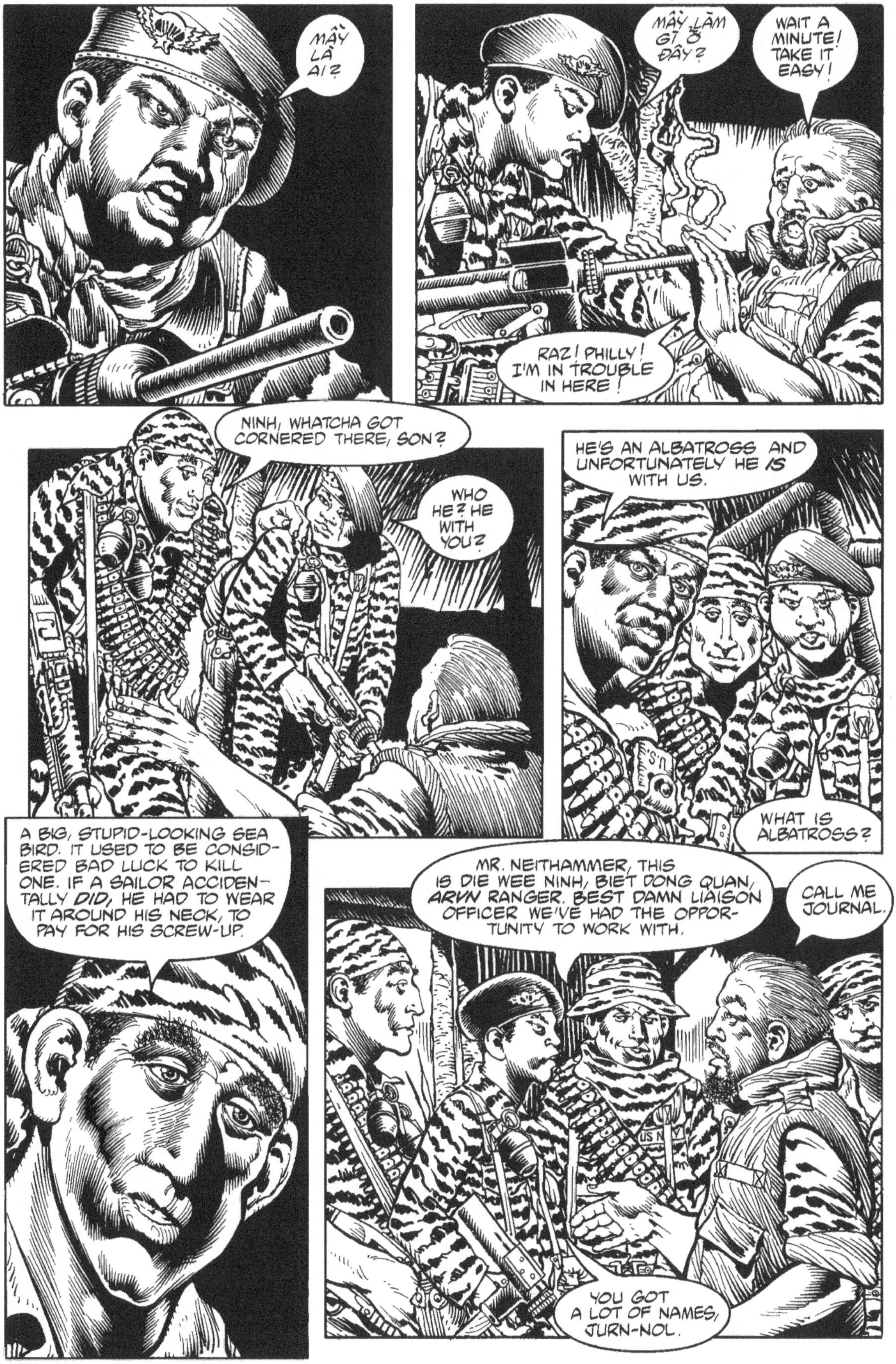
MẦY LÀ AI?
MẦY LÀM GÌ Ở ĐÂY?
WAIT A MINUTE! TAKE IT EASY!
RAZ! PHILLY! I'M IN TROUBLE IN HERE!
NINH, WHATCHA GOT CORNERED THERE, SON?
WHO HE? HE WITH YOU?
HE'S AN ALBATROSS AND UNFORTUNATELY HE *IS* WITH US.
WHAT IS ALBATROSS?
A BIG, STUPID-LOOKING SEA BIRD. IT USED TO BE CONSIDERED BAD LUCK TO KILL ONE. IF A SAILOR ACCIDENTALLY *DID*, HE HAD TO WEAR IT AROUND HIS NECK, TO PAY FOR HIS SCREW-UP.
MR. NEITHAMMER, THIS IS DIE WEE NINH, BIET DONG QUAN, *ARVN* RANGER. BEST DAMN LIAISON OFFICER WE'VE HAD THE OPPORTUNITY TO WORK WITH.
CALL ME JOURNAL.
YOU GOT A LOT OF NAMES, JURN-NOL.

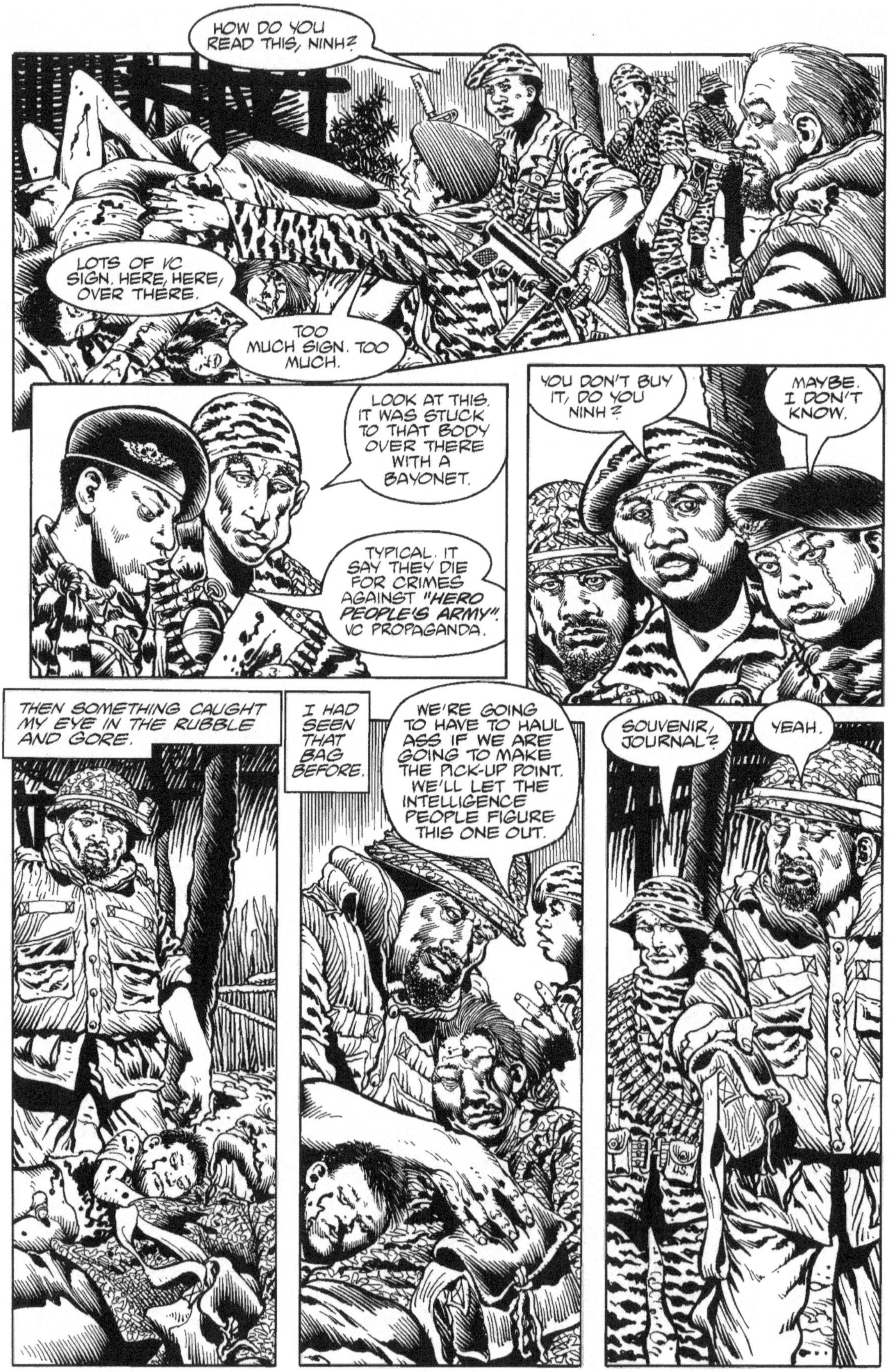
HOW DO YOU READ THIS, NINH?
LOTS OF VC SIGN. HERE, HERE, OVER THERE.
TOO MUCH SIGN. TOO MUCH.
LOOK AT THIS. IT WAS STUCK TO THAT BODY OVER THERE WITH A BAYONET.
TYPICAL. IT SAY THEY DIE FOR CRIMES AGAINST "HERO PEOPLE'S ARMY". VC PROPAGANDA.
YOU DON'T BUY IT, DO YOU NINH?
MAYBE. I DON'T KNOW.
THEN SOMETHING CAUGHT MY EYE IN THE RUBBLE AND GORE.
I HAD SEEN THAT BAG BEFORE.
WE'RE GOING TO HAVE TO HAUL ASS IF WE ARE GOING TO MAKE THE PICK-UP POINT. WE'LL LET THE INTELLIGENCE PEOPLE FIGURE THIS ONE OUT.
SOUVENIR, JOURNAL?
YEAH.

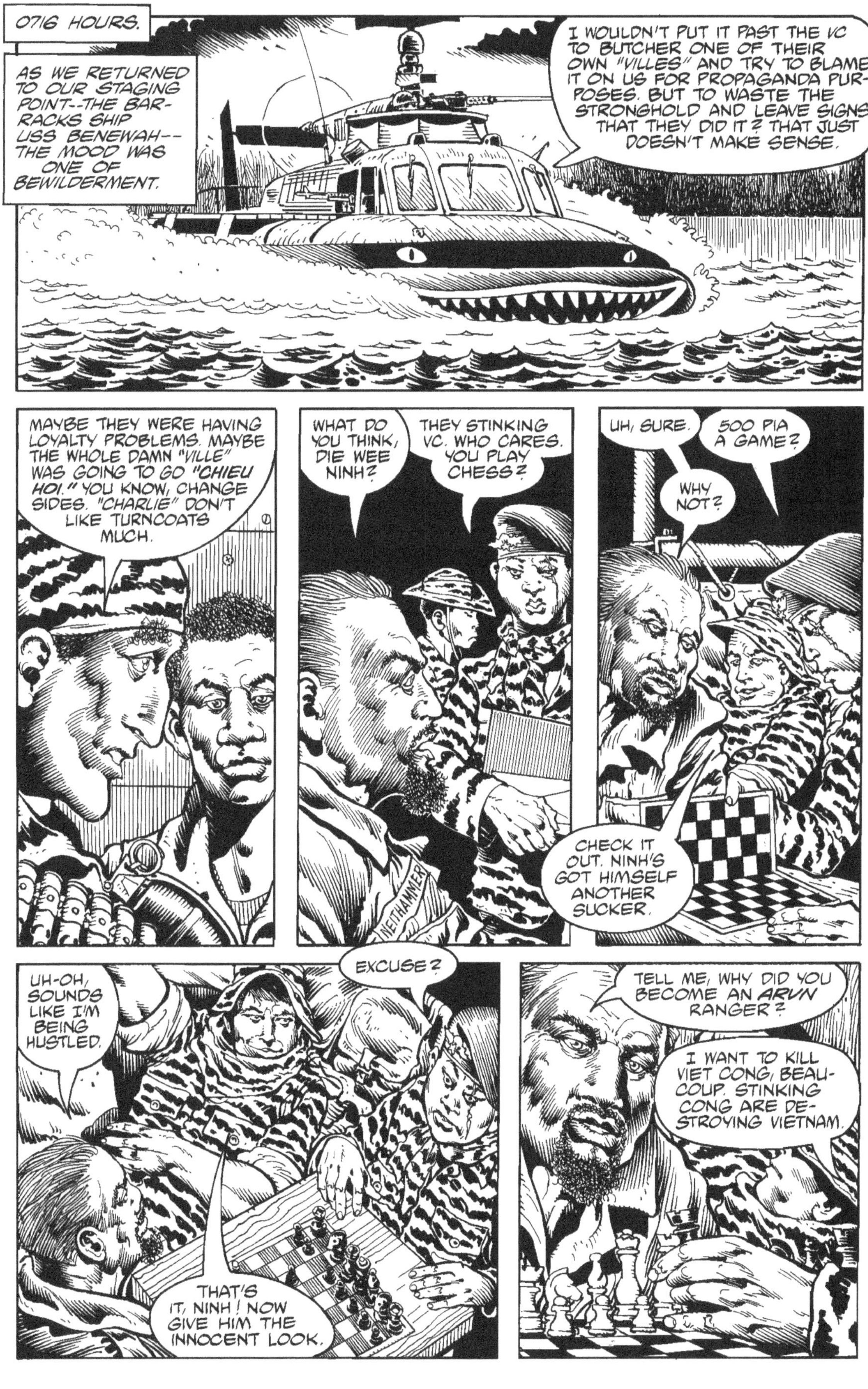
0716 HOURS.
AS WE RETURNED TO OUR STAGING POINT--THE BARRACKS SHIP USS BENEWAH--THE MOOD WAS ONE OF BEWILDERMENT.
I WOULDN'T PUT IT PAST THE VC TO BUTCHER ONE OF THEIR OWN "VILLES" AND TRY TO BLAME IT ON US FOR PROPAGANDA PURPOSES. BUT TO WASTE THE STRONGHOLD AND LEAVE SIGNS THAT THEY DID IT? THAT JUST DOESN'T MAKE SENSE.
MAYBE THEY WERE HAVING LOYALTY PROBLEMS. MAYBE THE WHOLE DAMN "VILLE" WAS GOING TO GO "CHIEU HOI." YOU KNOW, CHANGE SIDES. "CHARLIE" DON'T LIKE TURNCOATS MUCH.
WHAT DO YOU THINK, DIE WEE NINH?
THEY STINKING VC. WHO CARES. YOU PLAY CHESS?
NEITHAMMER
UH, SURE.
500 PIA A GAME?
WHY NOT?
CHECK IT OUT. NINH'S GOT HIMSELF ANOTHER SUCKER.
UH-OH, SOUNDS LIKE I'M BEING HUSTLED.
EXCUSE?
THAT'S IT, NINH! NOW GIVE HIM THE INNOCENT LOOK.
TELL ME, WHY DID YOU BECOME AN ARVN RANGER?
I WANT TO KILL VIET CONG, BEAUCOUP. STINKING CONG ARE DESTROYING VIETNAM.

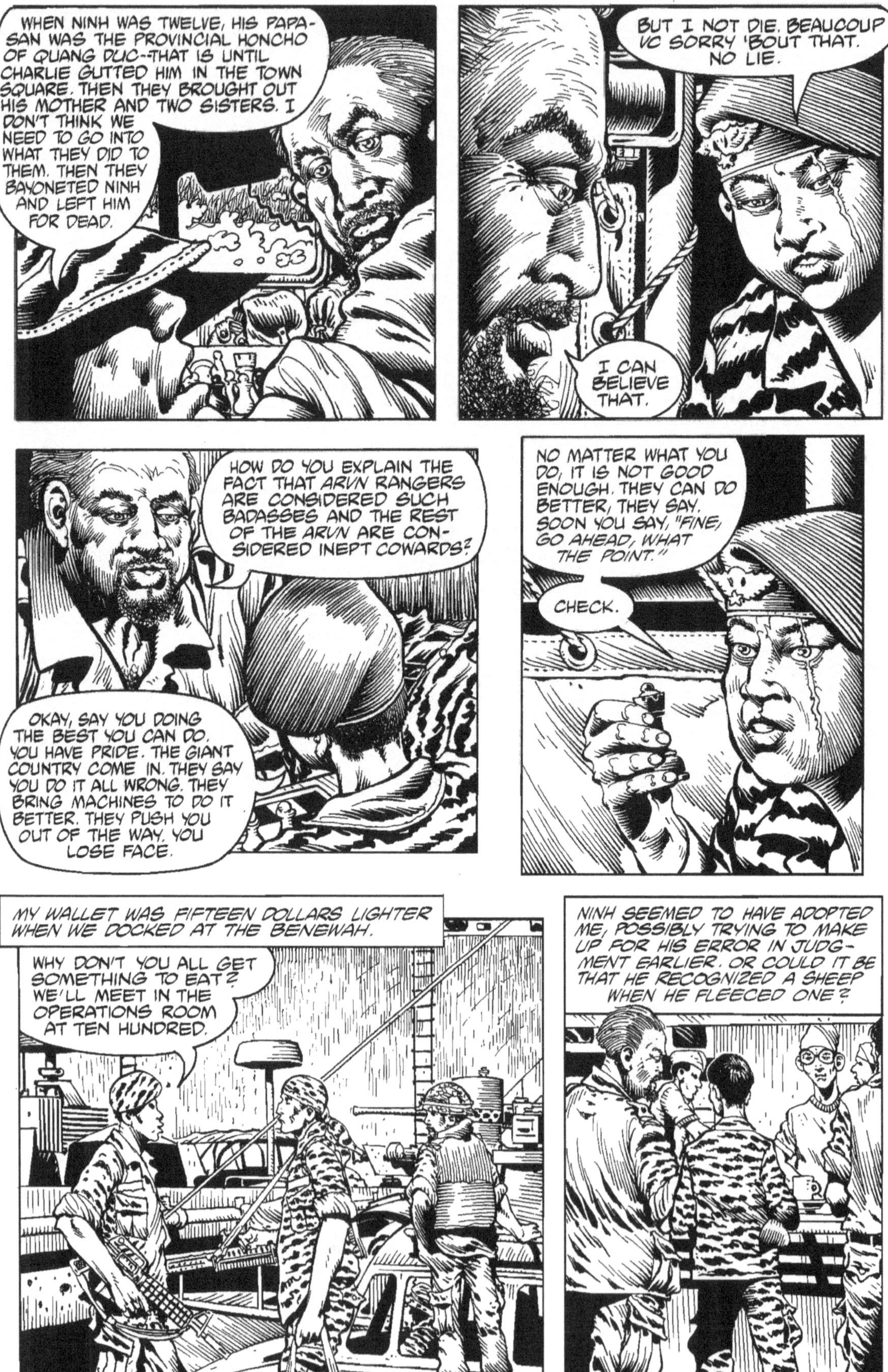
WHEN NINH WAS TWELVE, HIS PAPA-SAN WAS THE PROVINCIAL HONCHO OF QUANG DUC--THAT IS UNTIL CHARLIE GUTTED HIM IN THE TOWN SQUARE. THEN THEY BROUGHT OUT HIS MOTHER AND TWO SISTERS. I DON'T THINK WE NEED TO GO INTO WHAT THEY DID TO THEM. THEN THEY BAYONETED NINH AND LEFT HIM FOR DEAD.
BUT I NOT DIE. BEAUCOUP VC SORRY 'BOUT THAT. NO LIE.
I CAN BELIEVE THAT.
HOW DO YOU EXPLAIN THE FACT THAT ARVN RANGERS ARE CONSIDERED SUCH BADASSES AND THE REST OF THE ARVN ARE CONSIDERED INEPT COWARDS?
OKAY, SAY YOU DOING THE BEST YOU CAN DO. YOU HAVE PRIDE. THE GIANT COUNTRY COME IN. THEY SAY YOU DO IT ALL WRONG. THEY BRING MACHINES TO DO IT BETTER. THEY PUSH YOU OUT OF THE WAY. YOU LOSE FACE.
NO MATTER WHAT YOU DO, IT IS NOT GOOD ENOUGH. THEY CAN DO BETTER, THEY SAY. SOON YOU SAY, "FINE, GO AHEAD, WHAT THE POINT."
CHECK.
MY WALLET WAS FIFTEEN DOLLARS LIGHTER WHEN WE DOCKED AT THE BENEWAH.
WHY DON'T YOU ALL GET SOMETHING TO EAT? WE'LL MEET IN THE OPERATIONS ROOM AT TEN HUNDRED.
NINH SEEMED TO HAVE ADOPTED ME, POSSIBLY TRYING TO MAKE UP FOR HIS ERROR IN JUDGMENT EARLIER. OR COULD IT BE THAT HE RECOGNIZED A SHEEP WHEN HE FLEECED ONE?

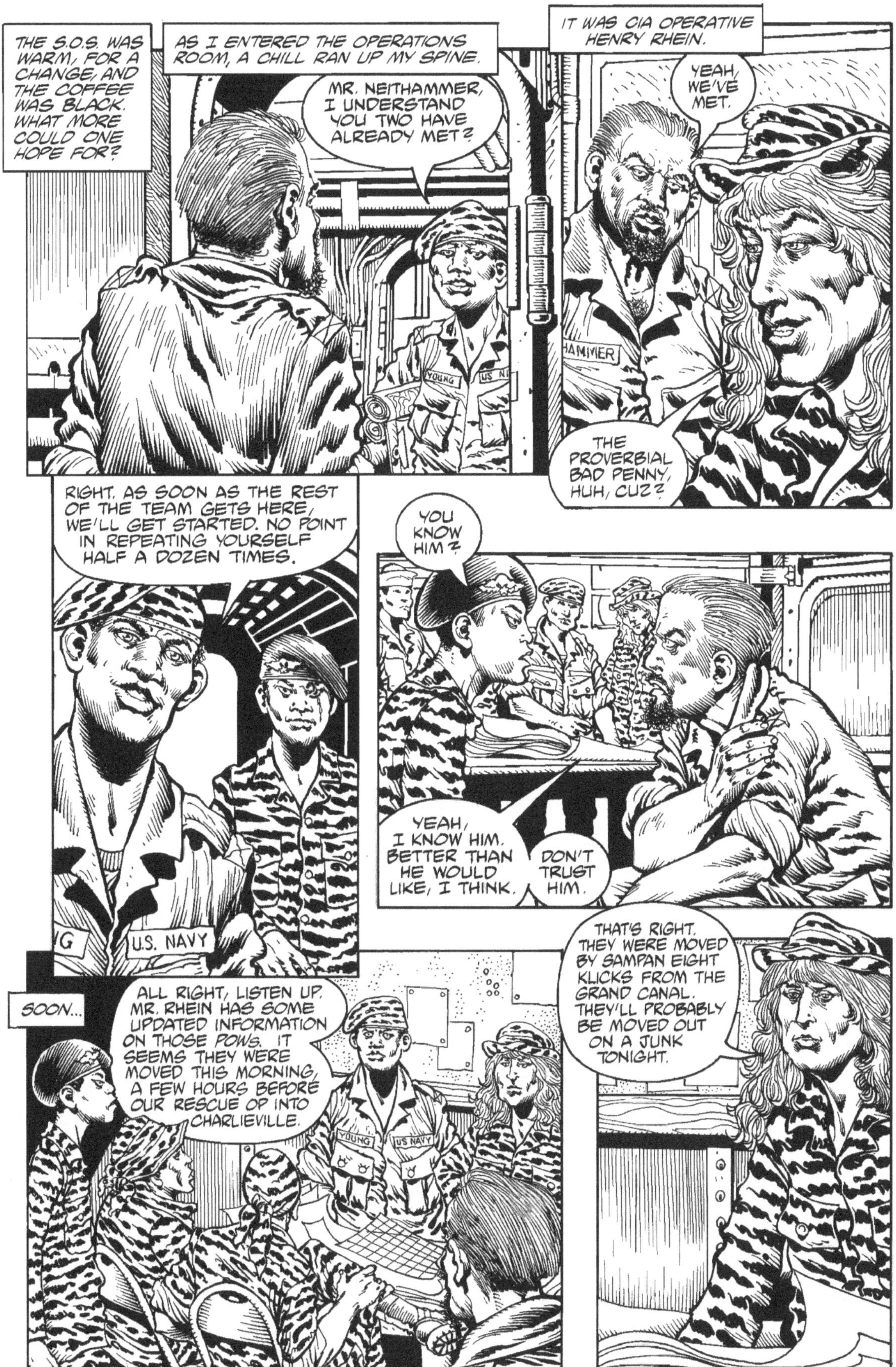
THE S.O.S. WAS WARM, FOR A CHANGE, AND THE COFFEE WAS BLACK. WHAT MORE COULD ONE HOPE FOR?
AS I ENTERED THE OPERATIONS ROOM, A CHILL RAN UP MY SPINE.
MR. NEITHAMMER, I UNDERSTAND YOU TWO HAVE ALREADY MET?
YOUNG
US N
IT WAS CIA OPERATIVE HENRY RHEIN.
YEAH, WE'VE MET.
HAMMER
THE PROVERBIAL BAD PENNY, HUH, CUZ?
RIGHT. AS SOON AS THE REST OF THE TEAM GETS HERE, WE'LL GET STARTED. NO POINT IN REPEATING YOURSELF HALF A DOZEN TIMES.
G
U.S. NAVY
YOU KNOW HIM?
YEAH, I KNOW HIM. BETTER THAN HE WOULD LIKE, I THINK.
DON'T TRUST HIM.
SOON...
ALL RIGHT, LISTEN UP. MR. RHEIN HAS SOME UPDATED INFORMATION ON THOSE POWS. IT SEEMS THEY WERE MOVED THIS MORNING, A FEW HOURS BEFORE OUR RESCUE OP INTO CHARLIEVILLE.
YOUNG
US NAVY
THAT'S RIGHT. THEY WERE MOVED BY SAMPAN EIGHT KLICKS FROM THE GRAND CANAL. THEY'LL PROBABLY BE MOVED OUT ON A JUNK TONIGHT.

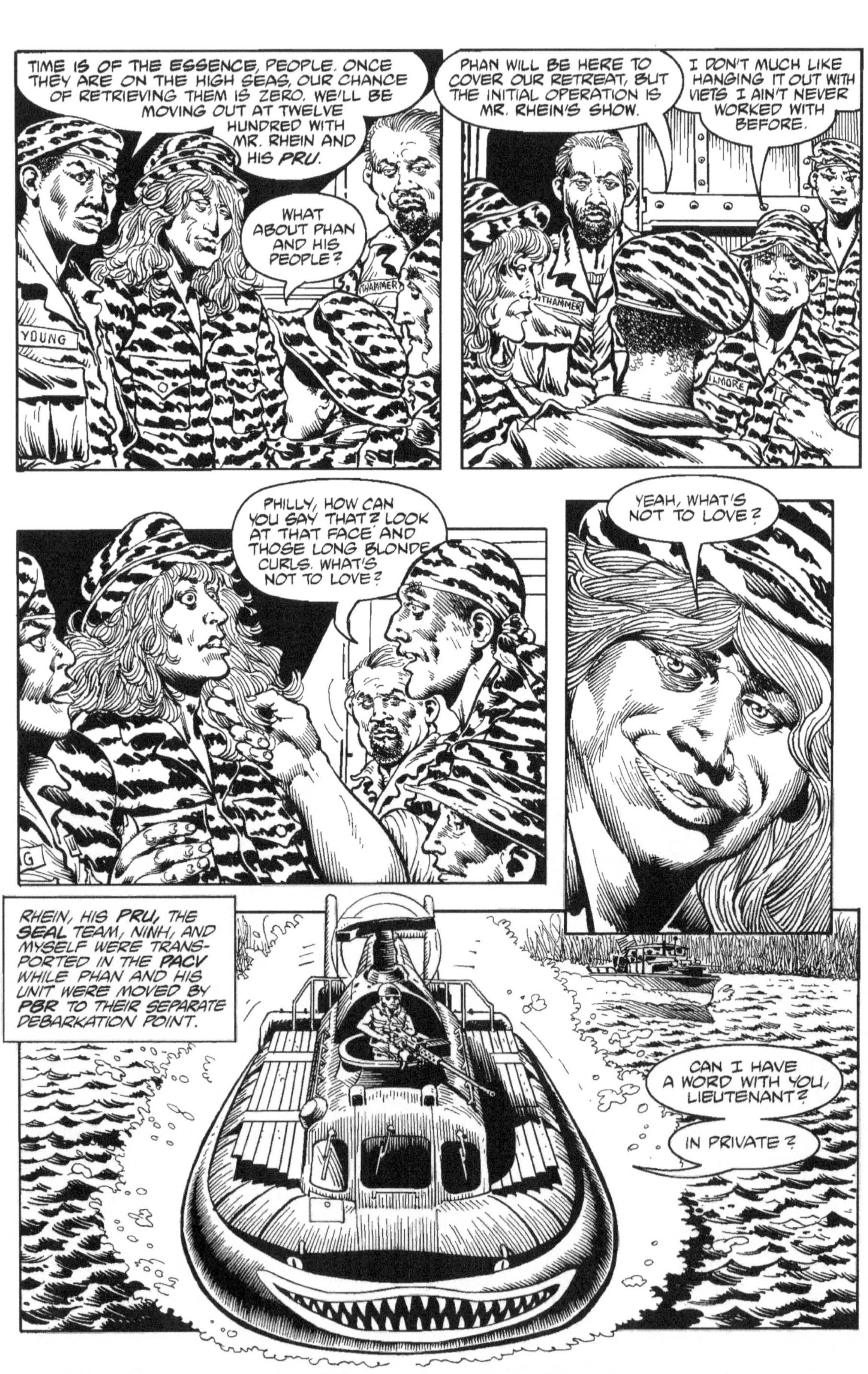

TIME IS OF THE ESSENCE, PEOPLE. ONCE THEY ARE ON THE HIGH SEAS, OUR CHANCE OF RETRIEVING THEM IS ZERO. WE'LL BE MOVING OUT AT TWELVE HUNDRED WITH MR. RHEIN AND HIS PRU.
WHAT ABOUT PHAN AND HIS PEOPLE?
YOUNG
THAMMER
PHAN WILL BE HERE TO COVER OUR RETREAT, BUT THE INITIAL OPERATION IS MR. RHEIN'S SHOW.
I DON'T MUCH LIKE HANGING IT OUT WITH VIETS I AIN'T NEVER WORKED WITH BEFORE.
THAMMER
PHILLY, HOW CAN YOU SAY THAT? LOOK AT THAT FACE AND THOSE LONG BLONDE CURLS. WHAT'S NOT TO LOVE?
YEAH, WHAT'S NOT TO LOVE?
RHEIN, HIS PRU, THE SEAL TEAM, NINH, AND MYSELF WERE TRANSPORTED IN THE PACV WHILE PHAN AND HIS UNIT WERE MOVED BY PBR TO THEIR SEPARATE DEBARKATION POINT.
CAN I HAVE A WORD WITH YOU, LIEUTENANT?
IN PRIVATE?

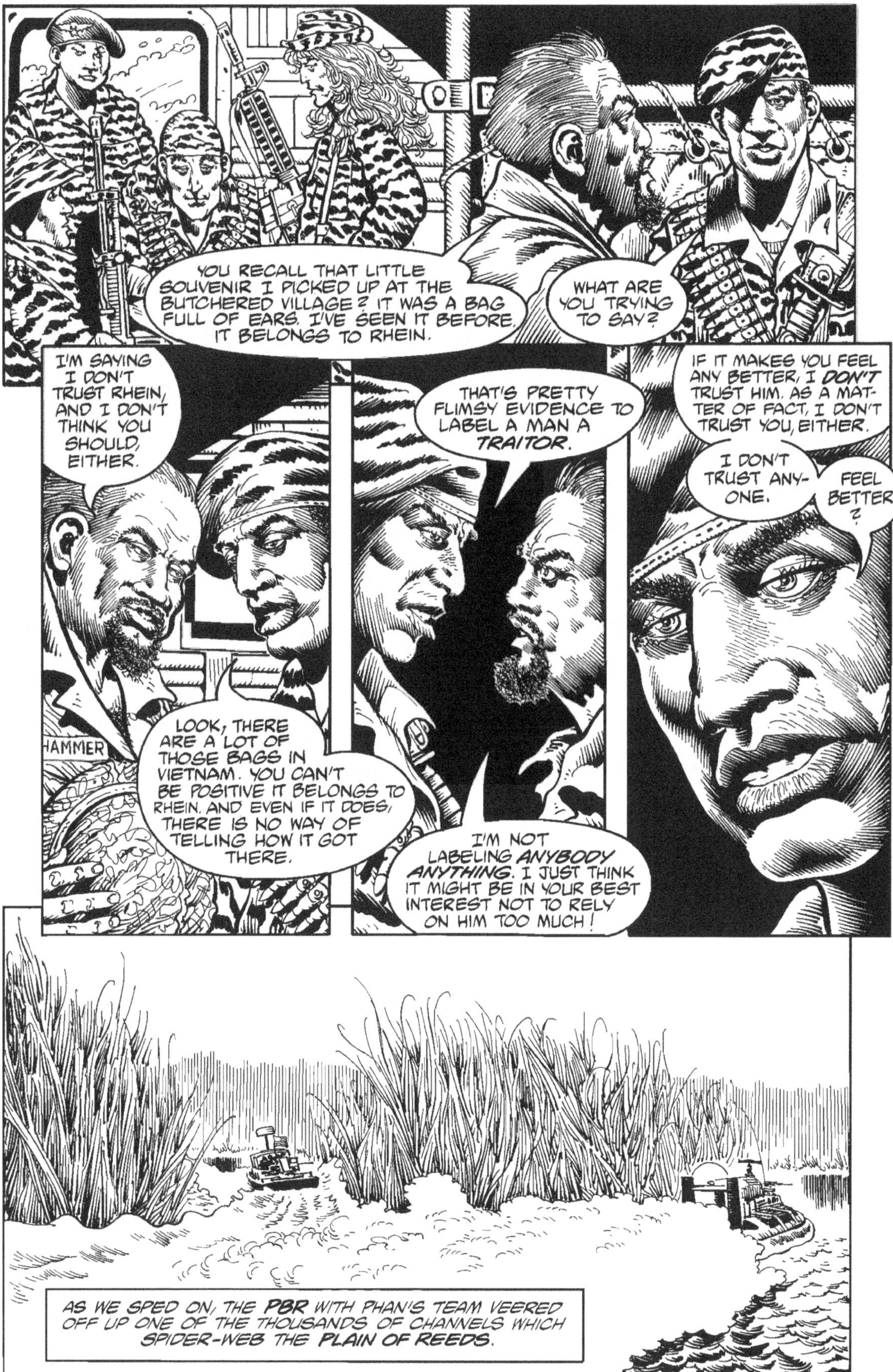
YOU RECALL THAT LITTLE SOUVENIR I PICKED UP AT THE BUTCHERED VILLAGE? IT WAS A BAG FULL OF EARS. I'VE SEEN IT BEFORE. IT BELONGS TO RHEIN.
WHAT ARE YOU TRYING TO SAY?
I'M SAYING I DON'T TRUST RHEIN, AND I DON'T THINK YOU SHOULD, EITHER.
HAMMER
LOOK, THERE ARE A LOT OF THOSE BAGS IN VIETNAM. YOU CAN'T BE POSITIVE IT BELONGS TO RHEIN. AND EVEN IF IT DOES, THERE IS NO WAY OF TELLING HOW IT GOT THERE.
THAT'S PRETTY FLIMSY EVIDENCE TO LABEL A MAN A TRAITOR.
I'M NOT LABELING ANYBODY ANYTHING. I JUST THINK IT MIGHT BE IN YOUR BEST INTEREST NOT TO RELY ON HIM TOO MUCH!
IF IT MAKES YOU FEEL ANY BETTER, I DON'T TRUST HIM. AS A MATTER OF FACT, I DON'T TRUST YOU, EITHER.
I DON'T TRUST ANYONE.
FEEL BETTER?
AS WE SPED ON, THE PBR WITH PHAN'S TEAM VEERED OFF UP ONE OF THE THOUSANDS OF CHANNELS WHICH SPIDER-WEB THE PLAIN OF REEDS.

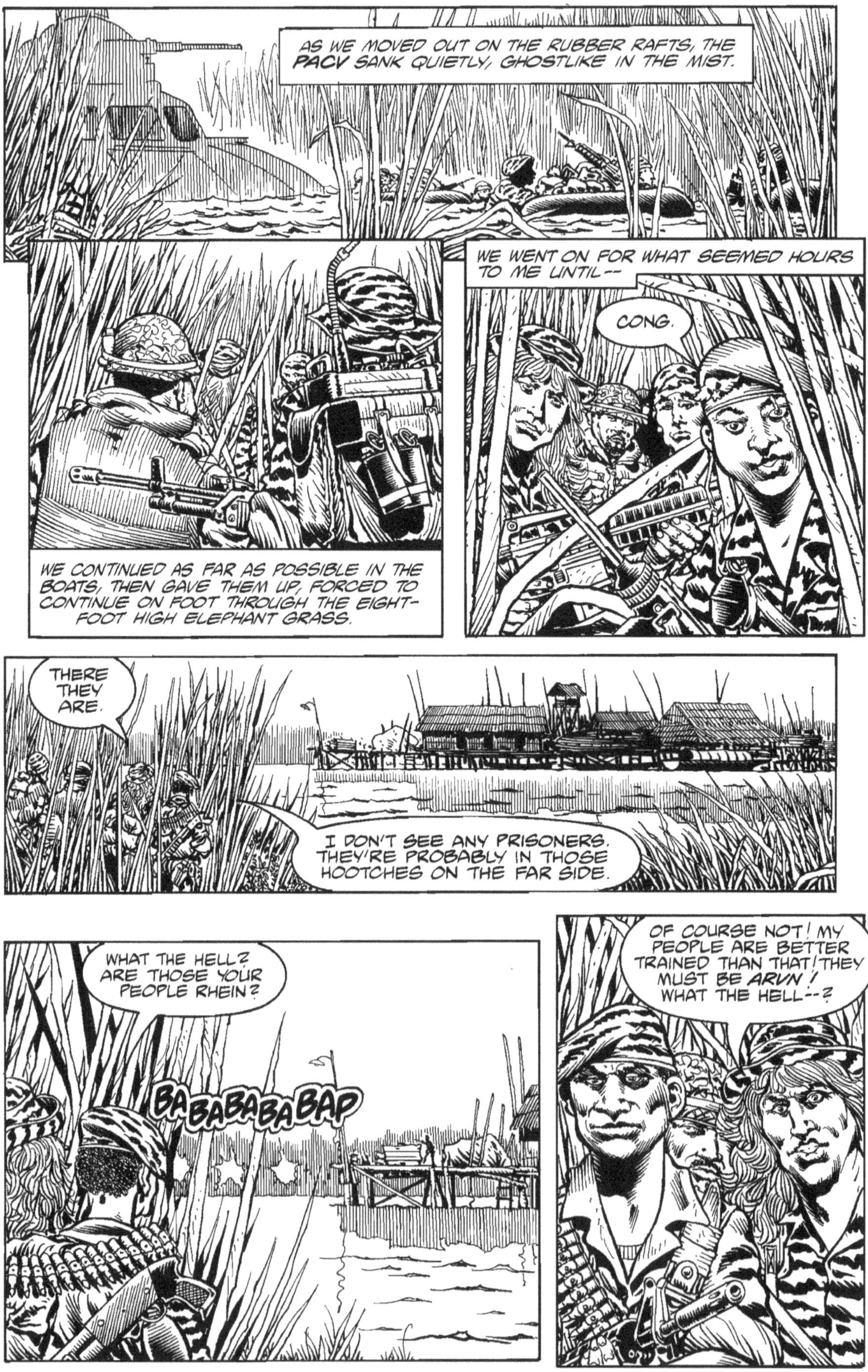
AS WE MOVED OUT ON THE RUBBER RAFTS, THE PACV SANK QUIETLY, GHOSTLIKE IN THE MIST.
WE CONTINUED AS FAR AS POSSIBLE IN THE BOATS, THEN GAVE THEM UP, FORCED TO CONTINUE ON FOOT THROUGH THE EIGHT-FOOT HIGH ELEPHANT GRASS.
WE WENT ON FOR WHAT SEEMED HOURS TO ME UNTIL--
CONG.
THERE THEY ARE.
I DON'T SEE ANY PRISONERS. THEY'RE PROBABLY IN THOSE HOOTCHES ON THE FAR SIDE.
WHAT THE HELL? ARE THOSE YOUR PEOPLE RHEIN?
BABABABABAP
OF COURSE NOT! MY PEOPLE ARE BETTER TRAINED THAN THAT! THEY MUST BE ARVN! WHAT THE HELL--?

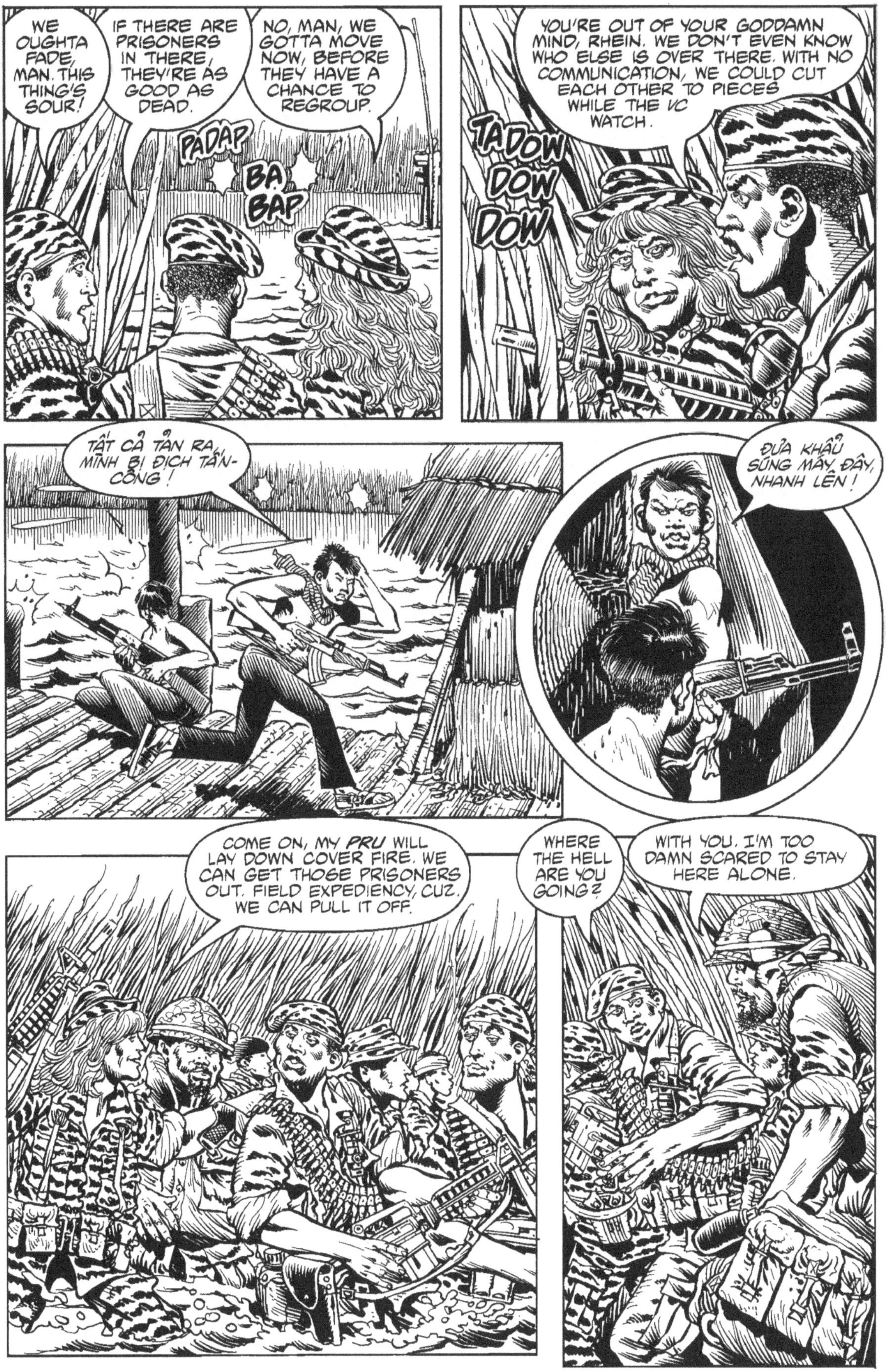
WE OUGHTA FADE, MAN. THIS THING'S SOUR!
IF THERE ARE PRISONERS IN THERE, THEY'RE AS GOOD AS DEAD.
NO, MAN, WE GOTTA MOVE NOW, BEFORE THEY HAVE A CHANCE TO REGROUP.
PADAP
BA BAP
YOU'RE OUT OF YOUR GODDAMN MIND, RHEIN. WE DON'T EVEN KNOW WHO ELSE IS OVER THERE. WITH NO COMMUNICATION, WE COULD CUT EACH OTHER TO PIECES WHILE THE VC WATCH.
TADOW DOW DOW
TẤT CẢ TẢN RA, MÌNH BỊ ĐỊCH TẤN-CÔNG !
ĐƯA KHẨU SÚNG MÁY ĐÂY, NHANH LÊN !
COME ON, MY *PRU* WILL LAY DOWN COVER FIRE. WE CAN GET THOSE PRISONERS OUT. FIELD EXPEDIENCY, CUZ. WE CAN PULL IT OFF.
WHERE THE HELL ARE YOU GOING?
WITH YOU. I'M TOO DAMN SCARED TO STAY HERE ALONE.

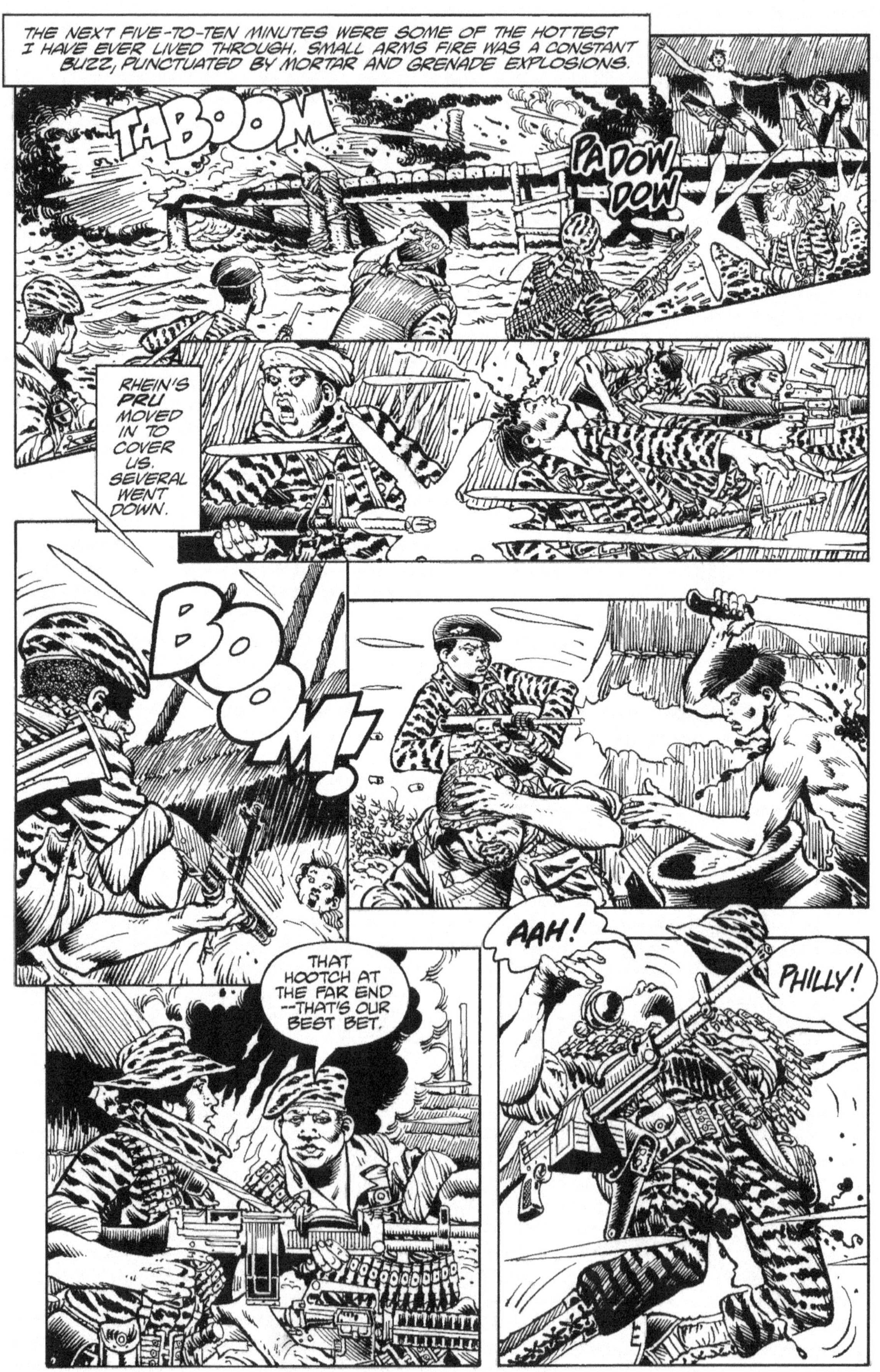
THE NEXT FIVE-TO-TEN MINUTES WERE SOME OF THE HOTTEST I HAVE EVER LIVED THROUGH. SMALL ARMS FIRE WAS A CONSTANT BUZZ, PUNCTUATED BY MORTAR AND GRENADE EXPLOSIONS.
TABOOM
PADOW DOW
RHEIN'S PRU MOVED IN TO COVER US. SEVERAL WENT DOWN.
BOOOM!
THAT HOOTCH AT THE FAR END --THAT'S OUR BEST BET.
AAH!
PHILLY!

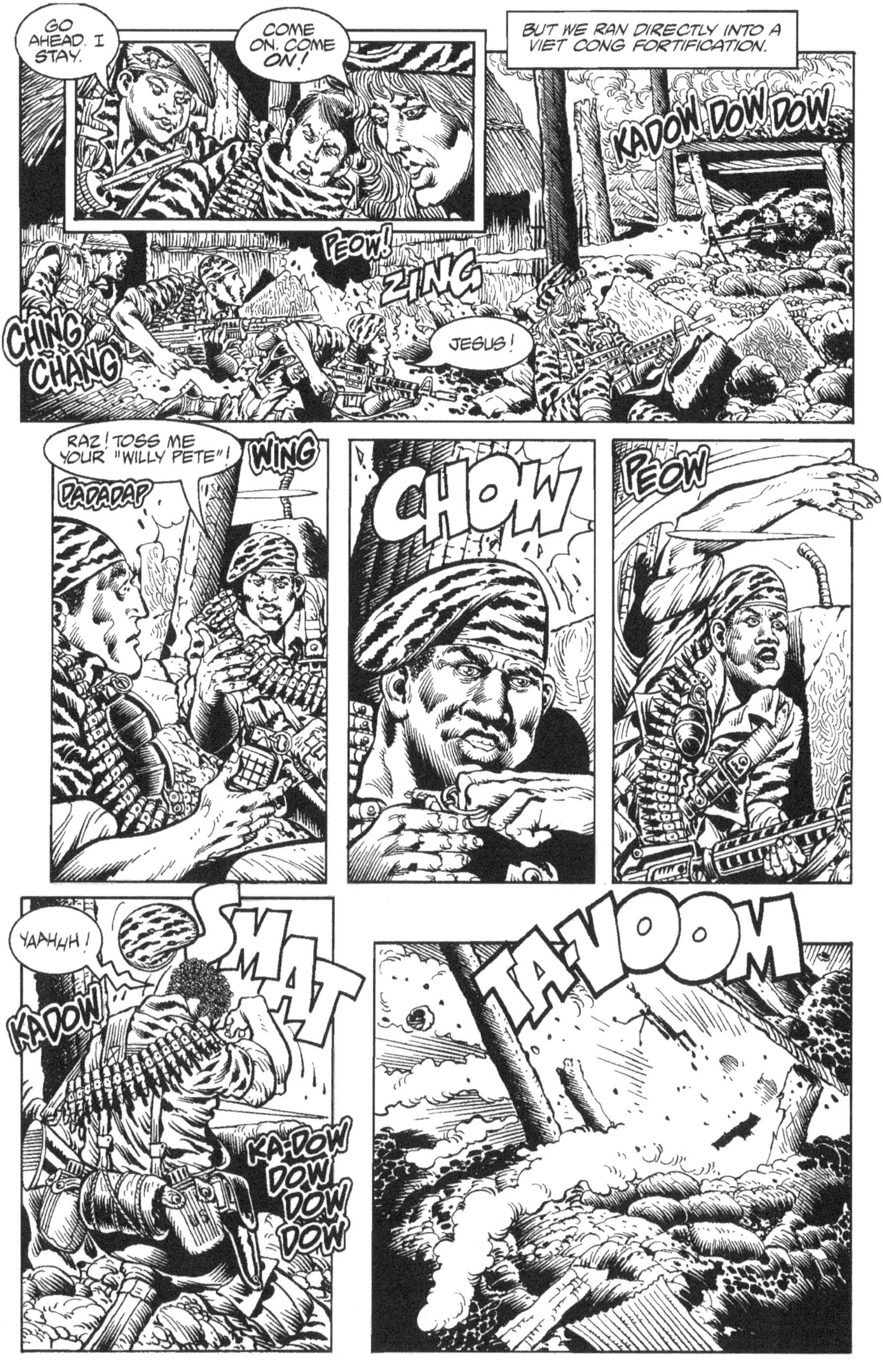

GO AHEAD. I STAY.
COME ON, COME ON!
BUT WE RAN DIRECTLY INTO A VIET CONG FORTIFICATION.
KADOW DOW DOW
PEOW!
ZING
CHING CHANG
JESUS!
RAZ! TOSS ME YOUR "WILLY PETE"!
WING
DADADAP
CHOW
PEOW
YAAHHH!
SMAT
KADOW
KA-DOW DOW DOW DOW
TA-VOOM

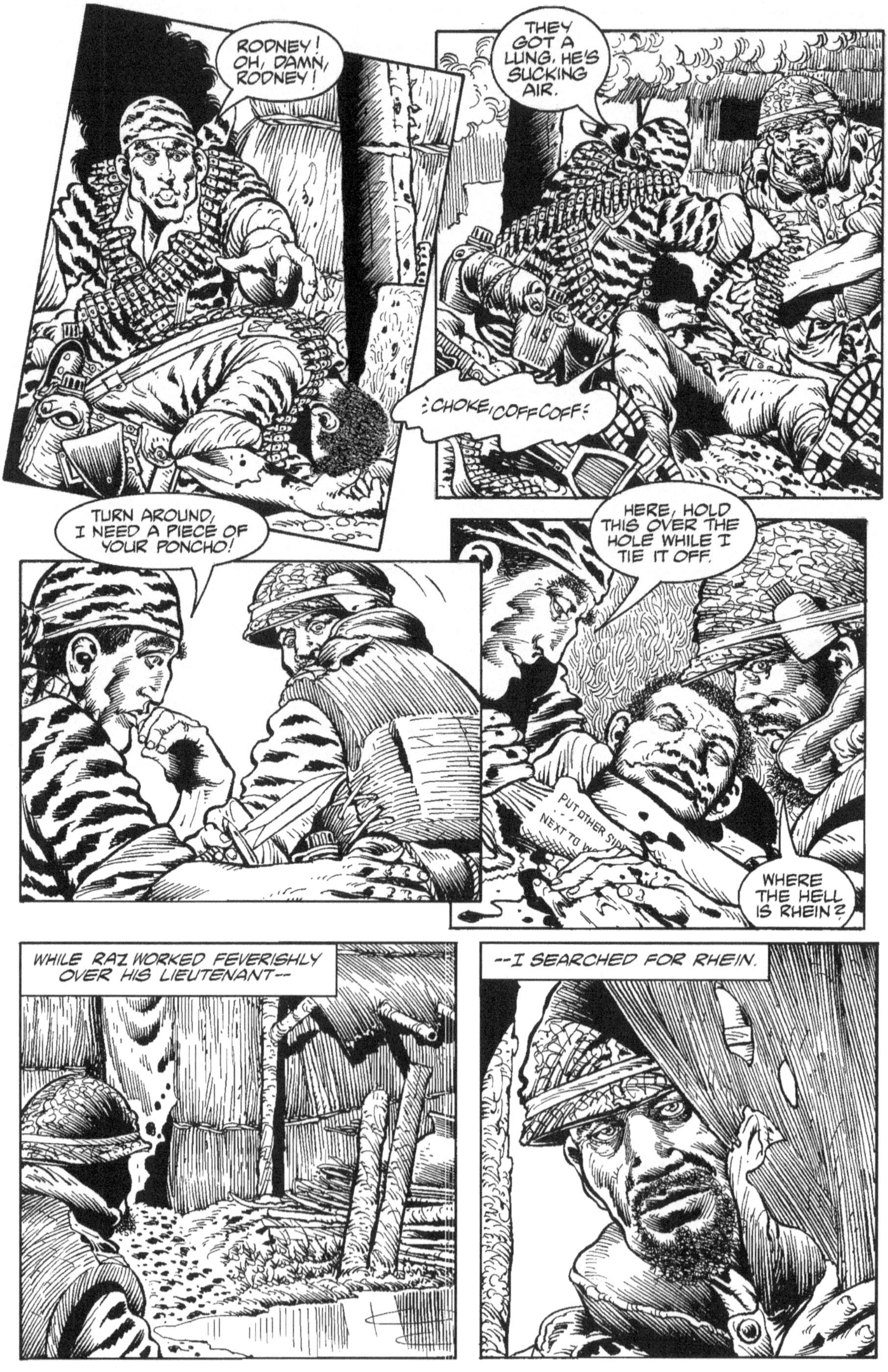
RODNEY! OH, DAMN, RODNEY!
THEY GOT A LUNG, HE'S SUCKING AIR.
CHOKE, COFF COFF
TURN AROUND, I NEED A PIECE OF YOUR PONCHO!
HERE, HOLD THIS OVER THE HOLE WHILE I TIE IT OFF.
PUT OTHER SIDE NEXT TO
WHERE THE HELL IS RHEIN?
WHILE RAZ WORKED FEVERISHLY OVER HIS LIEUTENANT--
--I SEARCHED FOR RHEIN.

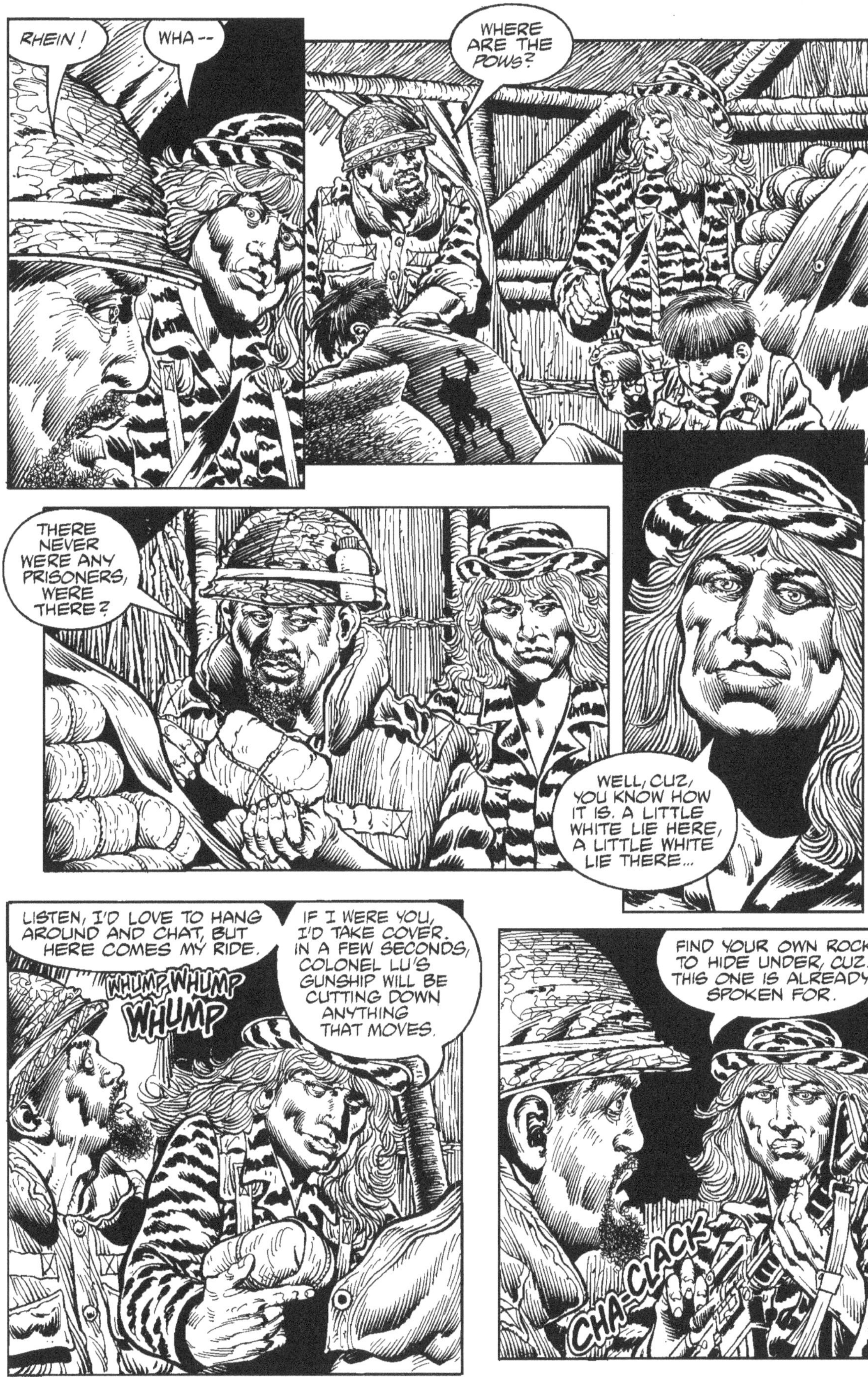
RHEIN!
WHA--
WHERE ARE THE POWS?
THERE NEVER WERE ANY PRISONERS, WERE THERE?
WELL, CUZ, YOU KNOW HOW IT IS. A LITTLE WHITE LIE HERE, A LITTLE WHITE LIE THERE...
LISTEN, I'D LOVE TO HANG AROUND AND CHAT, BUT HERE COMES MY RIDE.
WHUMP WHUMP
WHUMP
IF I WERE YOU, I'D TAKE COVER. IN A FEW SECONDS, COLONEL LU'S GUNSHIP WILL BE CUTTING DOWN ANYTHING THAT MOVES.
FIND YOUR OWN ROCK TO HIDE UNDER, CUZ. THIS ONE IS ALREADY SPOKEN FOR.
CHA-CLACK

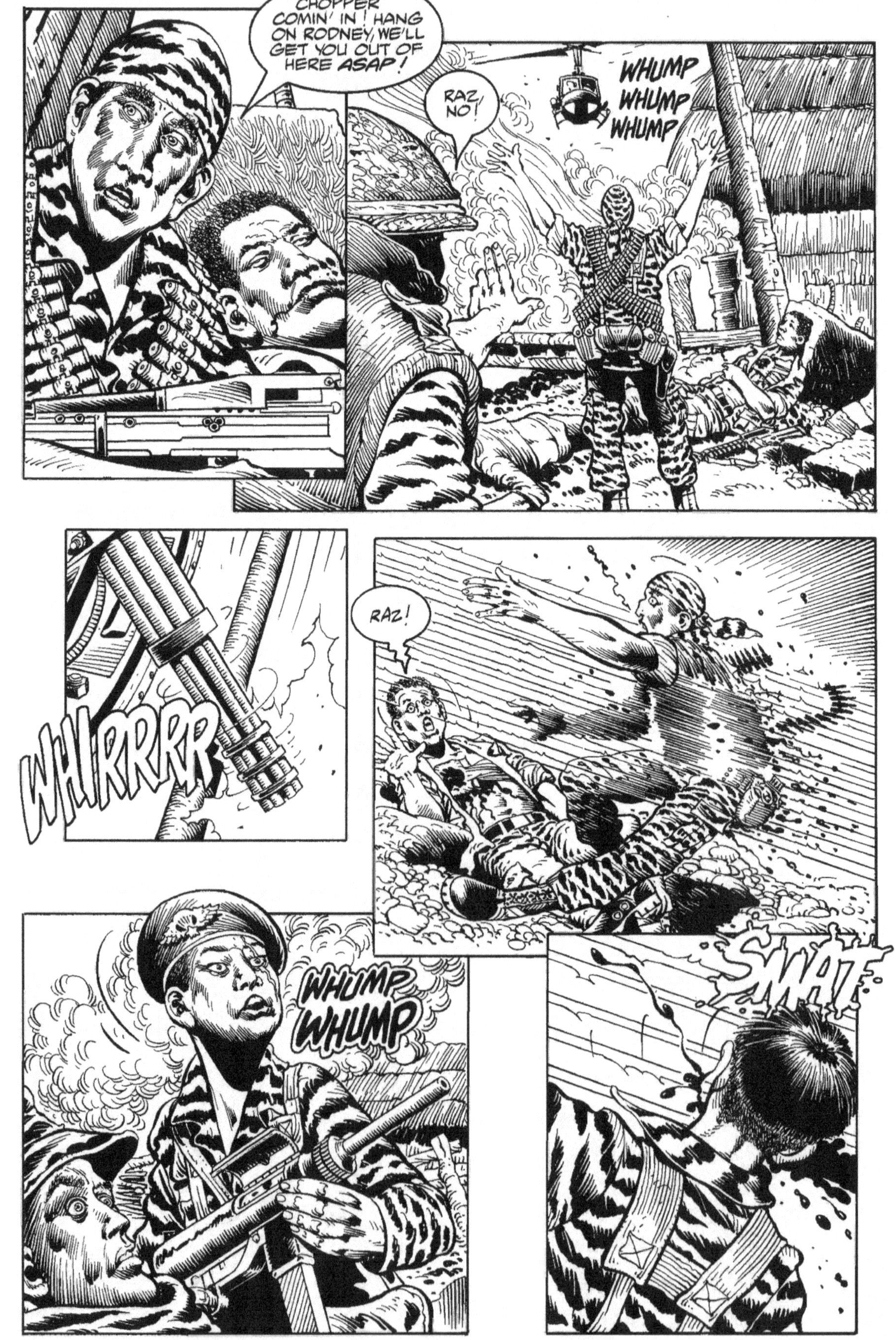
CHOPPER COMIN' IN! HANG ON RODNEY, WE'LL GET YOU OUT OF HERE ASAP!
RAZ, NO!
WHUMP WHUMP WHUMP
WHIRRRR
RAZ!
WHUMP WHUMP
SWAT

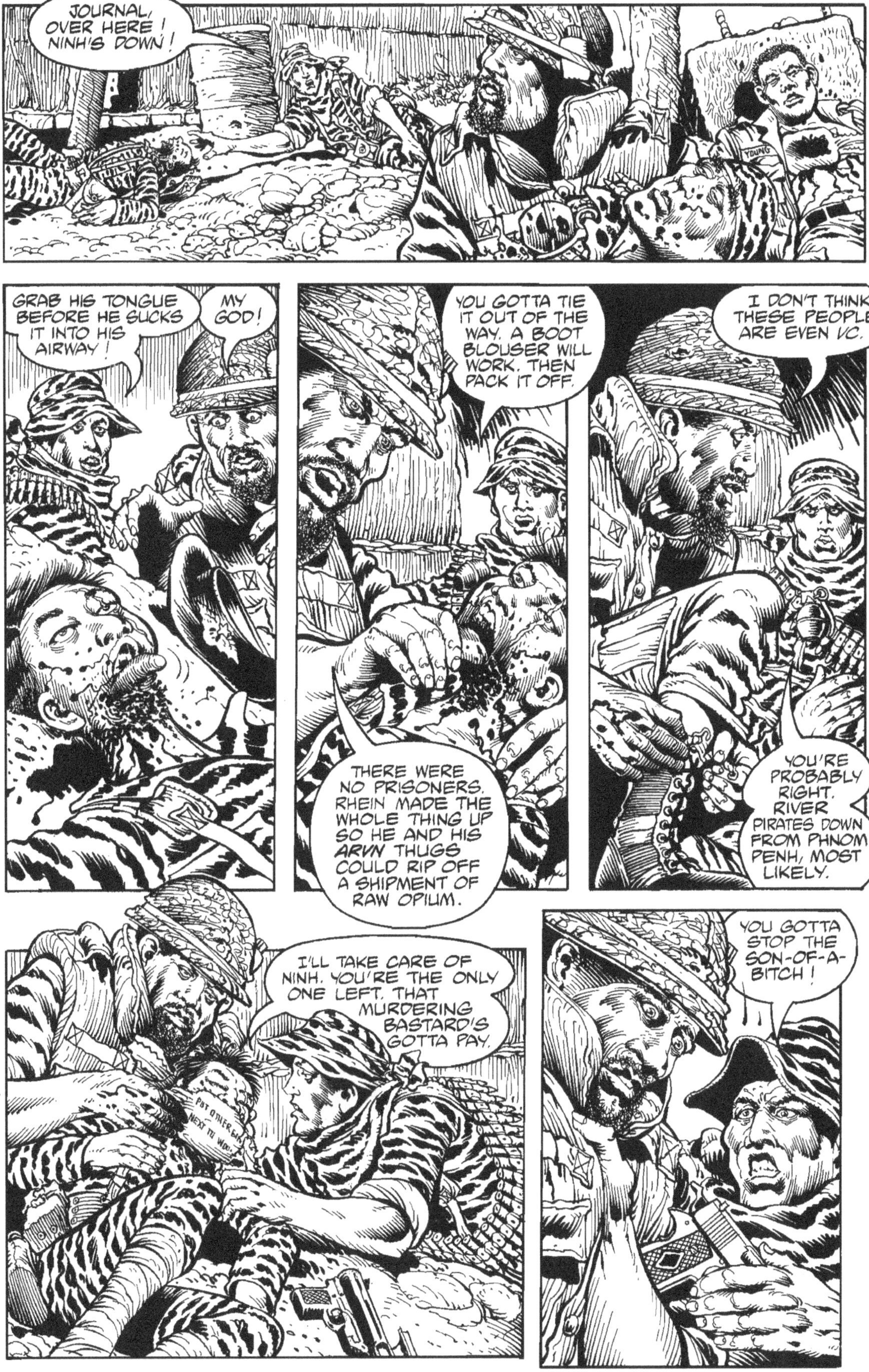
JOURNAL, OVER HERE! NINH'S DOWN!
GRAB HIS TONGUE BEFORE HE SUCKS IT INTO HIS AIRWAY!
MY GOD!
YOU GOTTA TIE IT OUT OF THE WAY. A BOOT BLOUSER WILL WORK. THEN PACK IT OFF.
THERE WERE NO PRISONERS. RHEIN MADE THE WHOLE THING UP SO HE AND HIS ARVN THUGS COULD RIP OFF A SHIPMENT OF RAW OPIUM.
I DON'T THINK THESE PEOPLE ARE EVEN VC.
YOU'RE PROBABLY RIGHT. RIVER PIRATES DOWN FROM PHNOM PENH, MOST LIKELY.
I'LL TAKE CARE OF NINH. YOU'RE THE ONLY ONE LEFT. THAT MURDERING BASTARD'S GOTTA PAY.
YOU GOTTA STOP THE SON-OF-A-BITCH!

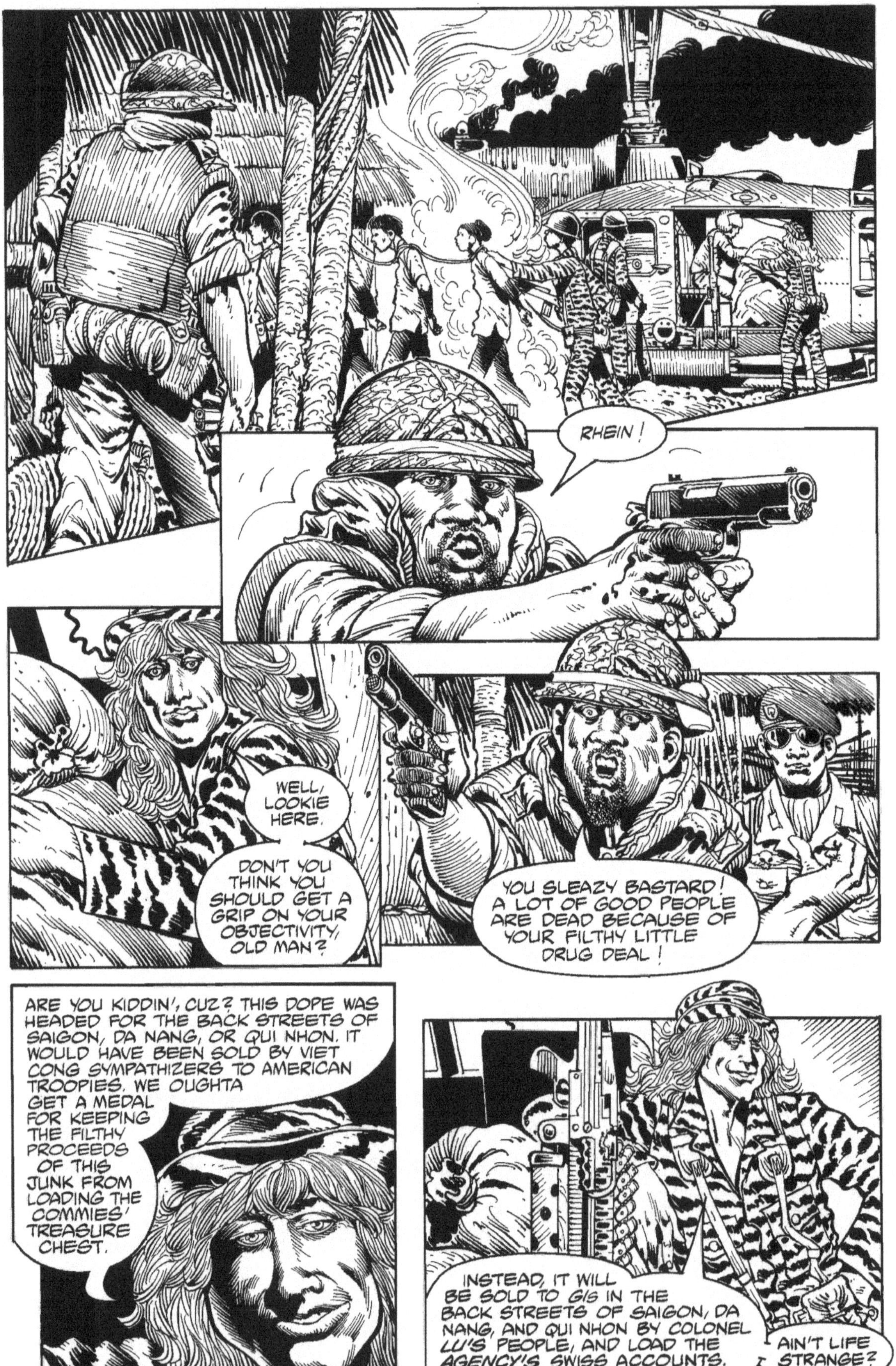
RHEIN!
WELL, LOOKIE HERE.
DON'T YOU THINK YOU SHOULD GET A GRIP ON YOUR OBJECTIVITY, OLD MAN?
YOU SLEAZY BASTARD! A LOT OF GOOD PEOPLE ARE DEAD BECAUSE OF YOUR FILTHY LITTLE DRUG DEAL!
ARE YOU KIDDIN', CUZ? THIS DOPE WAS HEADED FOR THE BACK STREETS OF SAIGON, DA NANG, OR QUI NHON. IT WOULD HAVE BEEN SOLD BY VIET CONG SYMPATHIZERS TO AMERICAN TROOPIES. WE OUGHTA GET A MEDAL FOR KEEPING THE FILTHY PROCEEDS OF THIS JUNK FROM LOADING THE COMMIES' TREASURE CHEST.
INSTEAD, IT WILL BE SOLD TO *GIs* IN THE BACK STREETS OF SAIGON, DA NANG, AND QUI NHON BY COLONEL *LU'S* PEOPLE, AND LOAD THE *AGENCY'S* SWISS ACCOUNTS.
AIN'T LIFE STRANGE?

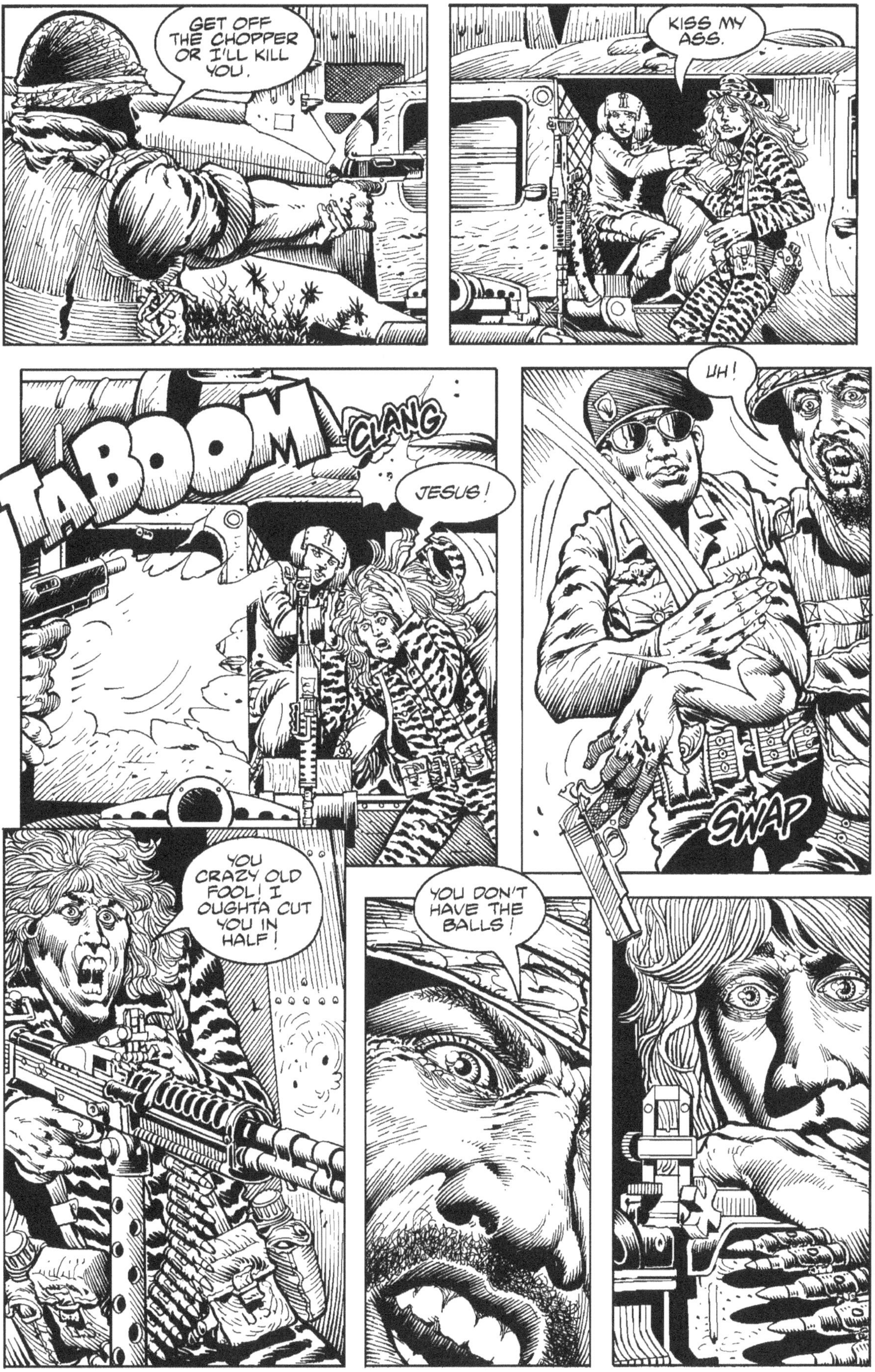
GET OFF THE CHOPPER OR I'LL KILL YOU.
KISS MY ASS.
TABOOM
CLANG
JESUS!
UH!
SWAP
YOU CRAZY OLD FOOL! I OUGHTA CUT YOU IN HALF!
YOU DON'T HAVE THE BALLS!

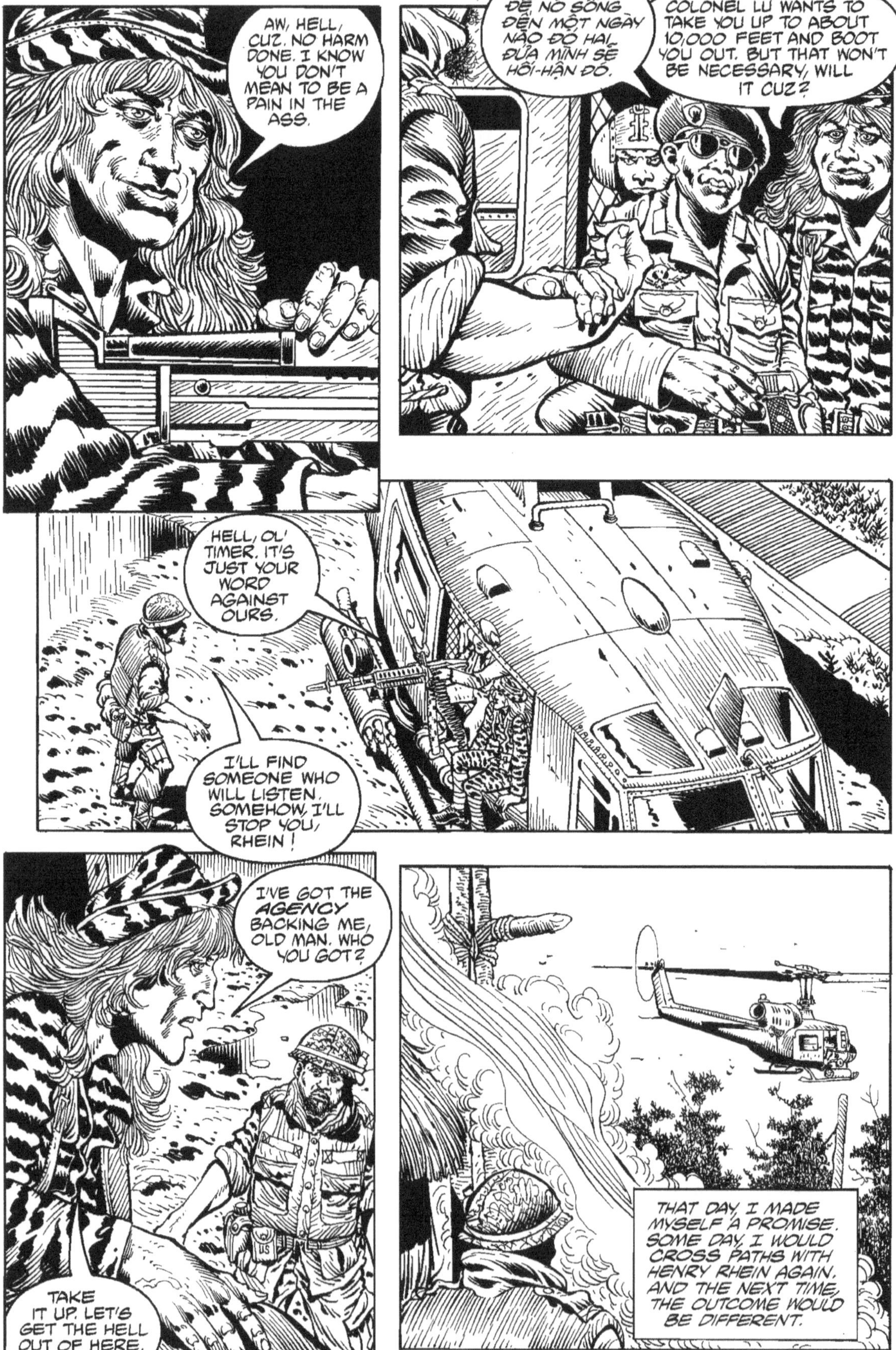
AW, HELL, CUZ. NO HARM DONE. I KNOW YOU DON'T MEAN TO BE A PAIN IN THE ASS.
NẾU ANH ĐỂ NÓ SỐNG ĐẾN MỘT NGÀY NÀO ĐÓ HAI ĐỨA MÌNH SẼ HỐI-HẬN ĐÓ.
COLONEL LU WANTS TO TAKE YOU UP TO ABOUT 10,000 FEET AND BOOT YOU OUT. BUT THAT WON'T BE NECESSARY, WILL IT CUZ?
HELL, OL' TIMER. IT'S JUST YOUR WORD AGAINST OURS.
I'LL FIND SOMEONE WHO WILL LISTEN. SOMEHOW, I'LL STOP YOU, RHEIN!
I'VE GOT THE AGENCY BACKING ME, OLD MAN. WHO YOU GOT?
TAKE IT UP. LET'S GET THE HELL OUT OF HERE.
THAT DAY, I MADE MYSELF A PROMISE. SOME DAY, I WOULD CROSS PATHS WITH HENRY RHEIN AGAIN. AND THE NEXT TIME, THE OUTCOME WOULD BE DIFFERENT.

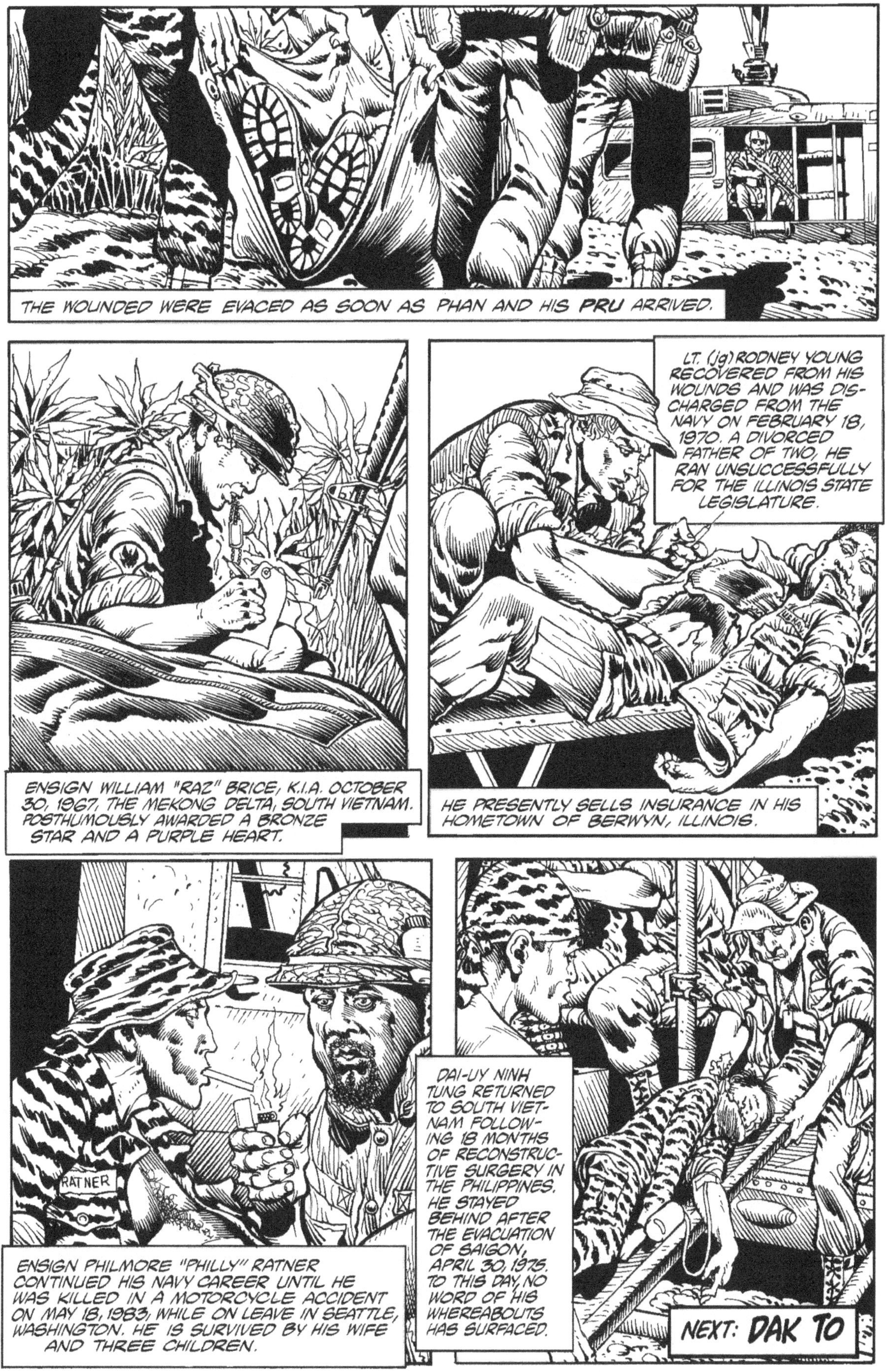
THE WOUNDED WERE EVACED AS SOON AS PHAN AND HIS **PRU** ARRIVED.
ENSIGN WILLIAM "RAZ" BRICE, K.I.A. OCTOBER 30, 1967, THE MEKONG DELTA, SOUTH VIETNAM. POSTHUMOUSLY AWARDED A BRONZE STAR AND A PURPLE HEART.
LT. (jg) RODNEY YOUNG RECOVERED FROM HIS WOUNDS AND WAS DISCHARGED FROM THE NAVY ON FEBRUARY 18, 1970. A DIVORCED FATHER OF TWO, HE RAN UNSUCCESSFULLY FOR THE ILLINOIS STATE LEGISLATURE.
HE PRESENTLY SELLS INSURANCE IN HIS HOMETOWN OF BERWYN, ILLINOIS.
RATNER
ENSIGN PHILMORE "PHILLY" RATNER CONTINUED HIS NAVY CAREER UNTIL HE WAS KILLED IN A MOTORCYCLE ACCIDENT ON MAY 18, 1983, WHILE ON LEAVE IN SEATTLE, WASHINGTON. HE IS SURVIVED BY HIS WIFE AND THREE CHILDREN.
DAI-UY NINH TUNG RETURNED TO SOUTH VIETNAM FOLLOWING 18 MONTHS OF RECONSTRUCTIVE SURGERY IN THE PHILIPPINES. HE STAYED BEHIND AFTER THE EVACUATION OF SAIGON, APRIL 30, 1975. TO THIS DAY, NO WORD OF HIS WHEREABOUTS HAS SURFACED.
NEXT: DAK TO

Missing Americans™

POW Forum: Why communist countries want to keep POWs after the shooting stops

On February 1, 1988, The Connecticut chapter of the National Forget-Me-Not Association sponsored a Prisoner-of-War Forum at Western Connecticut State University in Danbury, Connecticut.

Participants included Bill Paul, a reporter for The Wall Street Journal, *and U.S. Rep. John Rowland (R-Conn.), a leader in Congress on the issue of POWs abandoned in Vietnam. The Departments of Defense and State were invited to send representatives to participate, but declined, saying no one was available.*

We begin our edited transcript of the proceedings with Mr. Paul's opening remarks...

To start off, I am sorry that no one is here from the Defense Department or the State Department, because I think that this issue would be better served if all sides had a chance to address their point of view, even up, on this podium; and — given that this is really a global issue going back over the last three wars — in London, Moscow, and everywhere else.

But when you get right down to it, in my opinion at least, this is the flip side of the nuclear disarmament issue. This is a core peace issue. If it can be established that governments throughout the world have, over the last three [wars] systematically either 1) taken prisoners when the shooting has stopped, or 2) allowed them to be taken and then abandoned them, I think the people in the world might just say, "No more wars." It is at least a thought to cling to.

As to what I'd like to talk about, I'm neither a Republican nor a Democrat — there is no political agenda on my part.

For four years I have written about what I think is the overwhelming body of evidence that shows that men were indeed taken by the communists and abandoned by the West at the end of each of the last three wars. And frankly, it goes further back than that.

You might ask "Why would they want them? What possible purpose could it serve to keep men behind when the shooting stops?"

Just recently, there were news reports about how North Korean agents had snatched Japanese women off beaches in the late 1970s and taken them by motorboat back to North Korea. The State Department verified [the reports] and put North Korea back on its terrorist list.

Remember the plane that was blown up? — the North Korean agent who took the cyanide pill and the other one who tried to and it just didn't work? Well, under what I'm sure was intensive questioning in South Korea, this North Korean woman said that she had been trained in the Japanese language and in Japanese customs by Japanese women in North Korea.

She further said that it was her impression that these women had been taken from Japan specifically to teach North Korean agents how to be Japanese. The woman had trained for nearly a decade for her assignment to blow up that airplane and to fake her way out of it by saying she was Japanese.

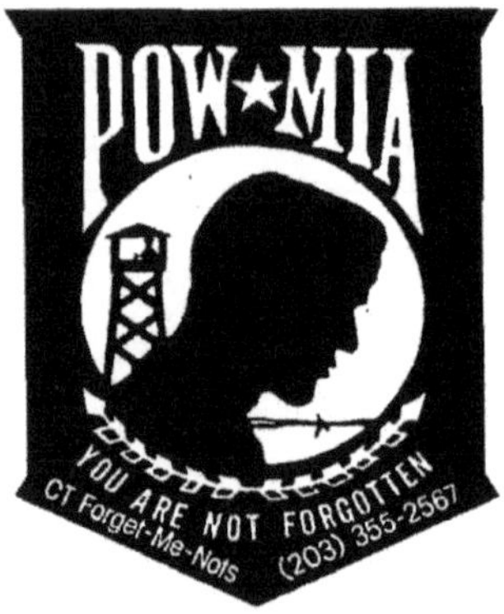
POW★MIA
YOU ARE NOT FORGOTTEN
CT Forget-Me-Nots (203) 355-2567

She was perfect, but she didn't get the cyanide pill down fast enough.

Ladies and gentlemen, that's why communists take people that you might not think are important.

They are living in closed societies. If you have someone available to you to teach you a language, to teach you customs, to do translations for you, to be your eye on the world, you take them.

Now imagine yourself — it's 1975 in Vietnam. You have American soldiers on your hands. Are you going to send them back? Or are you going to keep them because you say, "I can make use of these men. They can fix my airplanes, they can teach my kids English. They can be my eye on the world."

And in fact, they can also serve a very important propaganda purpose — namely, so that whenever Nicaraguans, Palestinians, or others come through Vietnam for terrorist training, you can parade your Americans forward and say "See? We did it to 'em, you can do it to 'em too."

That's why people are kept when the shooting is stopped. You're too human, you're too caring in this country. You don't realize that people are property — that they are worth their weight in gold when that nation is a communist nation and has no other way to learn this information.

[That's] point one.

continued...

Missing Americans™

POW Forum: Can we trust governments to tell us the truth about POW/MIAs?

On February 1, 1988, the Connecticut chapter of the National Forget-Me-Not Association sponsored a Prisoner-of-War Forum at Western Connecticut State University in Danbury, Connecticut.

Participants included Bill Paul, a reporter for The Wall Street Journal, *and U.S. Rep. John Rowland (R-Conn.), a leader in Congress on the issue of POWs abandoned in Vietnam. The Departments of Defense and State declined to participate.*

In part 2 of our edited transcript of the proceedings, Mr. Paul continues his historical overview of the issue...

Point two: should we trust our government to tell us the truth?

(Laughter and "no"s from the audience. Rep. Rowland: "Make a distinction.")

Excuse me. Should we be trusting each successive administration — each regime in the White House — to be telling us the truth, the whole truth, and nothing but the truth? No. And that's not just my opinion, that's also history's judgment.

Let me take you back now, for a moment, to 1943. In March of 1943, a rabbi, Stephen Wise, organized a protest at Madison Square Garden in New York. That night, he filled the Garden with 75,000 people and had tens of thousands in the streets who couldn't get in, according to the New York police. It was a rally to save Jews from the Holocaust.

That night, speaker after speaker came forward and said the American government must do something to prevent the slaughter of innocent people in Europe.

The next month, an American delegation went to Bermuda with a British delegation to work this out — or so they said. They didn't do anything — not a bloody thing.

There was an editorial in the *London Observer,* after the meeting was over, which said "Here on the leisurely beach hotels of this Atlantic luxury island, well-dressed men assemble to assure each other, in the best Geneva fashion, that nothing much can be done. The opening speeches of the conference have been widely noted in this country" — meaning England — "and noted with anger. We have been told that this problem is beyond the resources of Britain and America combined. What is so terrible about these speeches is not only their utter insensitiveness to human suffering, it is the implied readiness of the two greatest powers on Earth to humiliate themselves — to declare themselves bankrupt and impotent in order to evade the slight discomfort of charity.".

They turned their backs — and as a result, hundred of thousands, if not millions, of Jews couldn't be saved.

Now why was the real reason for no action at Bermuda? Well, it turned out, according to the diary of an Assistant Secretary of State who was there, that the real reason was that

"What a terrible human toll!" – Bill Paul
Photo by Carol Kaliff. Copyright©1988 The Danbury (Ct.) News-Times

they feared that if they came to the rescue of the Jews, that Nazi propagandists would turn this to get Turkey, Spain, and other neutral nations in the war on the side of the Nazis.

In other words — it wasn't worth it. They had another agenda which they thought was more important. But rather than tell us that, what it came out was "Jewish propaganda."

There was a poor gentleman who represented the World Jewish Congress in Switzerland. For two years, he sent back message after message detailing the horrors, including some of those pictures smuggled out of the Warsaw ghetto showing the killing. Our response was "Jewish Propaganda," "unsubstantiated reports," "we just don't know, we're going to have to look into it." Finally in 1944, they did look into it. Finally in 1944, they realized they had made a mistake and Raoul Wallenberg was enlisted by the State Department to do what he could. But by then — what a terrible human toll!

So first of all, why do they take 'em? They've got value. They're worth something to the North Koreans, to the Vietnamese, to the Chinese, to the Laotians, to the Russians. Second of all, can you trust your government to tell the truth? Not necessarily. Not if they think they know best, not if they think there's another reason which is more important for sacrificing a human life than for saving it.

DAK TO

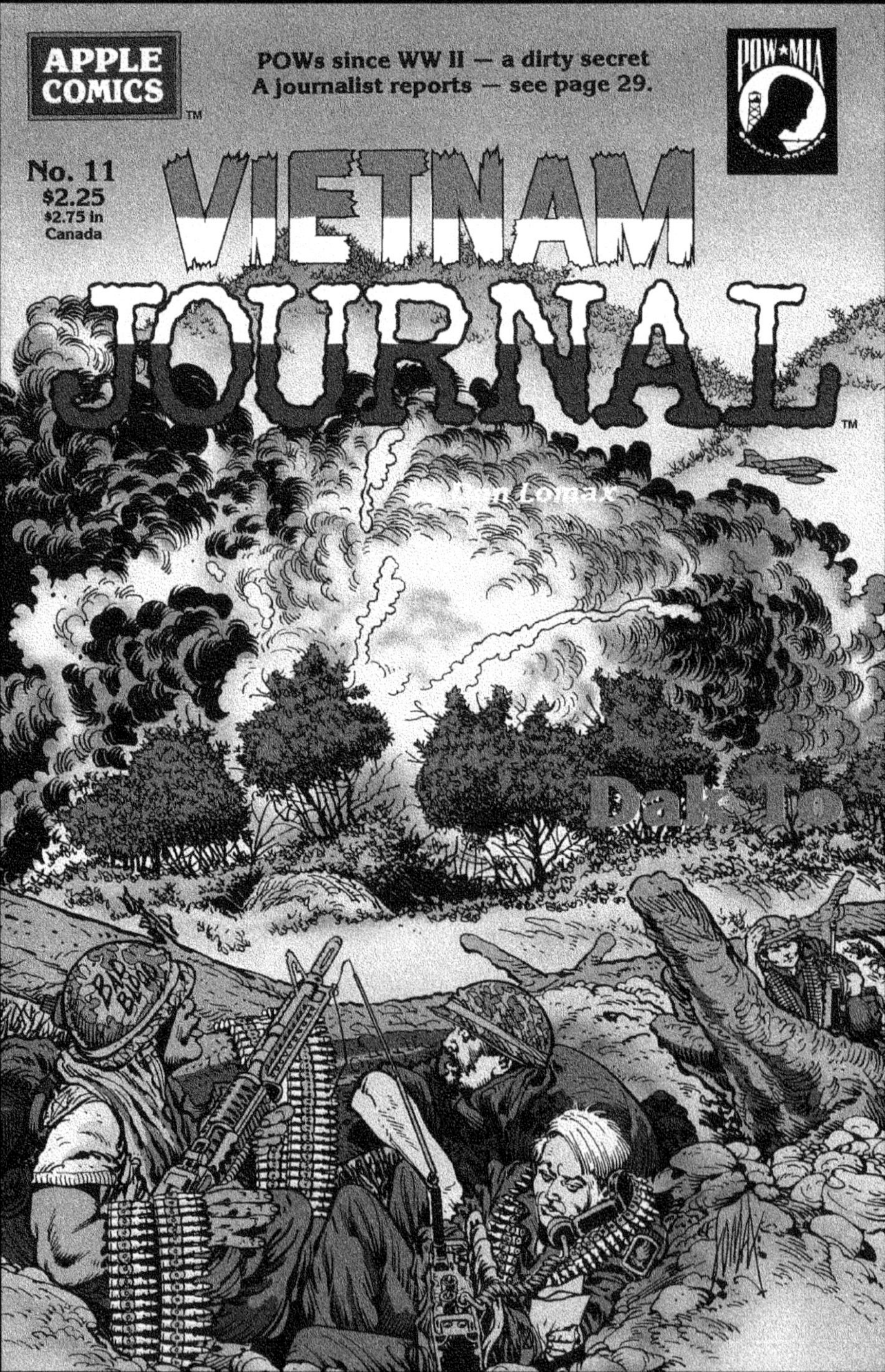

APPLE COMICS
TM
POWs since WW II — a dirty secret
A journalist reports — see page 29.
POW★MIA
No. 11
$2.25
$2.75 in Canada
VIETNAM JOURNAL
TM

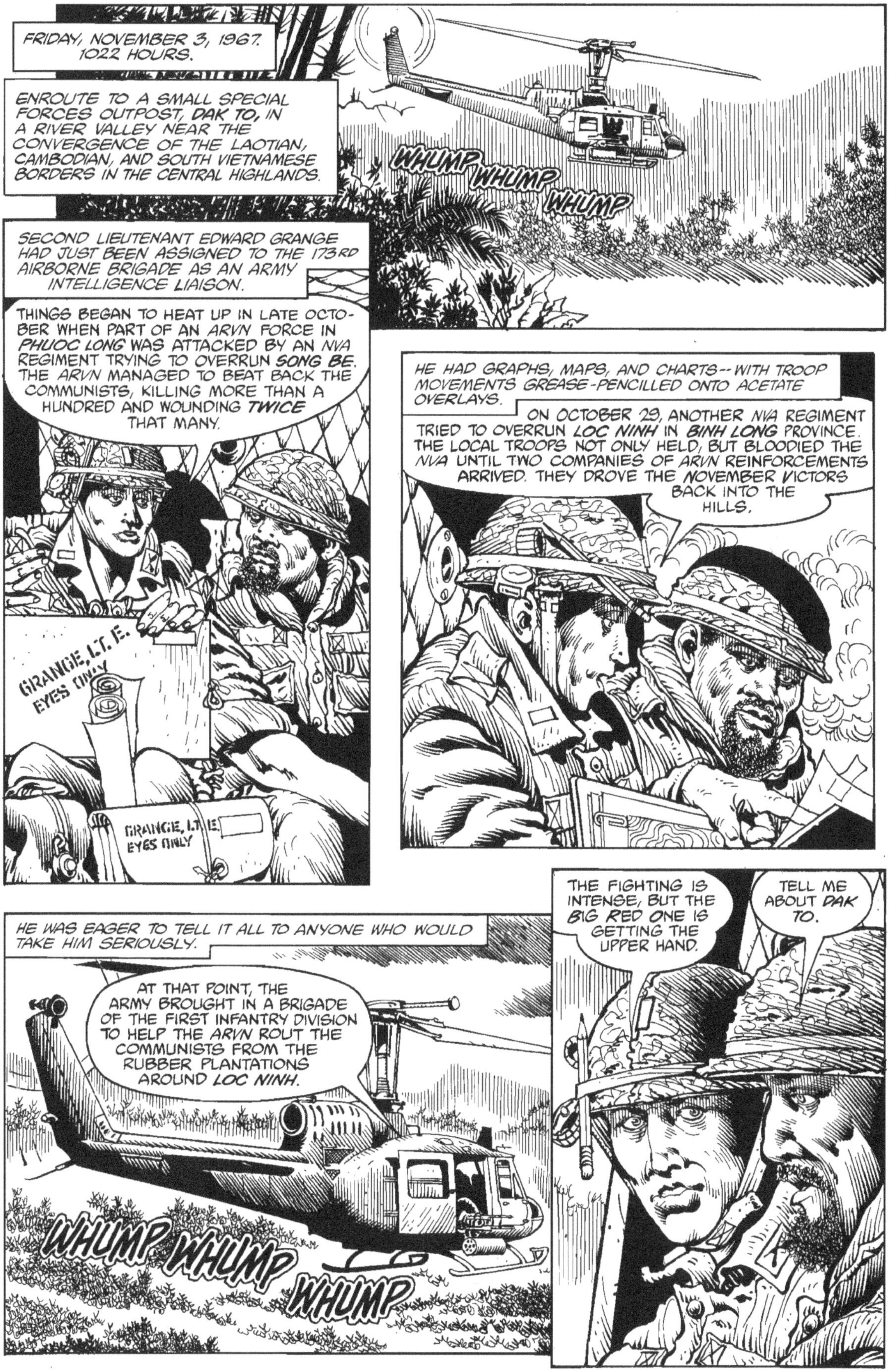
FRIDAY, NOVEMBER 3, 1967. 1022 HOURS.
ENROUTE TO A SMALL SPECIAL FORCES OUTPOST, DAK TO, IN A RIVER VALLEY NEAR THE CONVERGENCE OF THE LAOTIAN, CAMBODIAN, AND SOUTH VIETNAMESE BORDERS IN THE CENTRAL HIGHLANDS.
WHUMP WHUMP WHUMP
SECOND LIEUTENANT EDWARD GRANGE HAD JUST BEEN ASSIGNED TO THE 173RD AIRBORNE BRIGADE AS AN ARMY INTELLIGENCE LIAISON.
THINGS BEGAN TO HEAT UP IN LATE OCTOBER WHEN PART OF AN ARVN FORCE IN PHUOC LONG WAS ATTACKED BY AN NVA REGIMENT TRYING TO OVERRUN SONG BE. THE ARVN MANAGED TO BEAT BACK THE COMMUNISTS, KILLING MORE THAN A HUNDRED AND WOUNDING TWICE THAT MANY.
GRANGE, L.T. E. EYES ONLY
GRANGE, L.T. E. EYES ONLY
HE HAD GRAPHS, MAPS, AND CHARTS-- WITH TROOP MOVEMENTS GREASE-PENCILLED ONTO ACETATE OVERLAYS.
ON OCTOBER 29, ANOTHER NVA REGIMENT TRIED TO OVERRUN LOC NINH IN BINH LONG PROVINCE. THE LOCAL TROOPS NOT ONLY HELD, BUT BLOODIED THE NVA UNTIL TWO COMPANIES OF ARVN REINFORCEMENTS ARRIVED. THEY DROVE THE NOVEMBER VICTORS BACK INTO THE HILLS.
HE WAS EAGER TO TELL IT ALL TO ANYONE WHO WOULD TAKE HIM SERIOUSLY.
AT THAT POINT, THE ARMY BROUGHT IN A BRIGADE OF THE FIRST INFANTRY DIVISION TO HELP THE ARVN ROUT THE COMMUNISTS FROM THE RUBBER PLANTATIONS AROUND LOC NINH.
WHUMP WHUMP WHUMP
THE FIGHTING IS INTENSE, BUT THE BIG RED ONE IS GETTING THE UPPER HAND.
TELL ME ABOUT DAK TO.

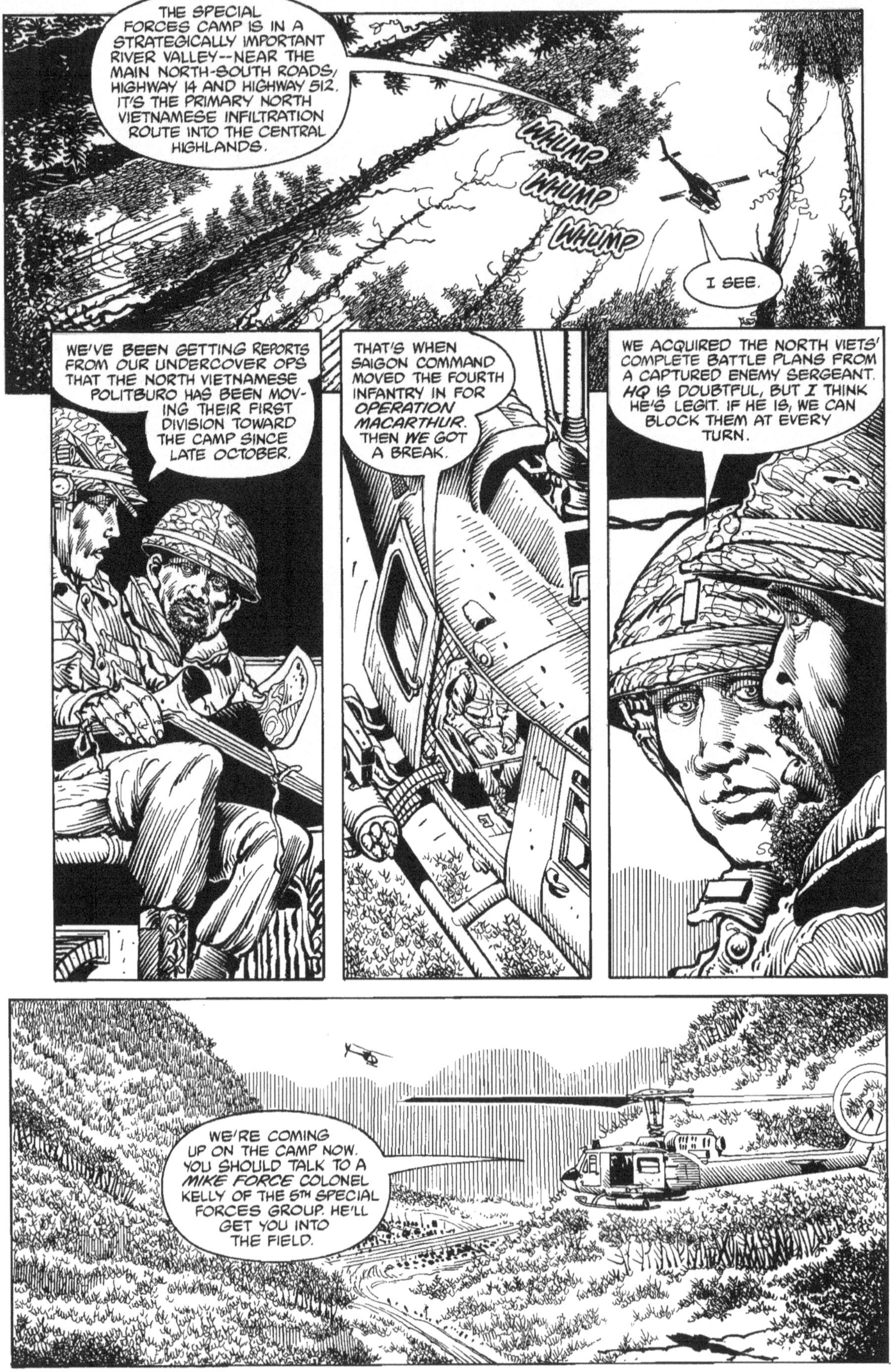

THE SPECIAL FORCES CAMP IS IN A STRATEGICALLY IMPORTANT RIVER VALLEY--NEAR THE MAIN NORTH-SOUTH ROADS, HIGHWAY 14 AND HIGHWAY 512. IT'S THE PRIMARY NORTH VIETNAMESE INFILTRATION ROUTE INTO THE CENTRAL HIGHLANDS.
WHUMP
WHUMP
WHUMP
I SEE.
WE'VE BEEN GETTING REPORTS FROM OUR UNDERCOVER OPS THAT THE NORTH VIETNAMESE POLITBURO HAS BEEN MOVING THEIR FIRST DIVISION TOWARD THE CAMP SINCE LATE OCTOBER.
THAT'S WHEN SAIGON COMMAND MOVED THE FOURTH INFANTRY IN FOR *OPERATION MACARTHUR*. THEN *WE* GOT A BREAK.
WE ACQUIRED THE NORTH VIETS' COMPLETE BATTLE PLANS FROM A CAPTURED ENEMY SERGEANT. *HQ* IS DOUBTFUL, BUT *I* THINK HE'S LEGIT. IF HE IS, WE CAN BLOCK THEM AT EVERY TURN.
WE'RE COMING UP ON THE CAMP NOW. YOU SHOULD TALK TO A *MIKE FORCE* COLONEL KELLY OF THE 5TH SPECIAL FORCES GROUP. HE'LL GET YOU INTO THE FIELD.

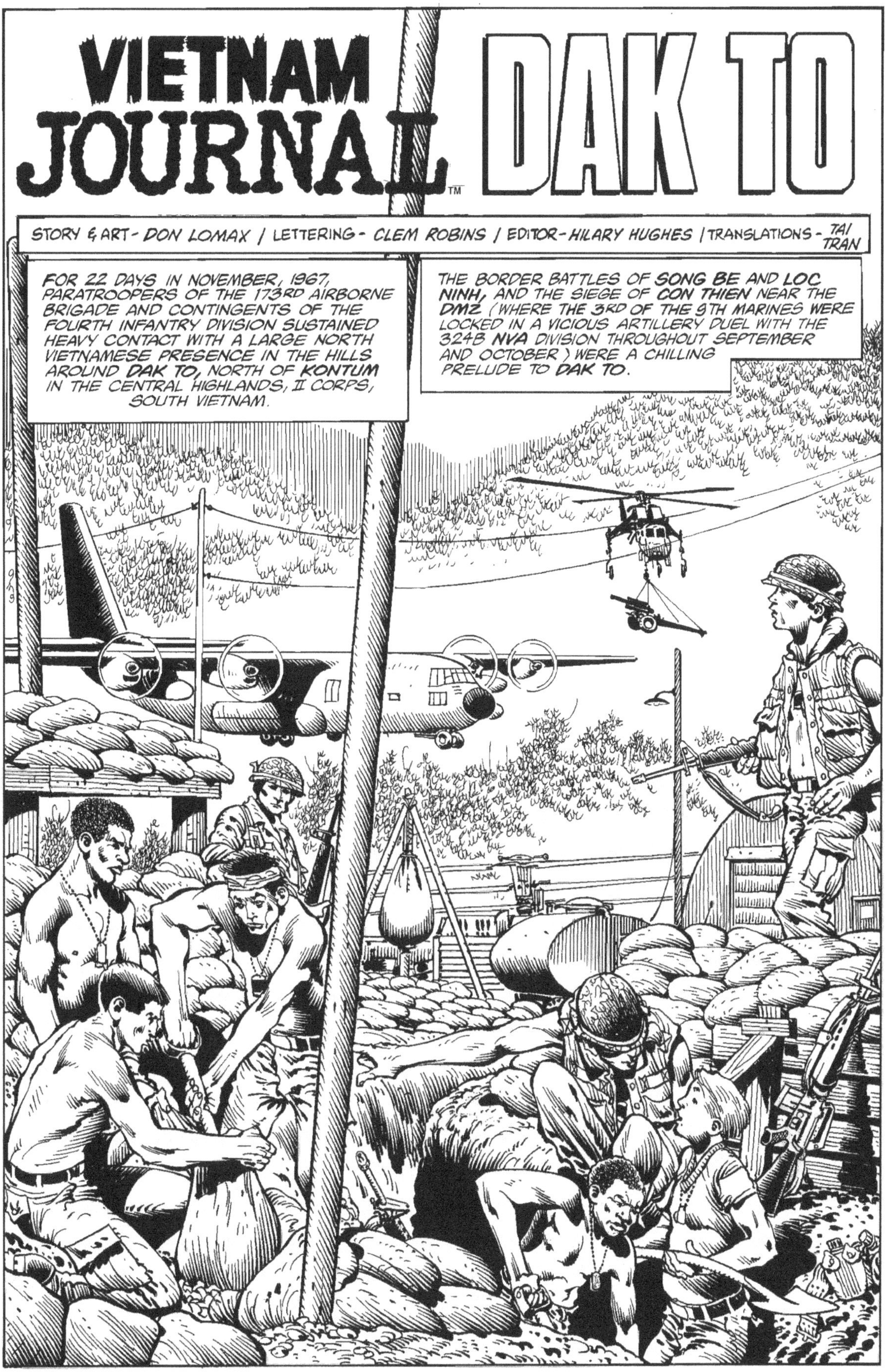
VIETNAM JOURNAL™
DAK TO
STORY & ART - DON LOMAX / LETTERING - CLEM ROBINS / EDITOR - HILARY HUGHES / TRANSLATIONS - TAI TRAN
FOR 22 DAYS IN NOVEMBER, 1967, PARATROOPERS OF THE 173RD AIRBORNE BRIGADE AND CONTINGENTS OF THE FOURTH INFANTRY DIVISION SUSTAINED HEAVY CONTACT WITH A LARGE NORTH VIETNAMESE PRESENCE IN THE HILLS AROUND DAK TO, NORTH OF KONTUM IN THE CENTRAL HIGHLANDS, II CORPS, SOUTH VIETNAM.
THE BORDER BATTLES OF SONG BE AND LOC NINH, AND THE SIEGE OF CON THIEN NEAR THE DMZ (WHERE THE 3RD OF THE 9TH MARINES WERE LOCKED IN A VICIOUS ARTILLERY DUEL WITH THE 324B NVA DIVISION THROUGHOUT SEPTEMBER AND OCTOBER) WERE A CHILLING PRELUDE TO DAK TO.

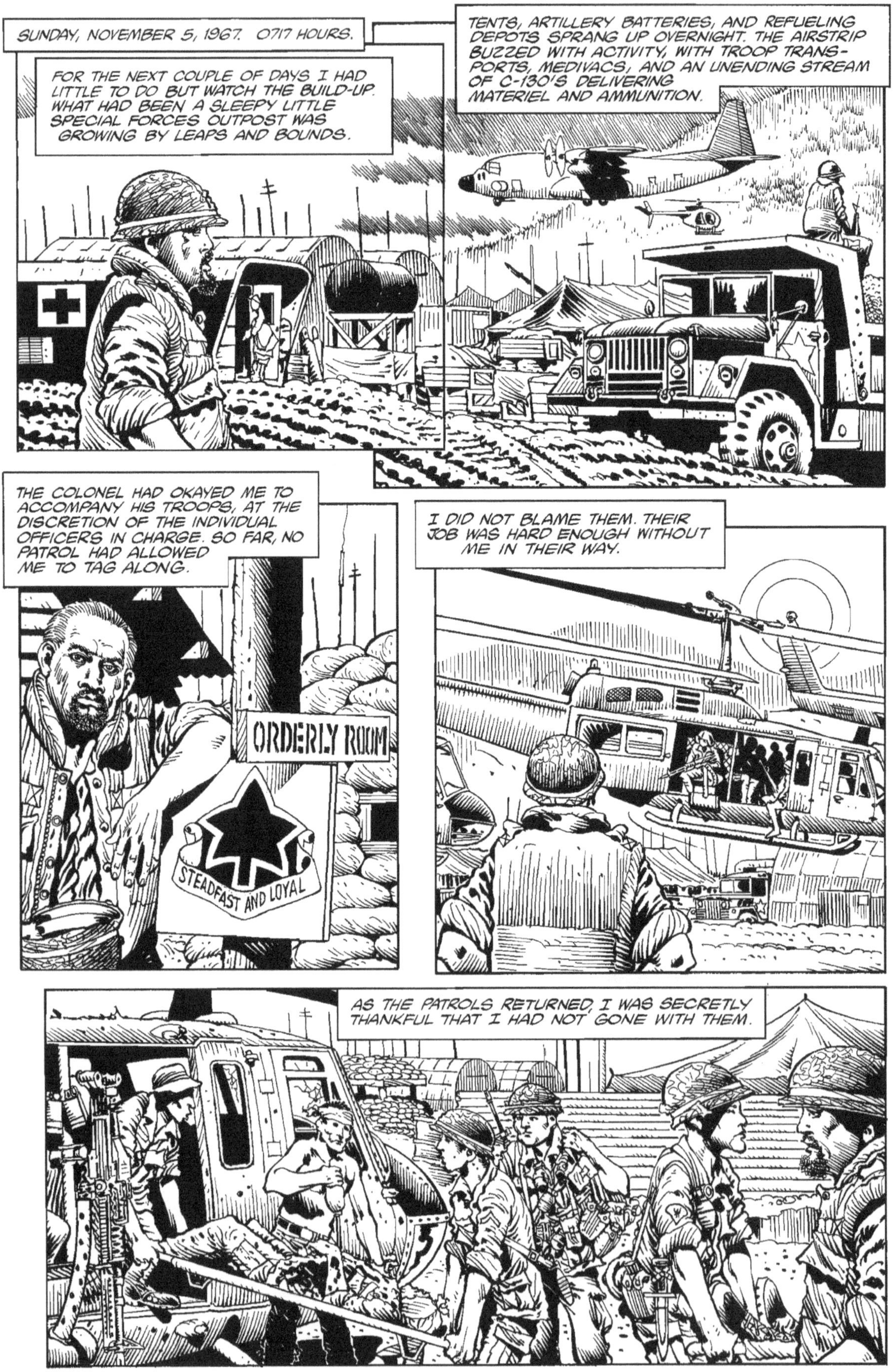
SUNDAY, NOVEMBER 5, 1967. 0717 HOURS.
FOR THE NEXT COUPLE OF DAYS I HAD LITTLE TO DO BUT WATCH THE BUILD-UP. WHAT HAD BEEN A SLEEPY LITTLE SPECIAL FORCES OUTPOST WAS GROWING BY LEAPS AND BOUNDS.
TENTS, ARTILLERY BATTERIES, AND REFUELING DEPOTS SPRANG UP OVERNIGHT. THE AIRSTRIP BUZZED WITH ACTIVITY, WITH TROOP TRANS-PORTS, MEDIVACS, AND AN UNENDING STREAM OF C-130'S DELIVERING MATERIEL AND AMMUNITION.
THE COLONEL HAD OKAYED ME TO ACCOMPANY HIS TROOPS, AT THE DISCRETION OF THE INDIVIDUAL OFFICERS IN CHARGE. SO FAR, NO PATROL HAD ALLOWED ME TO TAG ALONG.
ORDERLY ROOM
STEADFAST AND LOYAL
I DID NOT BLAME THEM. THEIR JOB WAS HARD ENOUGH WITHOUT ME IN THEIR WAY.
AS THE PATROLS RETURNED, I WAS SECRETLY THANKFUL THAT I HAD NOT GONE WITH THEM.

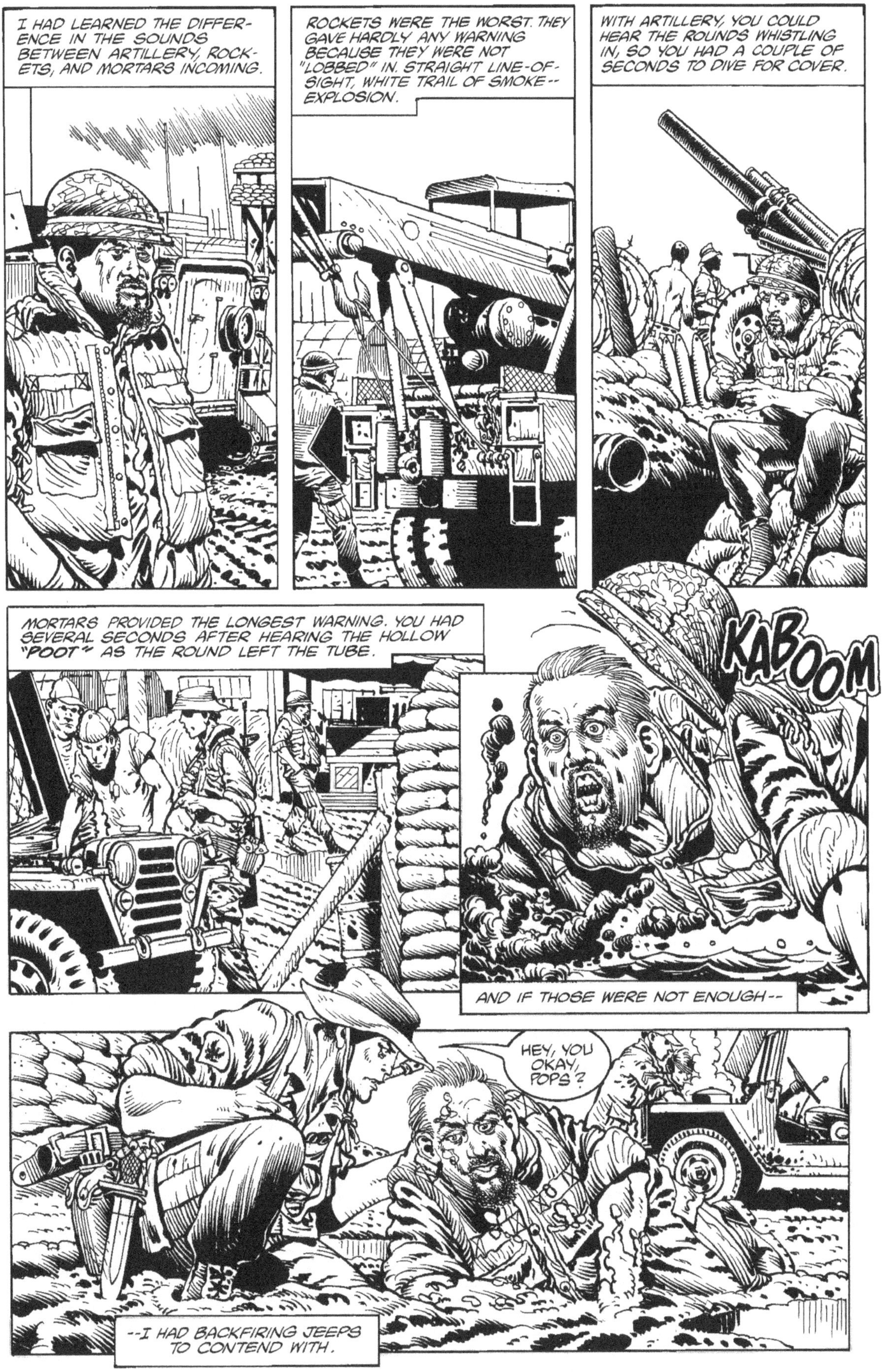
I HAD LEARNED THE DIFFERENCE IN THE SOUNDS BETWEEN ARTILLERY, ROCKETS, AND MORTARS INCOMING.
ROCKETS WERE THE WORST. THEY GAVE HARDLY ANY WARNING BECAUSE THEY WERE NOT "LOBBED" IN. STRAIGHT LINE-OF-SIGHT, WHITE TRAIL OF SMOKE--EXPLOSION.
WITH ARTILLERY, YOU COULD HEAR THE ROUNDS WHISTLING IN, SO YOU HAD A COUPLE OF SECONDS TO DIVE FOR COVER.
MORTARS PROVIDED THE LONGEST WARNING. YOU HAD SEVERAL SECONDS AFTER HEARING THE HOLLOW "POOT" AS THE ROUND LEFT THE TUBE.
KABOOM
AND IF THOSE WERE NOT ENOUGH--
HEY, YOU OKAY, POPS?
--I HAD BACKFIRING JEEPS TO CONTEND WITH.

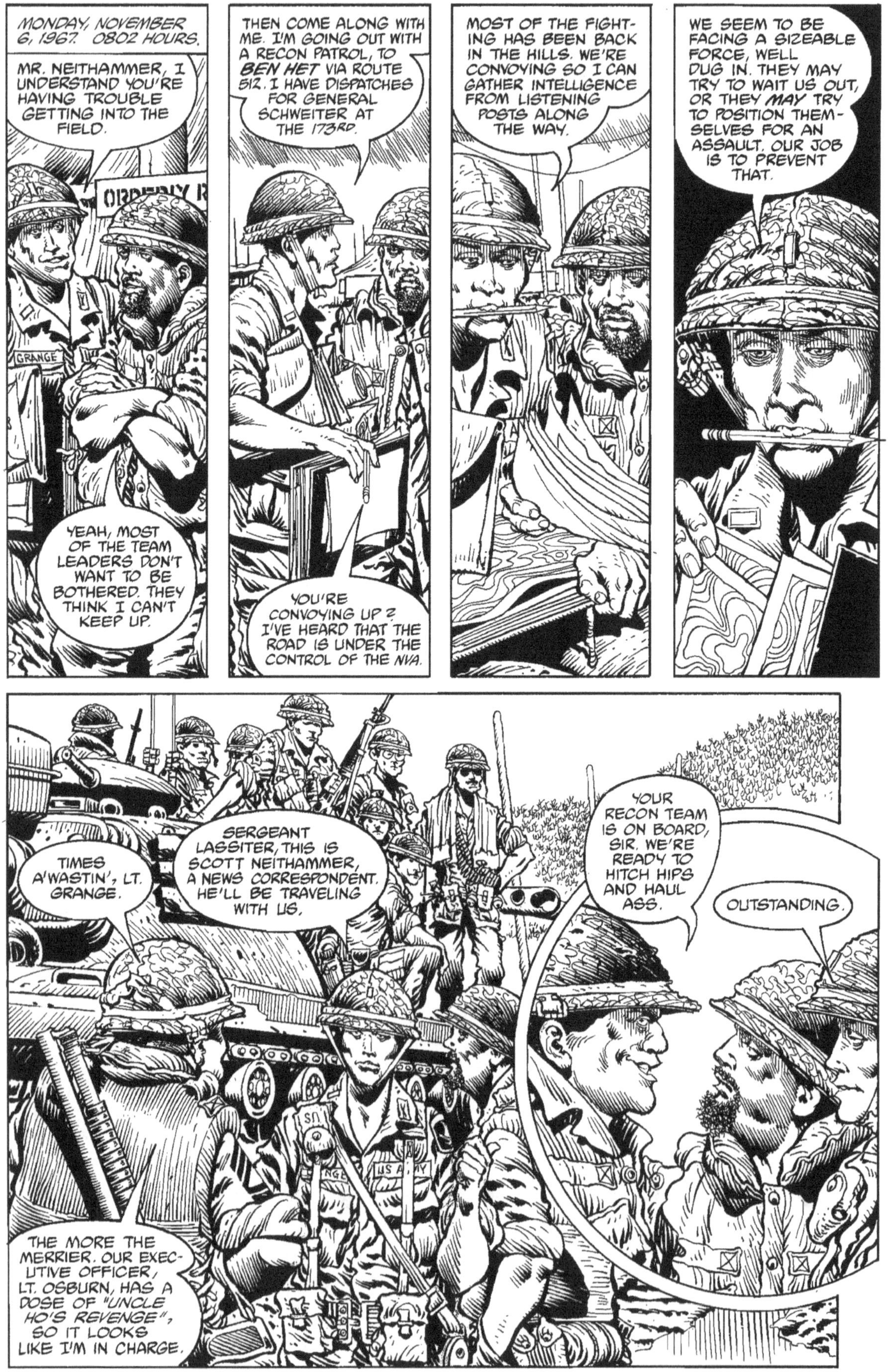
MONDAY, NOVEMBER 6, 1967. 0802 HOURS.
MR. NEITHAMMER, I UNDERSTAND YOU'RE HAVING TROUBLE GETTING INTO THE FIELD.
ORDERLY R
GRANGE
YEAH, MOST OF THE TEAM LEADERS DON'T WANT TO BE BOTHERED. THEY THINK I CAN'T KEEP UP.
THEN COME ALONG WITH ME. I'M GOING OUT WITH A RECON PATROL, TO BEN HET VIA ROUTE 512. I HAVE DISPATCHES FOR GENERAL SCHWEITER AT THE 173RD.
YOU'RE CONVOYING UP? I'VE HEARD THAT THE ROAD IS UNDER THE CONTROL OF THE NVA.
MOST OF THE FIGHTING HAS BEEN BACK IN THE HILLS. WE'RE CONVOYING SO I CAN GATHER INTELLIGENCE FROM LISTENING POSTS ALONG THE WAY.
WE SEEM TO BE FACING A SIZEABLE FORCE, WELL DUG IN. THEY MAY TRY TO WAIT US OUT, OR THEY MAY TRY TO POSITION THEMSELVES FOR AN ASSAULT. OUR JOB IS TO PREVENT THAT.
TIMES A'WASTIN', LT. GRANGE.
SERGEANT LASSITER, THIS IS SCOTT NEITHAMMER, A NEWS CORRESPONDENT. HE'LL BE TRAVELING WITH US.
THE MORE THE MERRIER. OUR EXECUTIVE OFFICER, LT. OSBURN, HAS A DOSE OF "UNCLE HO'S REVENGE", SO IT LOOKS LIKE I'M IN CHARGE.
US ARMY
YOUR RECON TEAM IS ON BOARD, SIR. WE'RE READY TO HITCH HIPS AND HAUL ASS.
OUTSTANDING.

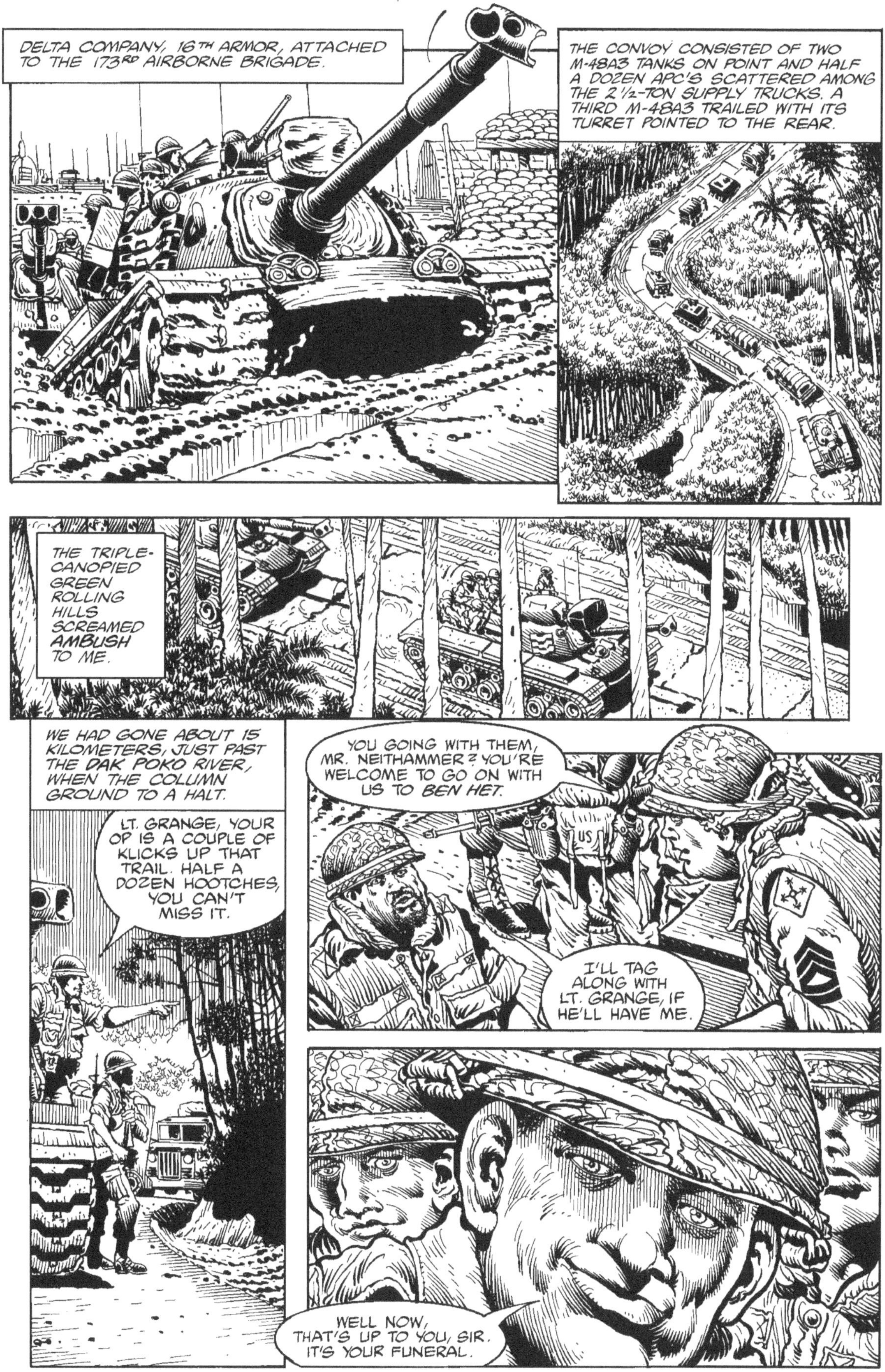
DELTA COMPANY, 16TH ARMOR, ATTACHED TO THE 173RD AIRBORNE BRIGADE.
THE CONVOY CONSISTED OF TWO M-48A3 TANKS ON POINT AND HALF A DOZEN APC'S SCATTERED AMONG THE 2 1/2-TON SUPPLY TRUCKS. A THIRD M-48A3 TRAILED WITH ITS TURRET POINTED TO THE REAR.
THE TRIPLE-CANOPIED GREEN ROLLING HILLS SCREAMED AMBUSH TO ME.
WE HAD GONE ABOUT 15 KILOMETERS, JUST PAST THE DAK POKO RIVER, WHEN THE COLUMN GROUND TO A HALT.
LT. GRANGE, YOUR OP IS A COUPLE OF KLICKS UP THAT TRAIL. HALF A DOZEN HOOTCHES, YOU CAN'T MISS IT.
YOU GOING WITH THEM, MR. NEITHAMMER? YOU'RE WELCOME TO GO ON WITH US TO BEN HET.
I'LL TAG ALONG WITH LT. GRANGE, IF HE'LL HAVE ME.
WELL NOW, THAT'S UP TO YOU, SIR. IT'S YOUR FUNERAL.

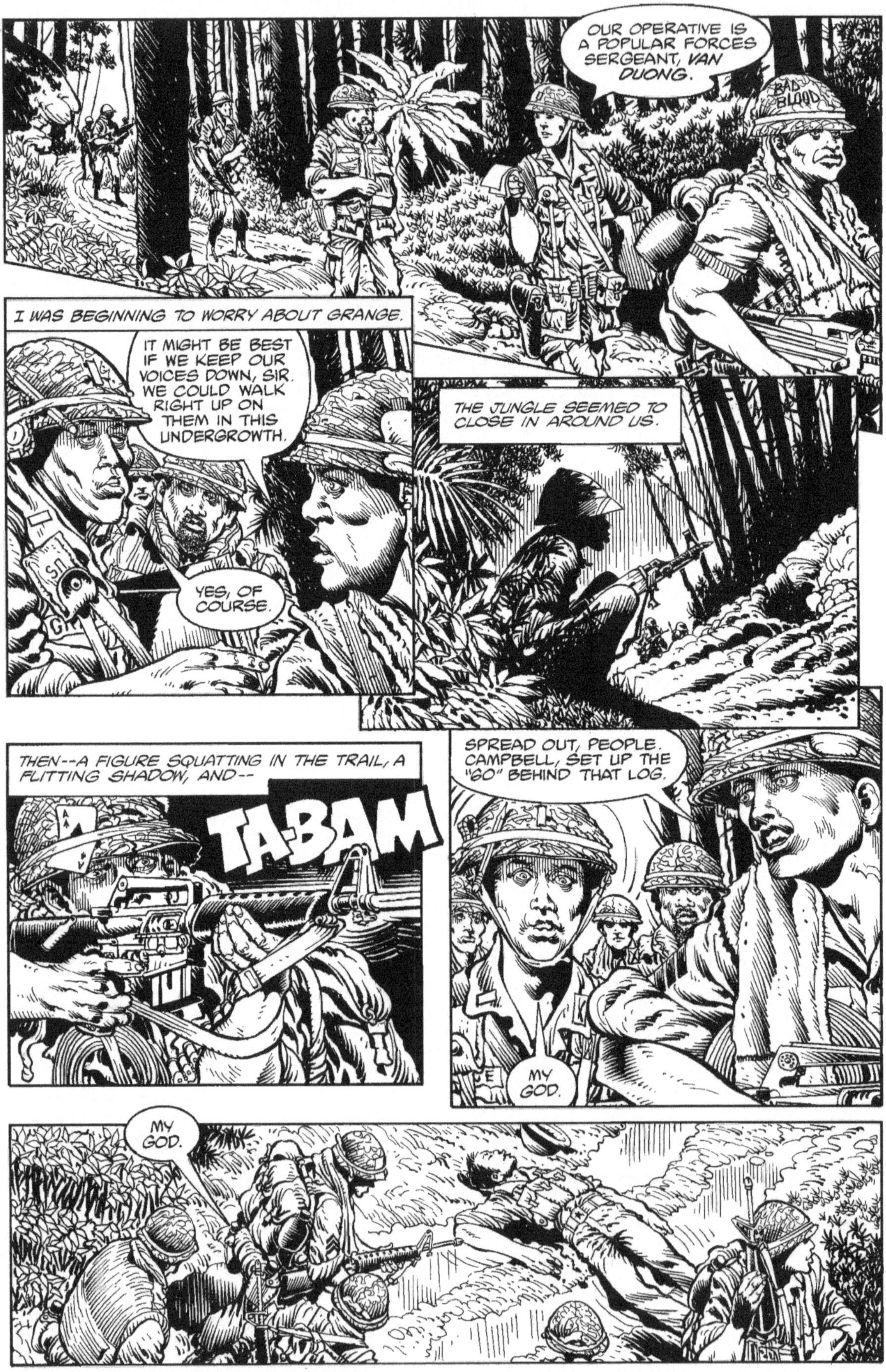

OUR OPERATIVE IS A POPULAR FORCES SERGEANT, VAN DUONG.
BAD BLOOD
I WAS BEGINNING TO WORRY ABOUT GRANGE.
IT MIGHT BE BEST IF WE KEEP OUR VOICES DOWN, SIR. WE COULD WALK RIGHT UP ON THEM IN THIS UNDERGROWTH.
YES, OF COURSE.
THE JUNGLE SEEMED TO CLOSE IN AROUND US.
THEN--A FIGURE SQUATTING IN THE TRAIL, A FLITTING SHADOW, AND--
TA-BAM
SPREAD OUT, PEOPLE. CAMPBELL, SET UP THE "60" BEHIND THAT LOG.
MY GOD.
MY GOD.

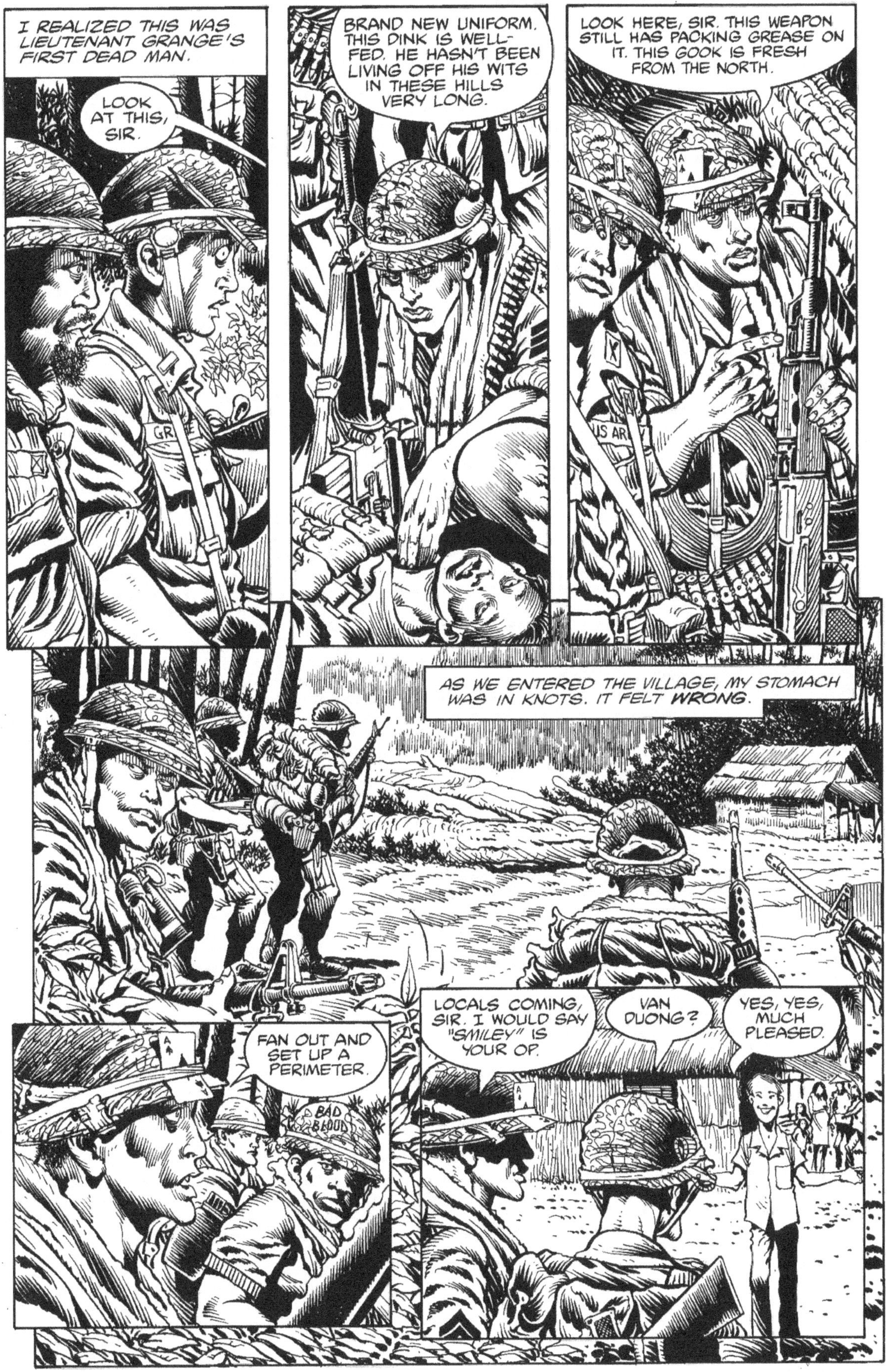
I REALIZED THIS WAS LIEUTENANT GRANGE'S FIRST DEAD MAN.
LOOK AT THIS, SIR.
GR
BRAND NEW UNIFORM. THIS DINK IS WELL-FED. HE HASN'T BEEN LIVING OFF HIS WITS IN THESE HILLS VERY LONG.
LOOK HERE, SIR. THIS WEAPON STILL HAS PACKING GREASE ON IT. THIS GOOK IS FRESH FROM THE NORTH.
US ARMY
AS WE ENTERED THE VILLAGE, MY STOMACH WAS IN KNOTS. IT FELT WRONG.
FAN OUT AND SET UP A PERIMETER.
BAD BLOOD
LOCALS COMING, SIR. I WOULD SAY "SMILEY" IS YOUR OP.
VAN DUONG?
YES, YES, MUCH PLEASED.

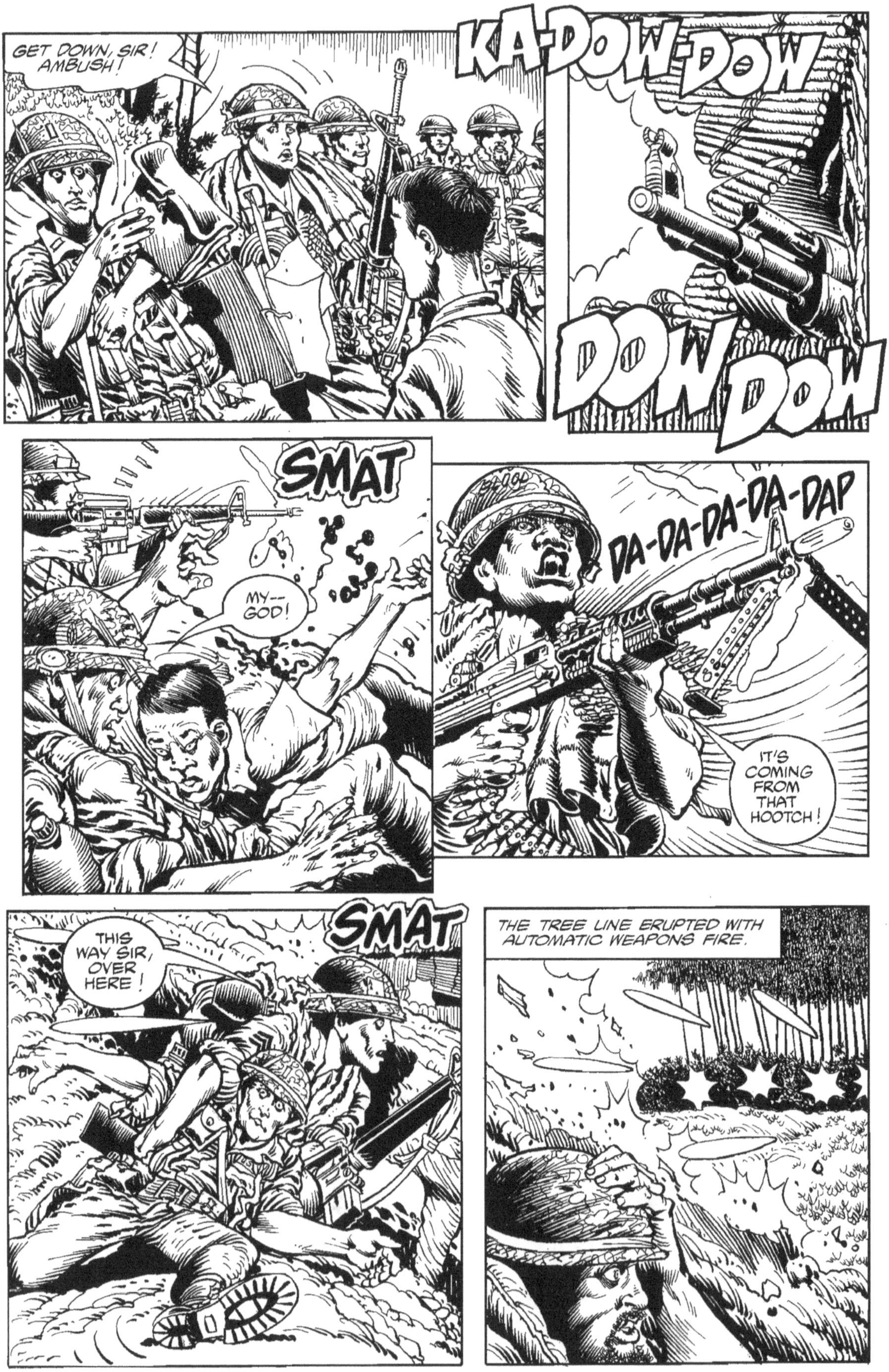
GET DOWN, SIR! AMBUSH!
KA-DOW-DOW-DOW
DOW DOW DOW
SMAT
MY--GOD!
DA-DA-DA-DA-DAP
IT'S COMING FROM THAT HOOTCH!
SMAT
THIS WAY SIR, OVER HERE!
THE TREE LINE ERUPTED WITH AUTOMATIC WEAPONS FIRE.

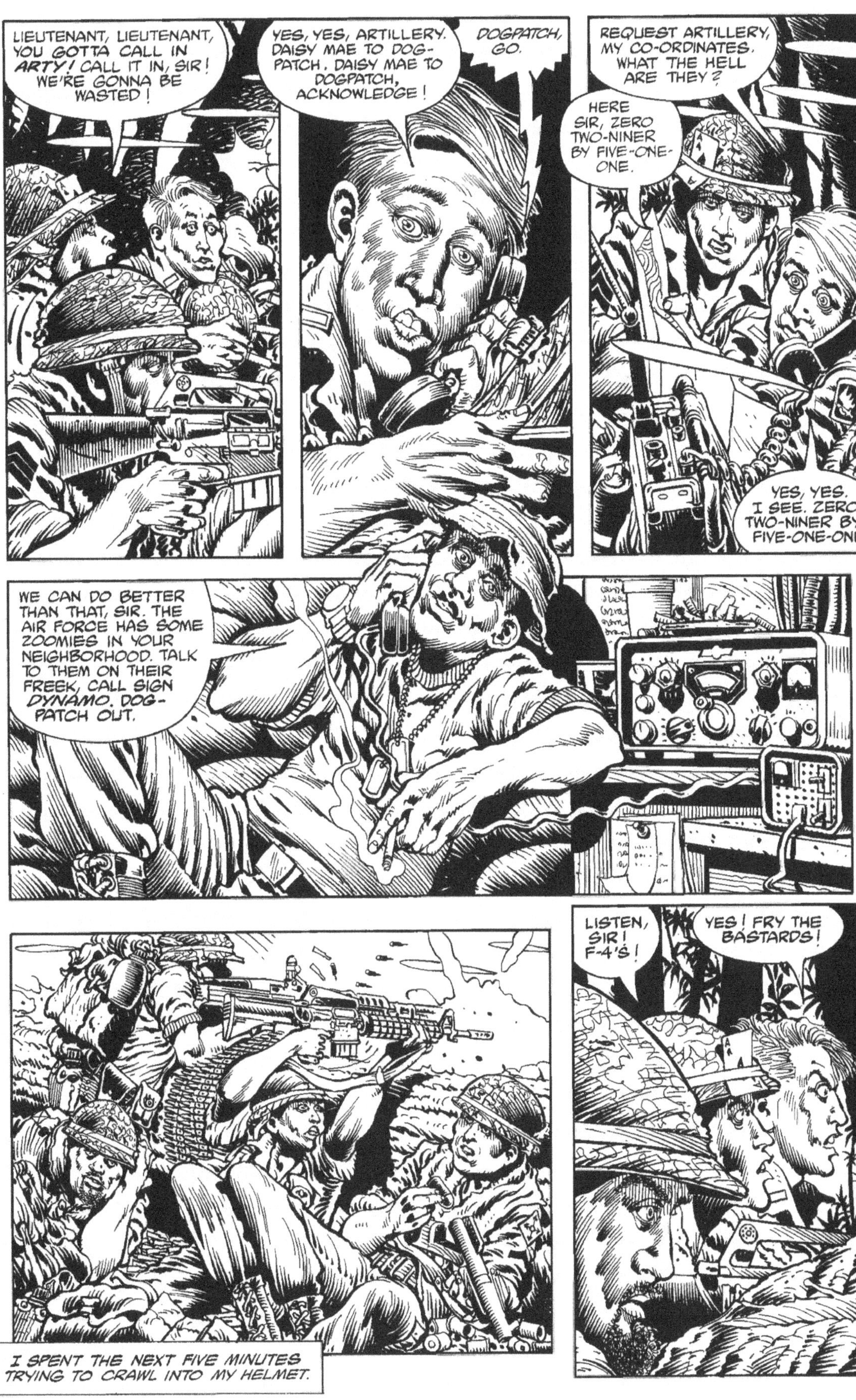
LIEUTENANT, LIEUTENANT, YOU GOTTA CALL IN ARTY! CALL IT IN, SIR! WE'RE GONNA BE WASTED!
YES, YES, ARTILLERY. DAISY MAE TO DOGPATCH. DAISY MAE TO DOGPATCH, ACKNOWLEDGE!
DOGPATCH, GO.
REQUEST ARTILLERY, MY CO-ORDINATES. WHAT THE HELL ARE THEY?
HERE SIR, ZERO TWO-NINER BY FIVE-ONE-ONE.
YES, YES. I SEE. ZERO TWO-NINER BY FIVE-ONE-ONE.
WE CAN DO BETTER THAN THAT, SIR. THE AIR FORCE HAS SOME ZOOMIES IN YOUR NEIGHBORHOOD. TALK TO THEM ON THEIR FREEK, CALL SIGN DYNAMO. DOGPATCH OUT.
I SPENT THE NEXT FIVE MINUTES TRYING TO CRAWL INTO MY HELMET.
LISTEN, SIR! F-4'S!
YES! FRY THE BASTARDS!

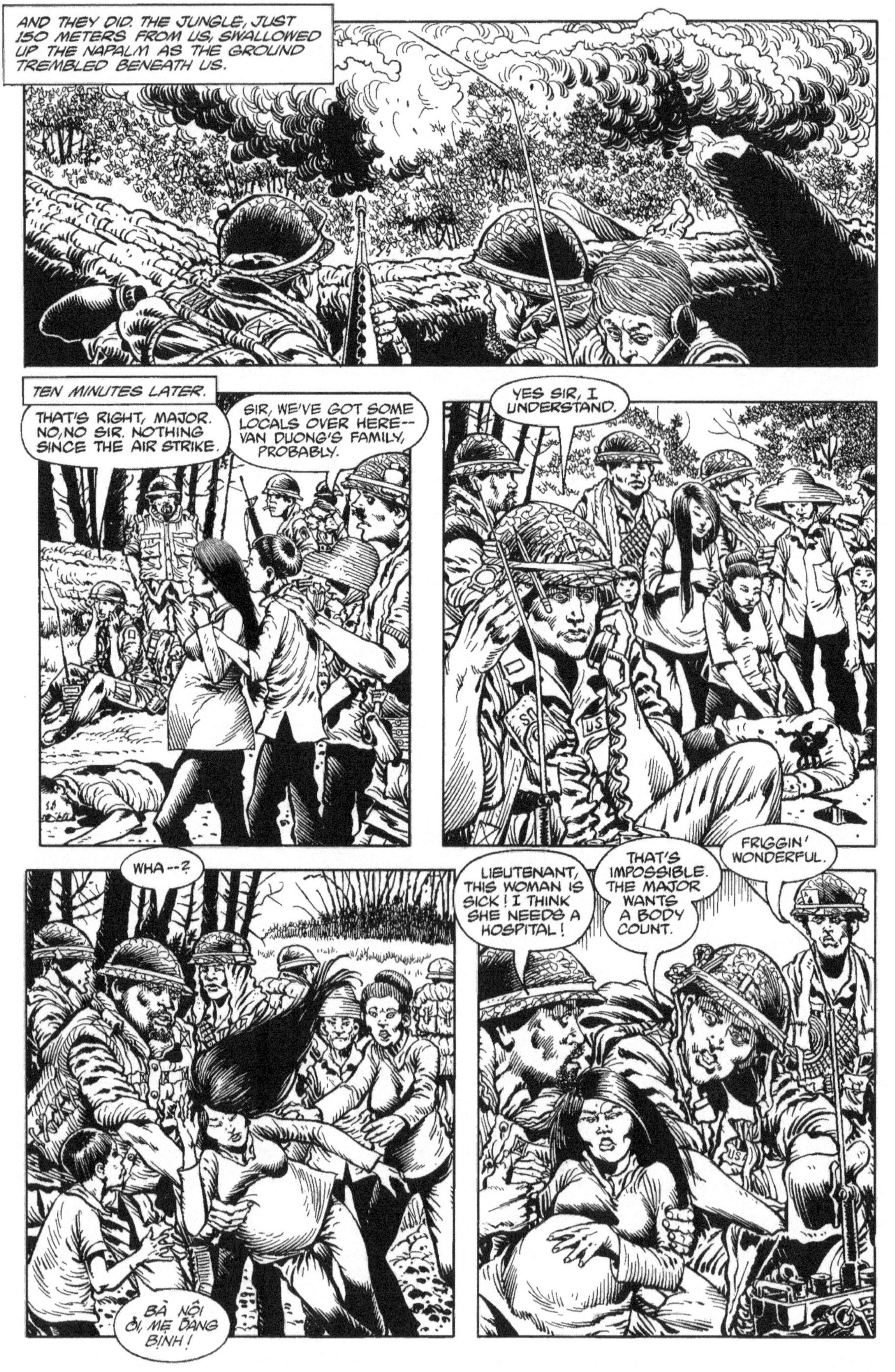
AND THEY DID. THE JUNGLE, JUST 150 METERS FROM US, SWALLOWED UP THE NAPALM AS THE GROUND TREMBLED BENEATH US.
TEN MINUTES LATER.
THAT'S RIGHT, MAJOR. NO, NO SIR. NOTHING SINCE THE AIR STRIKE.
SIR, WE'VE GOT SOME LOCALS OVER HERE-- VAN DUONG'S FAMILY, PROBABLY.
YES SIR, I UNDERSTAND.
WHA--?
BÀ NỘI ỜI, MẸ ĐANG BỊNH!
LIEUTENANT, THIS WOMAN IS SICK! I THINK SHE NEEDS A HOSPITAL!
THAT'S IMPOSSIBLE. THE MAJOR WANTS A BODY COUNT.
FRIGGIN' WONDERFUL.

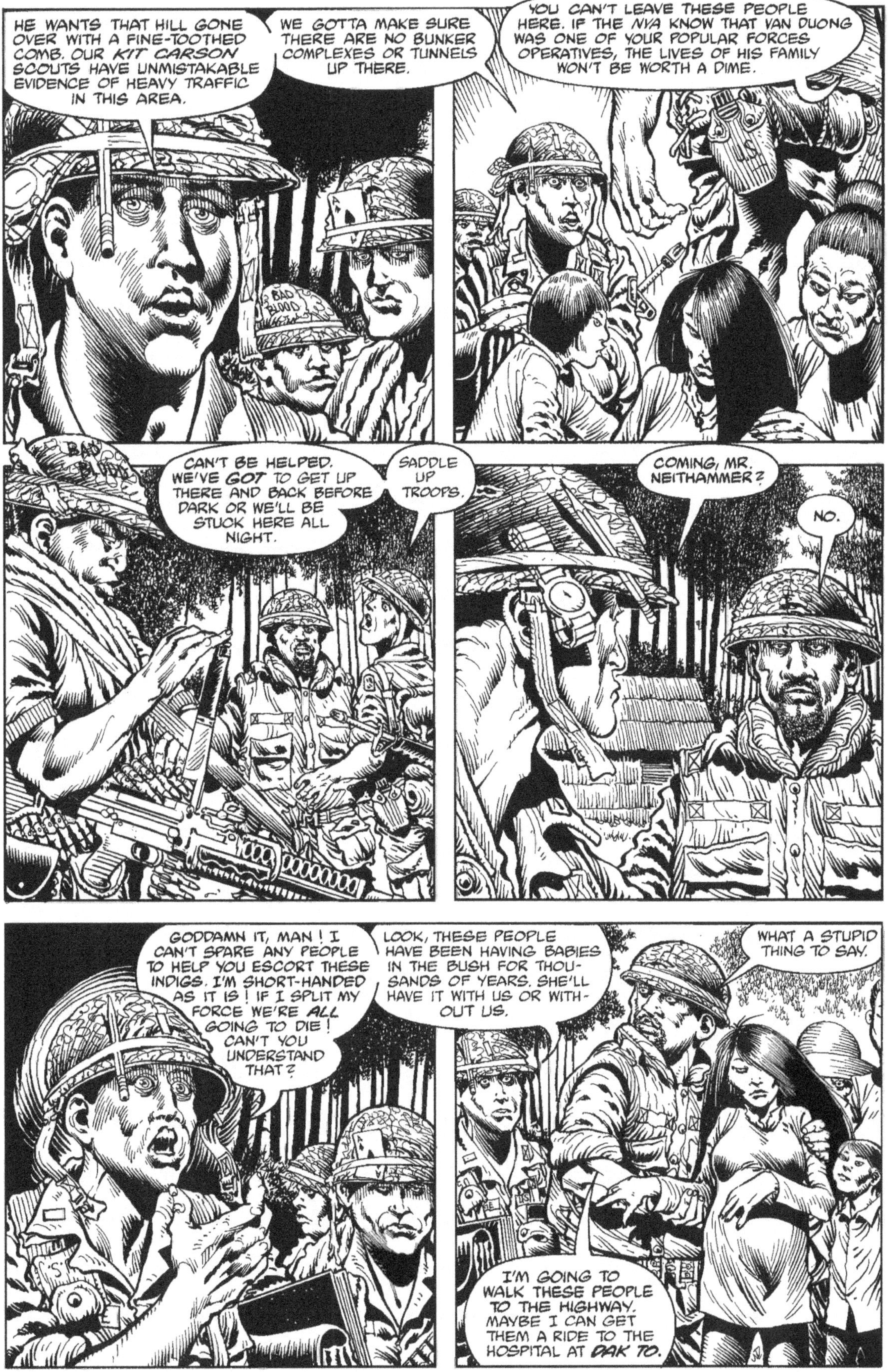
HE WANTS THAT HILL GONE OVER WITH A FINE-TOOTHED COMB. OUR *KIT CARSON* SCOUTS HAVE UNMISTAKABLE EVIDENCE OF HEAVY TRAFFIC IN THIS AREA.
WE GOTTA MAKE SURE THERE ARE NO BUNKER COMPLEXES OR TUNNELS UP THERE.
BAD BLOOD
YOU CAN'T LEAVE THESE PEOPLE HERE. IF THE *NVA* KNOW THAT VAN DUONG WAS ONE OF YOUR POPULAR FORCES OPERATIVES, THE LIVES OF HIS FAMILY WON'T BE WORTH A DIME.
CAN'T BE HELPED. WE'VE *GOT* TO GET UP THERE AND BACK BEFORE DARK OR WE'LL BE STUCK HERE ALL NIGHT.
SADDLE UP TROOPS.
COMING, MR. NEITHAMMER?
NO.
GODDAMN IT, MAN! I CAN'T SPARE ANY PEOPLE TO HELP YOU ESCORT THESE INDIGS. I'M SHORT-HANDED AS IT IS! IF I SPLIT MY FORCE WE'RE *ALL* GOING TO DIE! CAN'T YOU UNDERSTAND THAT?
LOOK, THESE PEOPLE HAVE BEEN HAVING BABIES IN THE BUSH FOR THOU-SANDS OF YEARS. SHE'LL HAVE IT WITH US OR WITH-OUT US.
WHAT A STUPID THING TO SAY.
I'M GOING TO WALK THESE PEOPLE TO THE HIGHWAY. MAYBE I CAN GET THEM A RIDE TO THE HOSPITAL AT *DAK TO*.

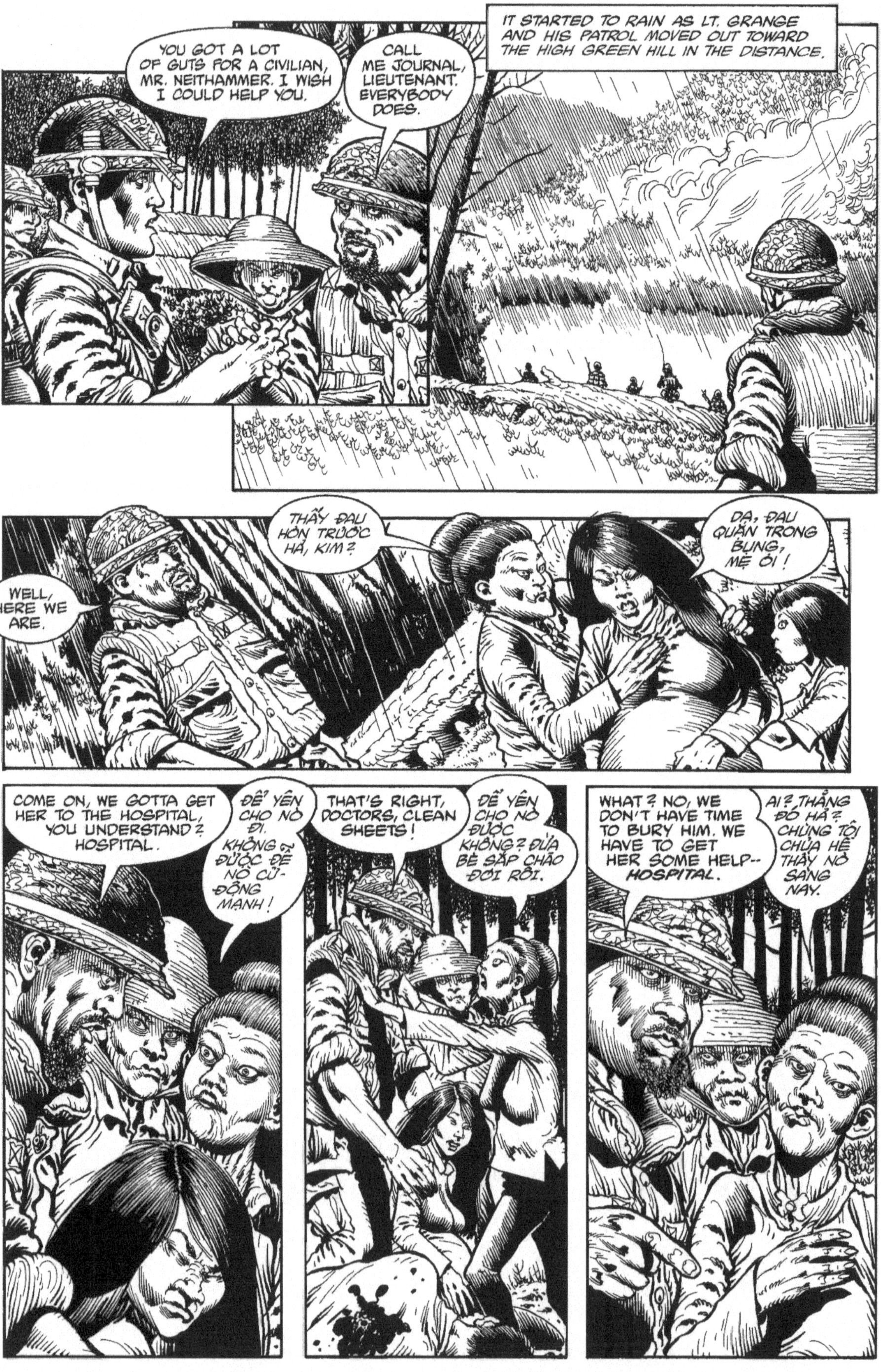
IT STARTED TO RAIN AS LT. GRANGE AND HIS PATROL MOVED OUT TOWARD THE HIGH GREEN HILL IN THE DISTANCE.
YOU GOT A LOT OF GUTS FOR A CIVILIAN, MR. NEITHAMMER. I WISH I COULD HELP YOU.
CALL ME JOURNAL, LIEUTENANT. EVERYBODY DOES.
THẤY ĐAU HƠN TRƯỚC HẢ, KIM?
DẠ, ĐAU QUẶN TRONG BỤNG, MẸ ƠI!
WELL, HERE WE ARE.
COME ON, WE GOTTA GET HER TO THE HOSPITAL, YOU UNDERSTAND? HOSPITAL.
ĐỂ YÊN CHO NÓ ĐI. KHÔNG ĐƯỢC ĐỂ NÓ CỬ-ĐỘNG MẠNH!
THAT'S RIGHT, DOCTORS, CLEAN SHEETS!
ĐỂ YÊN CHO NÓ ĐƯỢC KHÔNG? ĐỨA BÉ SẮP CHÀO ĐỜI RỒI.
WHAT? NO, WE DON'T HAVE TIME TO BURY HIM. WE HAVE TO GET HER SOME HELP-- HOSPITAL.
AI? THẰNG ĐÓ HẢ? CHÚNG TÔI CHƯA HỀ THẤY NÓ SÁNG NAY.

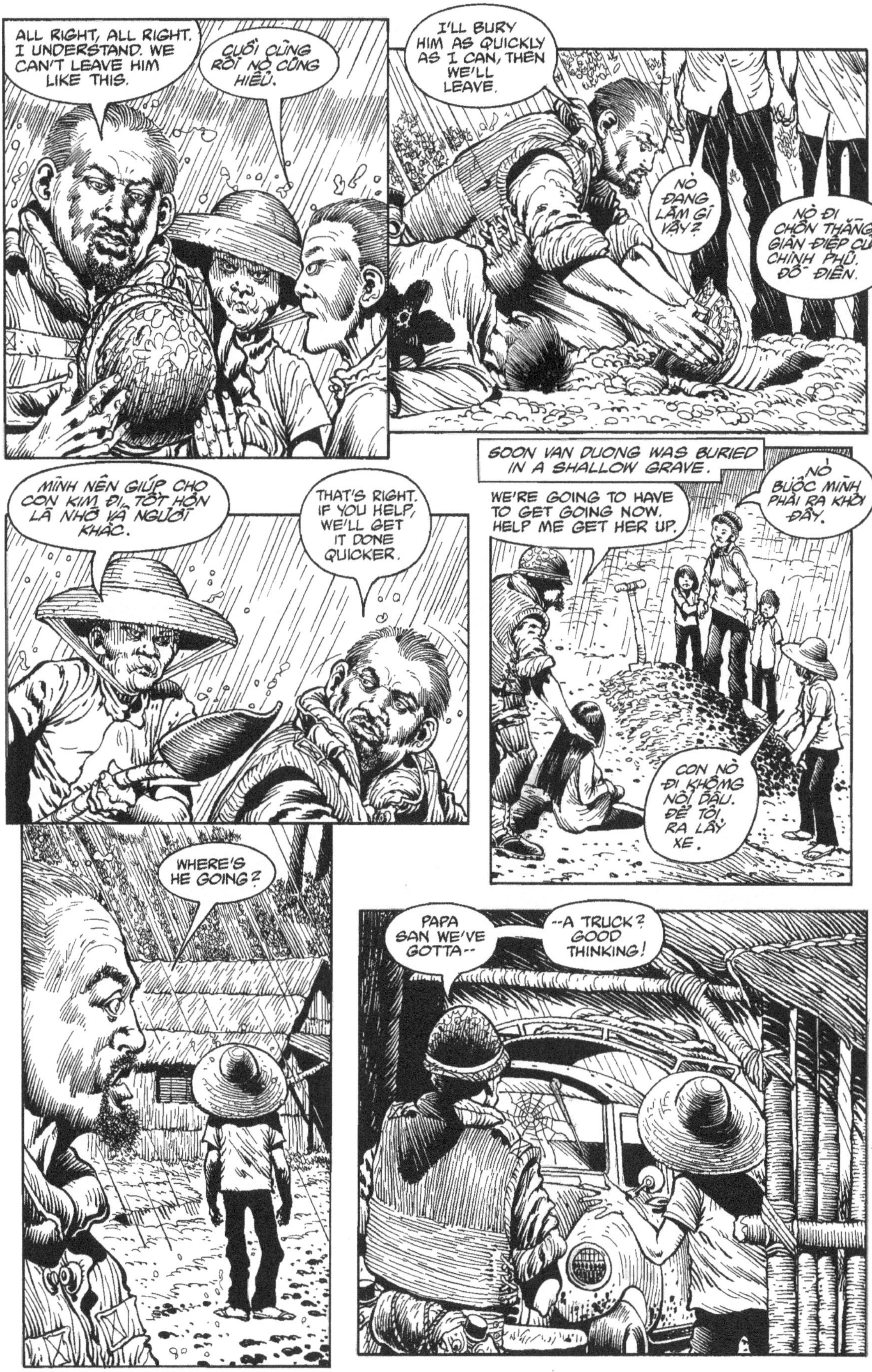
ALL RIGHT, ALL RIGHT. I UNDERSTAND. WE CAN'T LEAVE HIM LIKE THIS.
CUỐI CÙNG RỒI NỎ CŨNG HIỂU.
I'LL BURY HIM AS QUICKLY AS I CAN, THEN WE'LL LEAVE.
NỎ ĐANG LÃM GÌ VẬY?
NỎ ĐI CHÔN THẰNG GIÁN ĐIỆP CỦA CHÍNH PHỦ. ĐỒ ĐIÊN.
MÌNH NÊN GIÚP CHO CON KIM ĐI. TỐT HƠN LÃ NHỜ VẢ NGƯỜI KHÁC.
THAT'S RIGHT. IF YOU HELP, WE'LL GET IT DONE QUICKER.
SOON VAN DUONG WAS BURIED IN A SHALLOW GRAVE.
WE'RE GOING TO HAVE TO GET GOING NOW. HELP ME GET HER UP.
NỎ BUỘC MÌNH PHẢI RA KHỎI ĐẤY.
CON NỎ ĐI KHÔNG NỔI ĐÂU. ĐỂ TÔI RA LẤY XE.
WHERE'S HE GOING?
PAPA SAN WE'VE GOTTA--
--A TRUCK? GOOD THINKING!

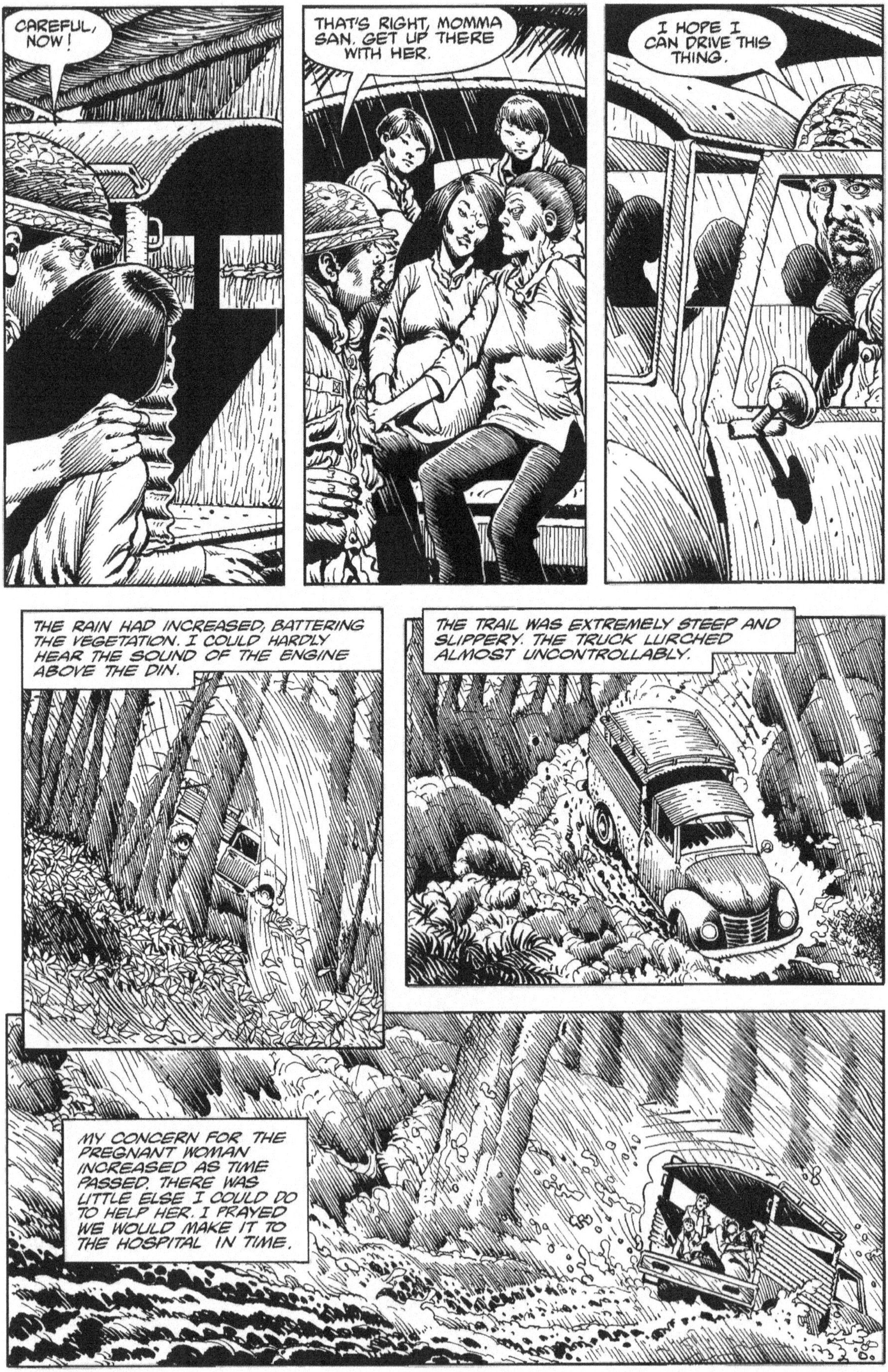
CAREFUL, NOW!
THAT'S RIGHT, MOMMA SAN. GET UP THERE WITH HER.
I HOPE I CAN DRIVE THIS THING.
THE RAIN HAD INCREASED, BATTERING THE VEGETATION. I COULD HARDLY HEAR THE SOUND OF THE ENGINE ABOVE THE DIN.
THE TRAIL WAS EXTREMELY STEEP AND SLIPPERY. THE TRUCK LURCHED ALMOST UNCONTROLLABLY.
MY CONCERN FOR THE PREGNANT WOMAN INCREASED AS TIME PASSED. THERE WAS LITTLE ELSE I COULD DO TO HELP HER. I PRAYED WE WOULD MAKE IT TO THE HOSPITAL IN TIME.

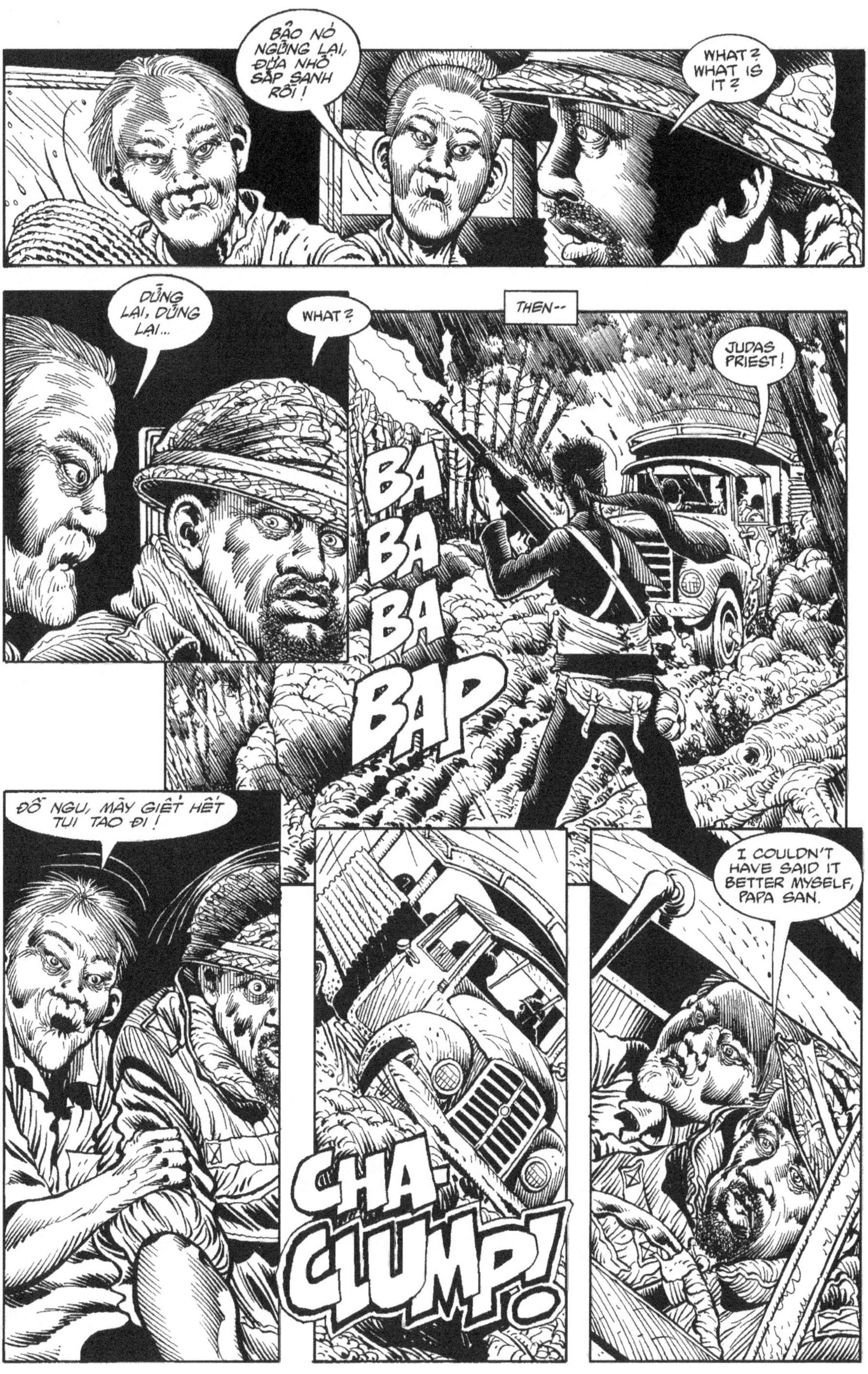
BẢO NÓ NGỪNG LẠI, ĐỨA NHỎ SẮP SANH RỒI!
WHAT? WHAT IS IT?
DỪNG LẠI, DỪNG LẠI...
WHAT?
THEN--
JUDAS PRIEST!
BA BA BA BAP
ĐỒ NGU, MÀY GIẾT HẾT TỤI TAO ĐI!
CHA-CLUMP!
I COULDN'T HAVE SAID IT BETTER MYSELF, PAPA SAN.

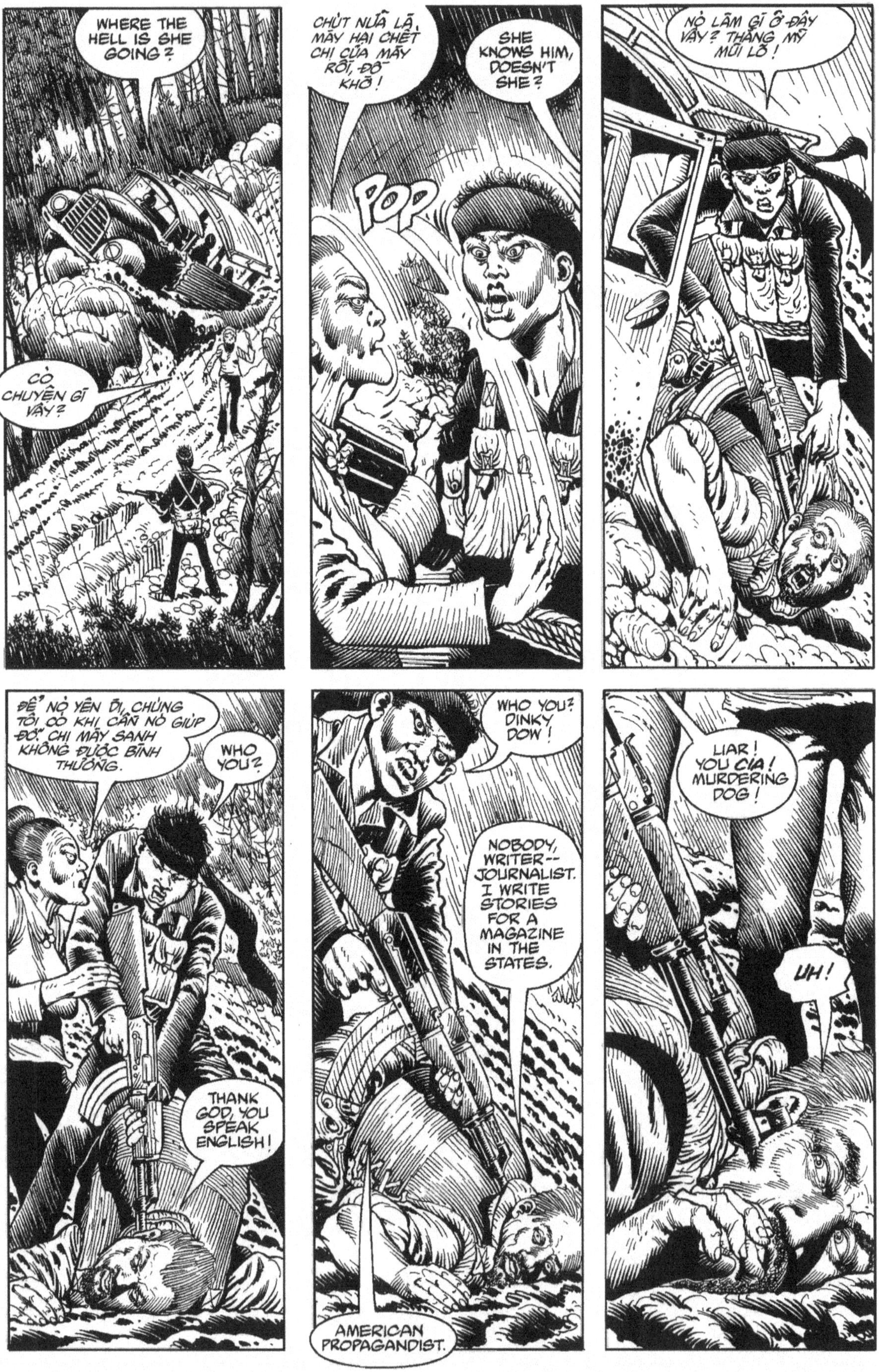
WHERE THE HELL IS SHE GOING?
CÓ CHUYỆN GÌ VẬY?
CHỦT NỮA LẬ, MÃY HẠI CHẾT CHỊ CỦA MÃY RỒI, ĐỒ KHỜ!
SHE KNOWS HIM, DOESN'T SHE?
POP
NỎ LÀM GÌ Ở ĐÂY VẬY? THẰNG MỸ MŨI LÕ!
ĐỂ NỌ YÊN ĐI, CHỦNG TÔI CÓ KHI CẦN NÓ GIÚP ĐỠ. CHỊ MÃY SANH KHÔNG ĐƯỢC BÌNH THƯỜNG.
WHO YOU?
THANK GOD, YOU SPEAK ENGLISH!
WHO YOU? DINKY DOW!
NOBODY, WRITER-- JOURNALIST. I WRITE STORIES FOR A MAGAZINE IN THE STATES.
AMERICAN PROPAGANDIST.
LIAR! YOU CIA! MURDERING DOG!
UH!

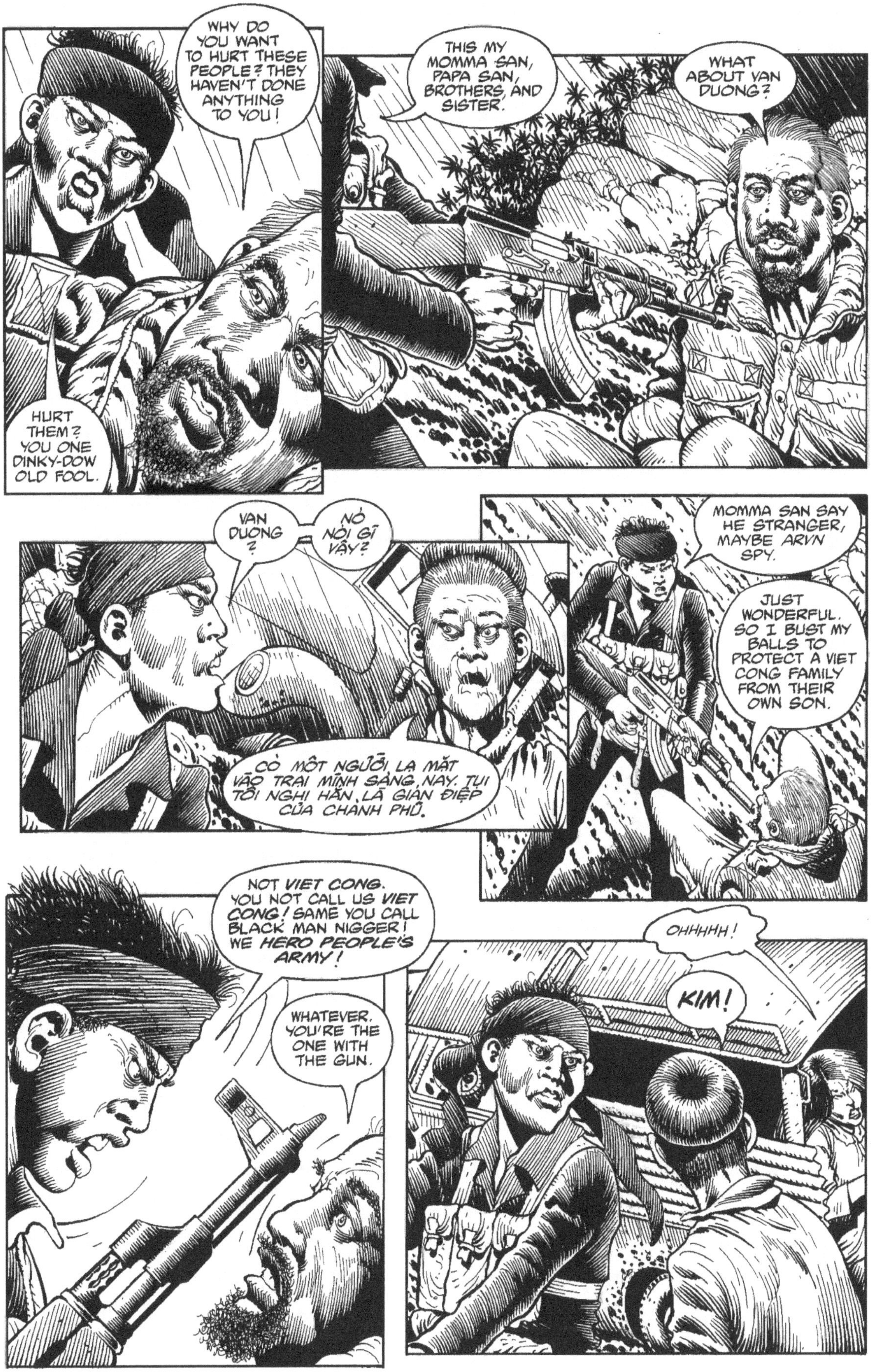
WHY DO YOU WANT TO HURT THESE PEOPLE? THEY HAVEN'T DONE ANYTHING TO YOU!
HURT THEM? YOU ONE DINKY-DOW OLD FOOL.
THIS MY MOMMA SAN, PAPA SAN, BROTHERS, AND SISTER.
WHAT ABOUT VAN DUONG?
VAN DUONG?
NÓ NÓI GÌ VẬY?
CÓ MỘT NGƯỜI LẠ MẶT VÀO TRẠI MÌNH SÁNG NAY. TỤI TÔI NGHI HẮN LÀ GIÁN ĐIỆP CỦA CHÁNH PHỦ.
MOMMA SAN SAY HE STRANGER, MAYBE ARVN SPY.
JUST WONDERFUL. SO I BUST MY BALLS TO PROTECT A VIET CONG FAMILY FROM THEIR OWN SON.
NOT VIET CONG. YOU NOT CALL US VIET CONG! SAME YOU CALL BLACK MAN NIGGER! WE HERO PEOPLE'S ARMY!
WHATEVER. YOU'RE THE ONE WITH THE GUN.
OHHHHH!
KIM!

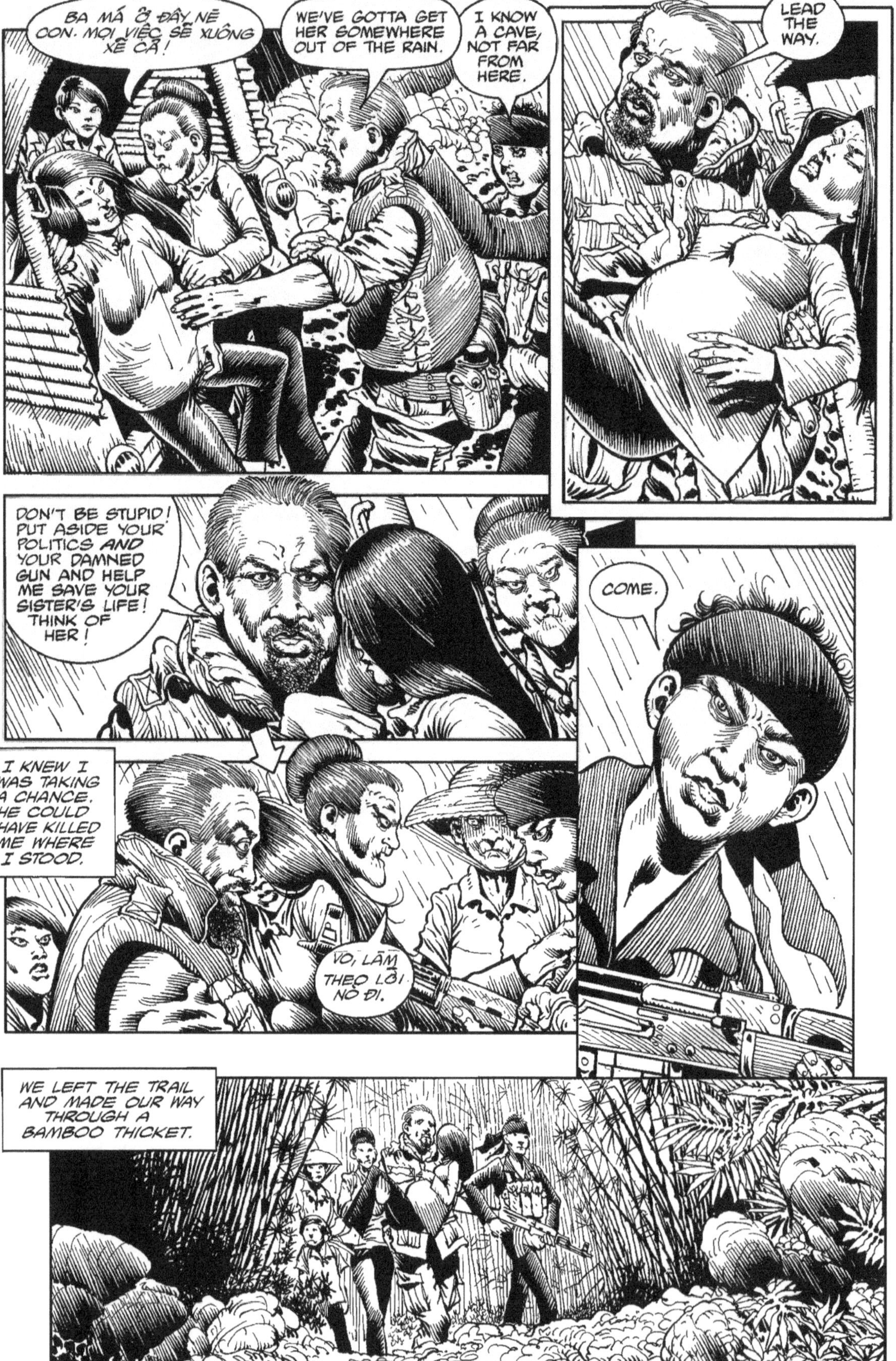
BA MÁ Ở ĐÂY NÈ CON. MỌI VIỆC SẼ XUÔNG XẾ CẢ!
WE'VE GOTTA GET HER SOMEWHERE OUT OF THE RAIN.
I KNOW A CAVE, NOT FAR FROM HERE.
LEAD THE WAY.
DON'T BE STUPID! PUT ASIDE YOUR POLITICS AND YOUR DAMNED GUN AND HELP ME SAVE YOUR SISTER'S LIFE! THINK OF HER!
COME.
I KNEW I WAS TAKING A CHANCE. HE COULD HAVE KILLED ME WHERE I STOOD.
VO, LÀM THEO LỜI NÓ ĐI.
WE LEFT THE TRAIL AND MADE OUR WAY THROUGH A BAMBOO THICKET.

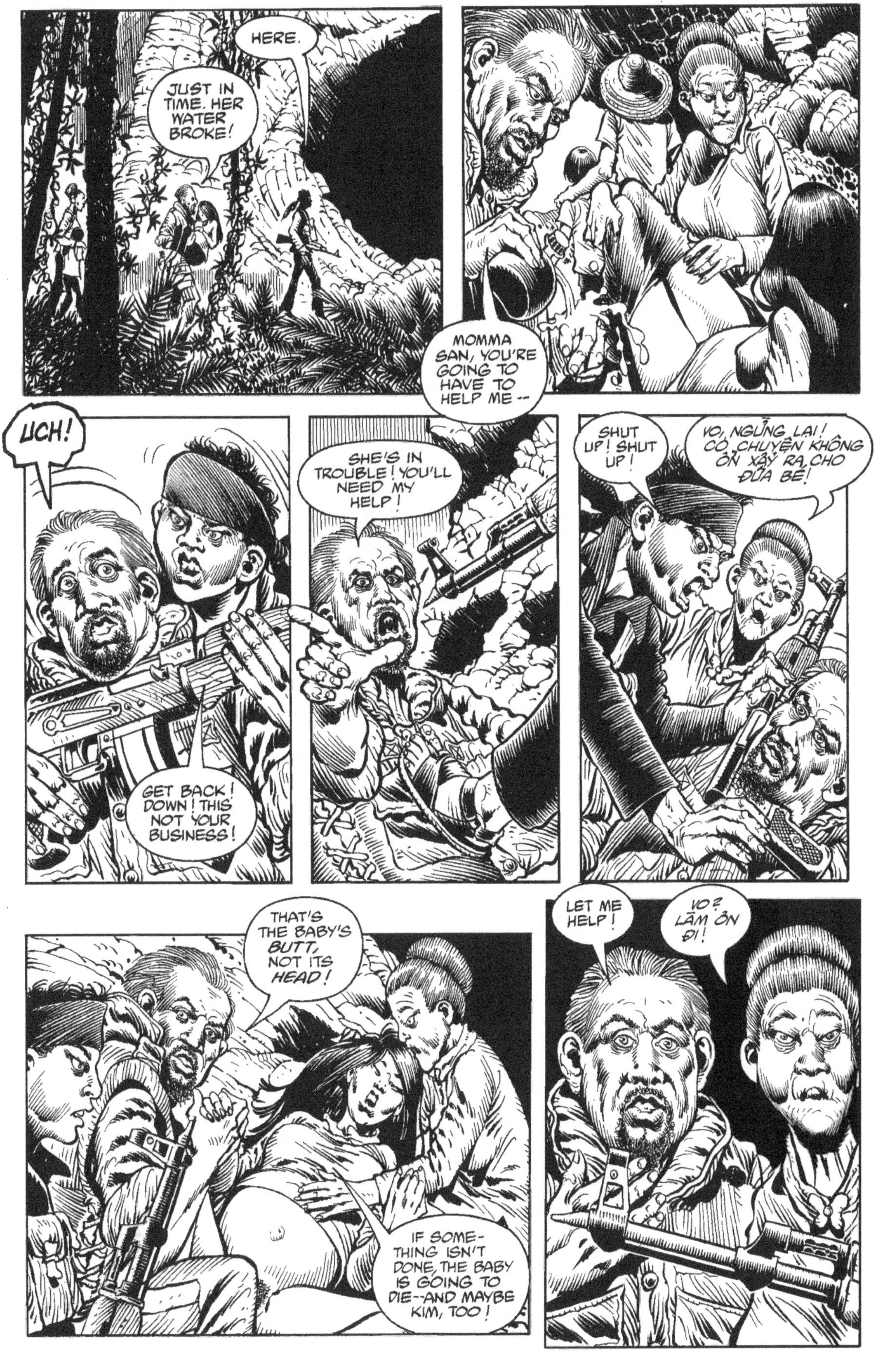
HERE.
JUST IN TIME. HER WATER BROKE!
MOMMA SAN, YOU'RE GOING TO HAVE TO HELP ME --
UCH!
GET BACK! DOWN! THIS NOT YOUR BUSINESS!
SHE'S IN TROUBLE! YOU'LL NEED MY HELP!
SHUT UP! SHUT UP!
VO, NGỪNG LẠI! CÓ CHUYỆN KHÔNG ỔN XẢY RA CHO ĐỨA BÉ!
THAT'S THE BABY'S *BUTT*, NOT ITS *HEAD*!
IF SOMETHING ISN'T DONE, THE BABY IS GOING TO DIE--AND MAYBE KIM, TOO!
LET ME HELP!
VO? LÃM ỔN ĐI!

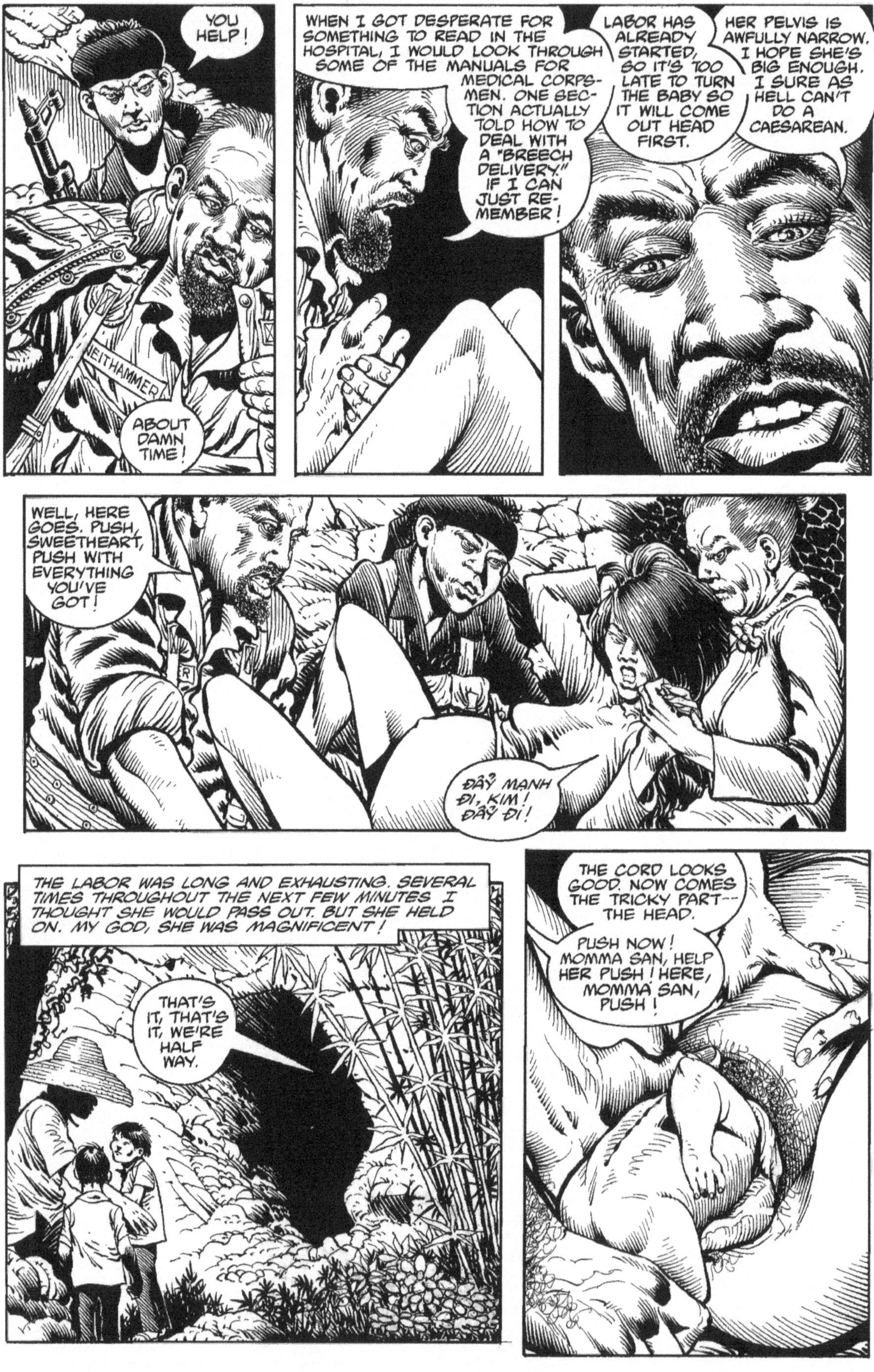
YOU HELP!
NEITHAMMER
ABOUT DAMN TIME!
WHEN I GOT DESPERATE FOR SOMETHING TO READ IN THE HOSPITAL, I WOULD LOOK THROUGH SOME OF THE MANUALS FOR MEDICAL CORPSMEN. ONE SECTION ACTUALLY TOLD HOW TO DEAL WITH A "BREECH DELIVERY." IF I CAN JUST REMEMBER!
LABOR HAS ALREADY STARTED, SO IT'S TOO LATE TO TURN THE BABY SO IT WILL COME OUT HEAD FIRST.
HER PELVIS IS AWFULLY NARROW. I HOPE SHE'S BIG ENOUGH. I SURE AS HELL CAN'T DO A CAESAREAN.
WELL, HERE GOES. PUSH, SWEETHEART, PUSH WITH EVERYTHING YOU'VE GOT!
ĐẨY MẠNH ĐI, KIM! ĐẨY ĐI!
THE LABOR WAS LONG AND EXHAUSTING. SEVERAL TIMES THROUGHOUT THE NEXT FEW MINUTES I THOUGHT SHE WOULD PASS OUT. BUT SHE HELD ON. MY GOD, SHE WAS MAGNIFICENT!
THAT'S IT, THAT'S IT, WE'RE HALF WAY.
THE CORD LOOKS GOOD. NOW COMES THE TRICKY PART-- THE HEAD.
PUSH NOW! MOMMA SAN, HELP HER PUSH! HERE, MOMMA SAN, PUSH!

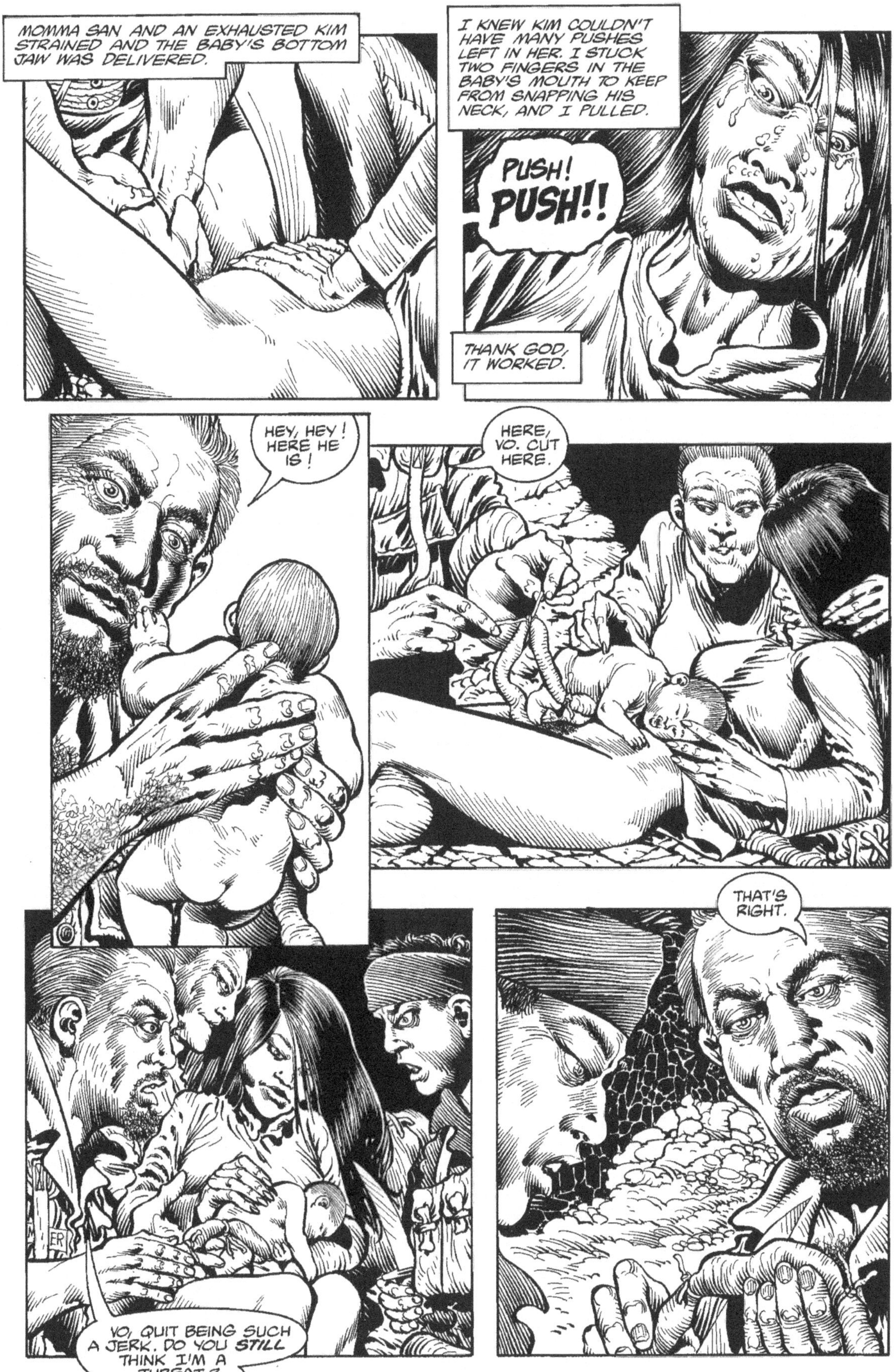
MOMMA SAN AND AN EXHAUSTED KIM STRAINED AND THE BABY'S BOTTOM JAW WAS DELIVERED.
I KNEW KIM COULDN'T HAVE MANY PUSHES LEFT IN HER. I STUCK TWO FINGERS IN THE BABY'S MOUTH TO KEEP FROM SNAPPING HIS NECK, AND I PULLED.
PUSH! PUSH!!
THANK GOD, IT WORKED.
HEY, HEY! HERE HE IS!
HERE, VO. CUT HERE.
VO, QUIT BEING SUCH A JERK. DO YOU STILL THINK I'M A THREAT?
THAT'S RIGHT.

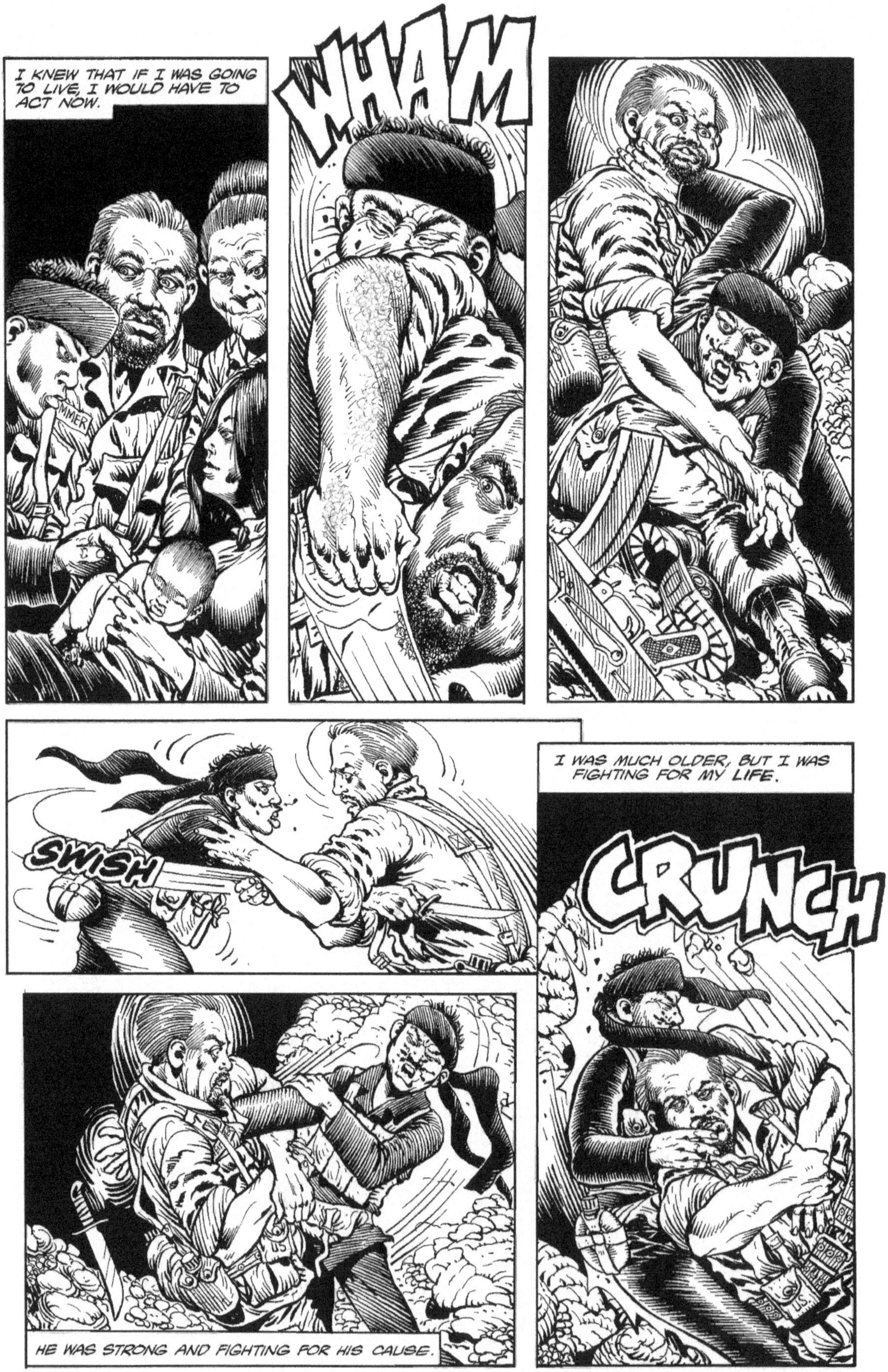
I KNEW THAT IF I WAS GOING TO LIVE, I WOULD HAVE TO ACT NOW.
WHAM
SWISH
HE WAS STRONG AND FIGHTING FOR HIS CAUSE.
I WAS MUCH OLDER, BUT I WAS FIGHTING FOR MY LIFE.
CRUNCH

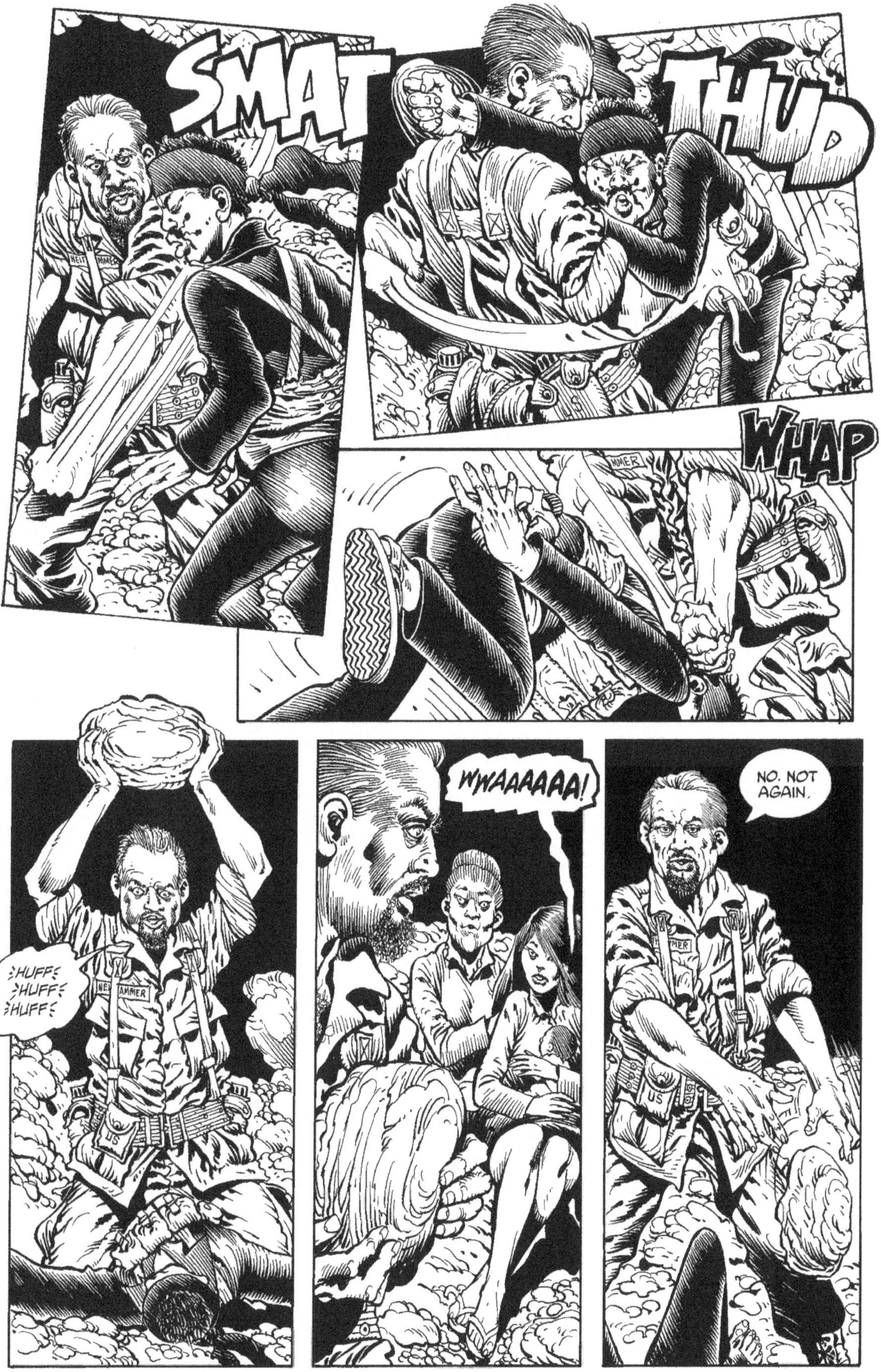
SMAT
THUD
WHAP
HUFF HUFF HUFF
WWAAAAAA!
NO. NOT AGAIN.

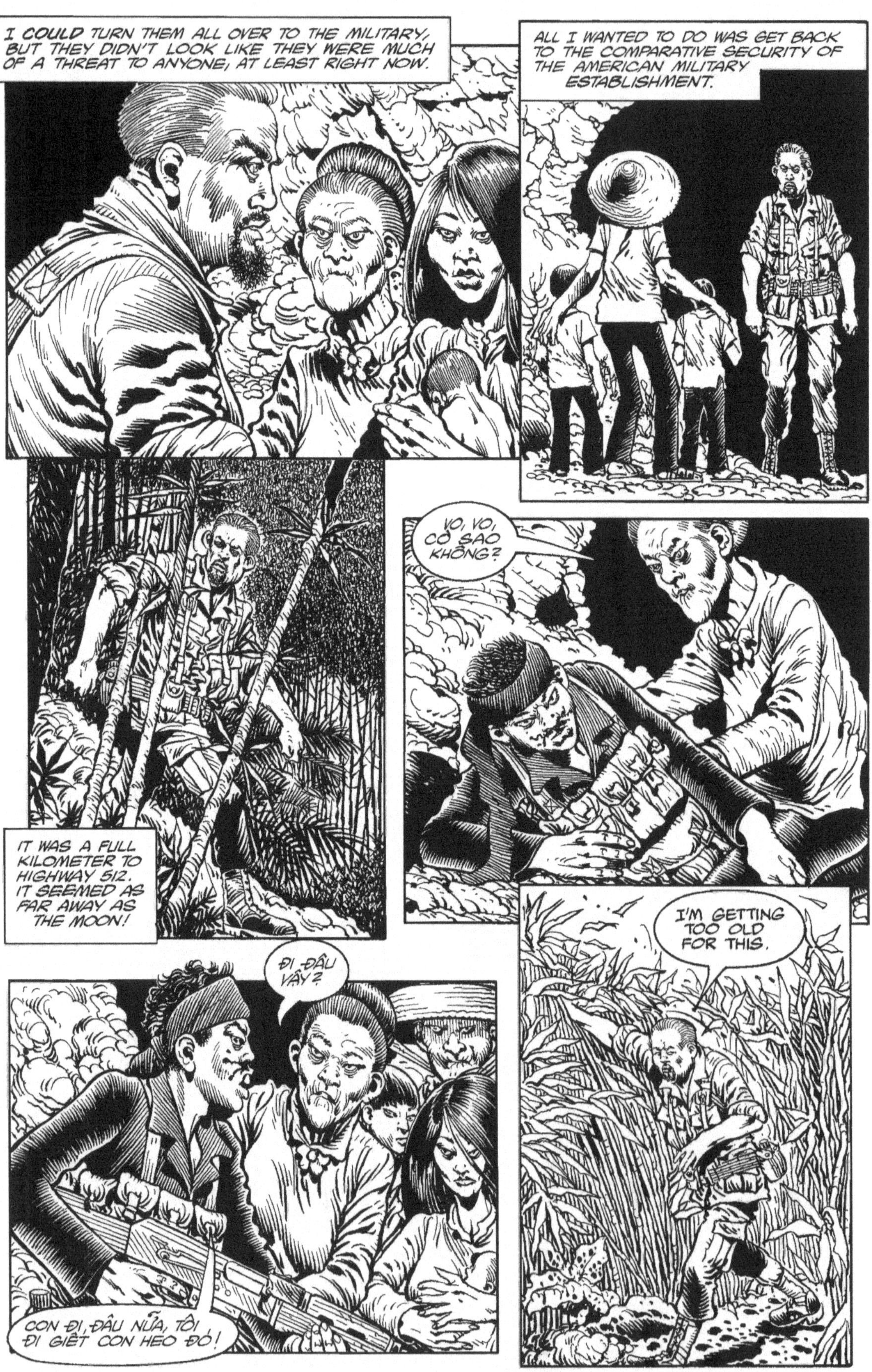
I **COULD** TURN THEM ALL OVER TO THE MILITARY, BUT THEY DIDN'T LOOK LIKE THEY WERE MUCH OF A THREAT TO ANYONE, AT LEAST RIGHT NOW.
ALL I WANTED TO DO WAS GET BACK TO THE COMPARATIVE SECURITY OF THE AMERICAN MILITARY ESTABLISHMENT.
IT WAS A FULL KILOMETER TO HIGHWAY 512. IT SEEMED AS FAR AWAY AS THE MOON!
VO, VO, CÒ SAO KHÔNG?
ĐI ĐÂU VẬY?
CON ĐI, ĐÂU NỮA, TÔI ĐI GIẾT CON HEO ĐÓ!
I'M GETTING TOO OLD FOR THIS.

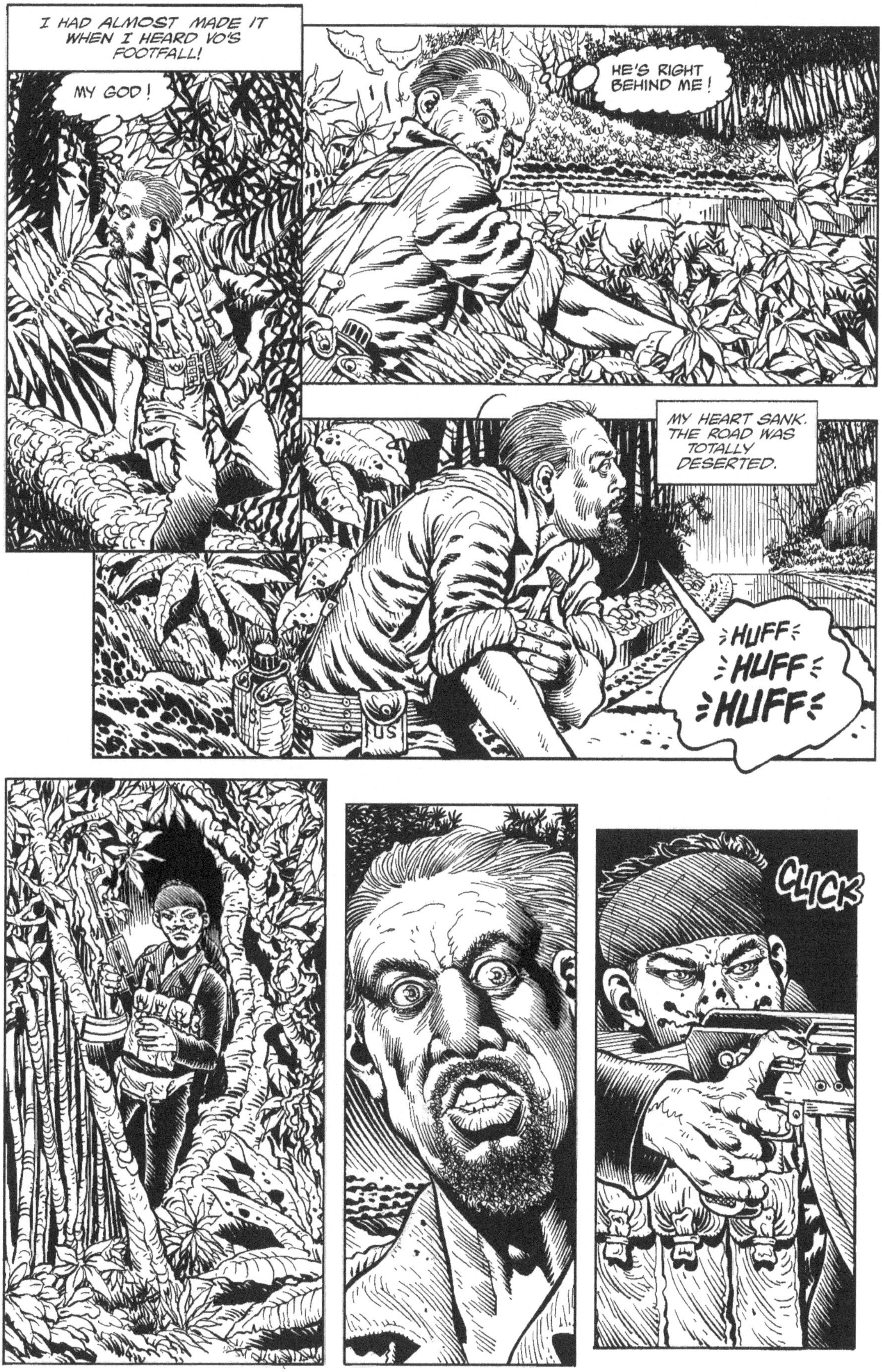
I HAD ALMOST MADE IT WHEN I HEARD VO'S FOOTFALL!
MY GOD!
HE'S RIGHT BEHIND ME!
MY HEART SANK. THE ROAD WAS TOTALLY DESERTED.
HUFF HUFF HUFF
CLICK

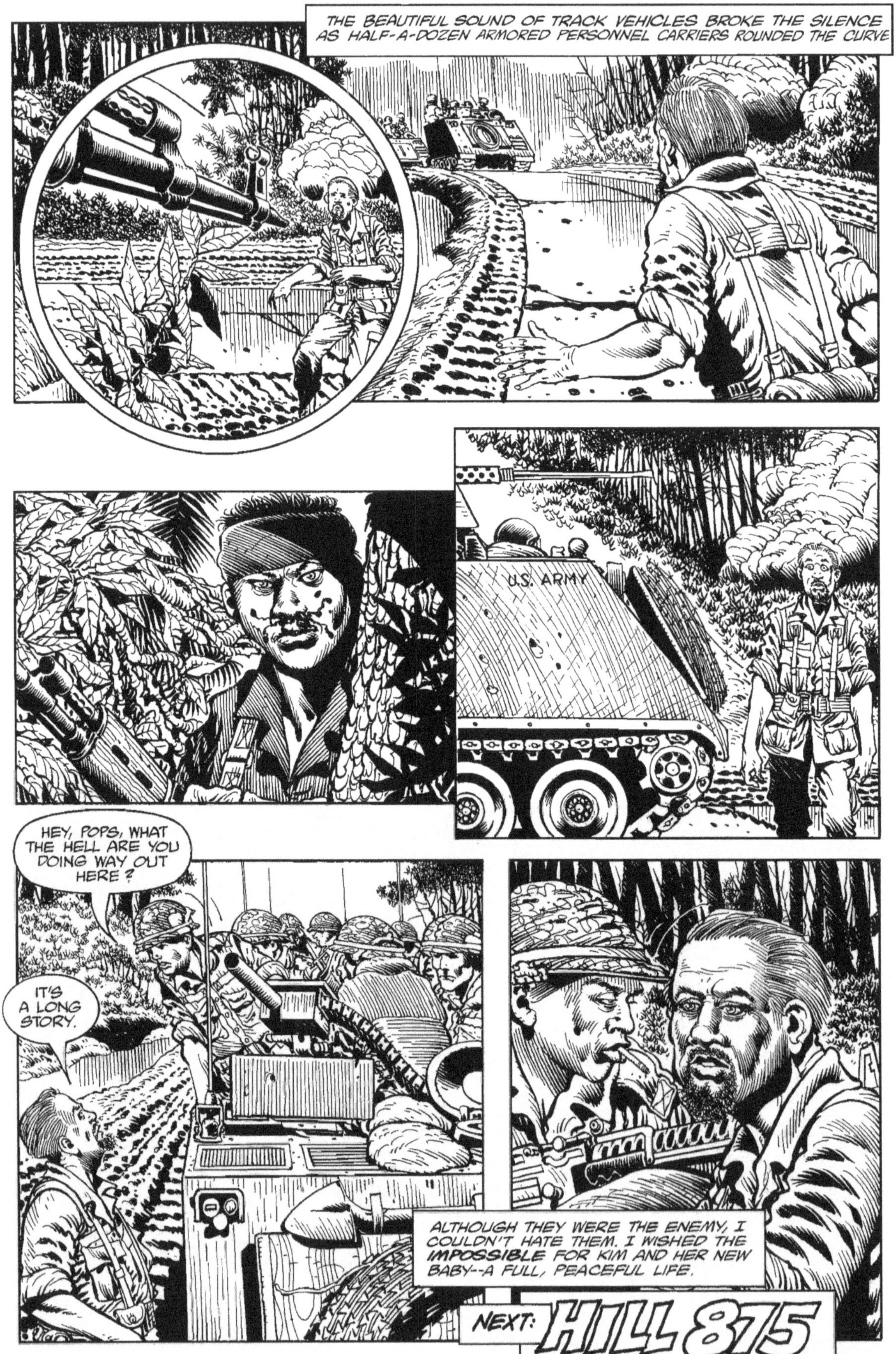
THE BEAUTIFUL SOUND OF TRACK VEHICLES BROKE THE SILENCE AS HALF-A-DOZEN ARMORED PERSONNEL CARRIERS ROUNDED THE CURVE
U.S. ARMY
HEY, POPS, WHAT THE HELL ARE YOU DOING WAY OUT HERE?
IT'S A LONG STORY.
ALTHOUGH THEY WERE THE ENEMY, I COULDN'T HATE THEM. I WISHED THE IMPOSSIBLE FOR KIM AND HER NEW BABY--A FULL, PEACEFUL LIFE.
NEXT: HILL 875

Missing American ™

Major Hugh M. Fanning, USMC
U.S. hides sighting report, returns wrong body

When the U.S. ended its involvement in the Vietnam War, many questions remained unanswered. But the most agonizing questions were those asked by the families of some 2,400 Americans listed as "Missing in Action."

The following is the information we have on just one of those missing Americans.

The story of Major Hugh Michael Fanning is at least as intriguing for what has happened since he was lost as for what had occurred before — and that may or may not be related to the questions surrounding his disappearance.

His wife, Kathryn, has never been able to uncover the details. She does know that his A6 Intruder was shot down over North Vietnam about 2:00 a.m., October 31, 1967.

Beyond that, details are sketchy. The sky was overcast in the area in which Hugh's plane went down. The pilot of the accompanying plane — whom Mrs. Fanning has never been permitted to speak with — is reported to have said that he saw an orange flash and then lost radio contact.

The duty officer described Hugh's last flight as a "kamikaze" mission and one for which Hugh volunteered. Mrs. Fanning has not been told what that mission was, but speculates that it may have been to mine Haiphong harbor.

Hugh was 26 years old at the time of his disappearance. He was a graduate of the University of Dallas and had attended graduate school at Texas Christian University. He joined the Marine Corps in 1964. Hugh was listed as missing in action until September, 1976, when his status was changed to presumed dead. His family was told that no information existed about Hugh's whereabouts, an assertion which later proved to be false.

On July 17, 1984, remains purported to be his were returned by the North Vietnamese. Kathryn Fanning and their three children — Kelly, Michael, and Erin — buried the remains in Oklahoma City, August 8, 1984.

In 1985, Mrs. Fanning attended a meeting of the National League of Families in Washington, D.C. and requested her husband's files from the government. Though she had seen those files before on several occasions, she was shocked to find live sighting reports on her husband that had never before been released to her.

According to the reports, Hugh survived the crash of his fighter plane, though the bombardier-navigator, Major Steve Kott, did not. One of the reports said a North Vietnamese deserter had given a description of Hugh, including his age and rank, and picked his photo out of a stack of 20 others.

She was further surprised to find a list of the bones she buried — it did not match the description given by her casualty assistance officer. She also learned that the casualty officer had concealed the forensic report in his home rather than make the report available to her.

Mrs. Fanning obtained a court order to exhume the remains and have them evaluated by board-certified anthropologists. The bones were examined by Drs. Clyde Snow and Michael

Charney, who agreed that the remains could not be identified as Major Fanning's or anyone else's.

Dr. Charney later testified before the House Armed Services Subcommittee on Investigations that 19 other families had asked him to evaluate the government's identification of returned remains. His conclusion was that only two could be scientifically substantiated.

The Armed Services Graves Registration Office decided that the identification of remains as Major Fanning, made by the Central Identification Laboratory of Hawaii, could not be upheld — either forensically or by process of elimination. Kathryn Fanning returned the remains to the U.S. government in July, 1987.

As a result of the Congressional investigations, the Central Identification Laboratory was forced to add basic equipment and staff, and to make a number of policy and procedural improvements. However, a number of questionable identifications have been made since Mrs. Fanning's victory — and the government has failed to comply with all the suggestions made by the Congressional subcommittee.

Mrs. Fanning, represented by attorney Mark Waple of Fayetteville, North Carolina, was a plaintiff in the class action lawsuit on behalf of live prisoners of war in Southeast Asia, seeking compliance with the Federal Hostage Act. The Supreme Court refused to review the suit after it was dismissed by the Fourth Circuit Court of Appeals.

While Mrs. Fanning considers further action, the real fate of her husband remains shrouded in mystery.

HILL 875

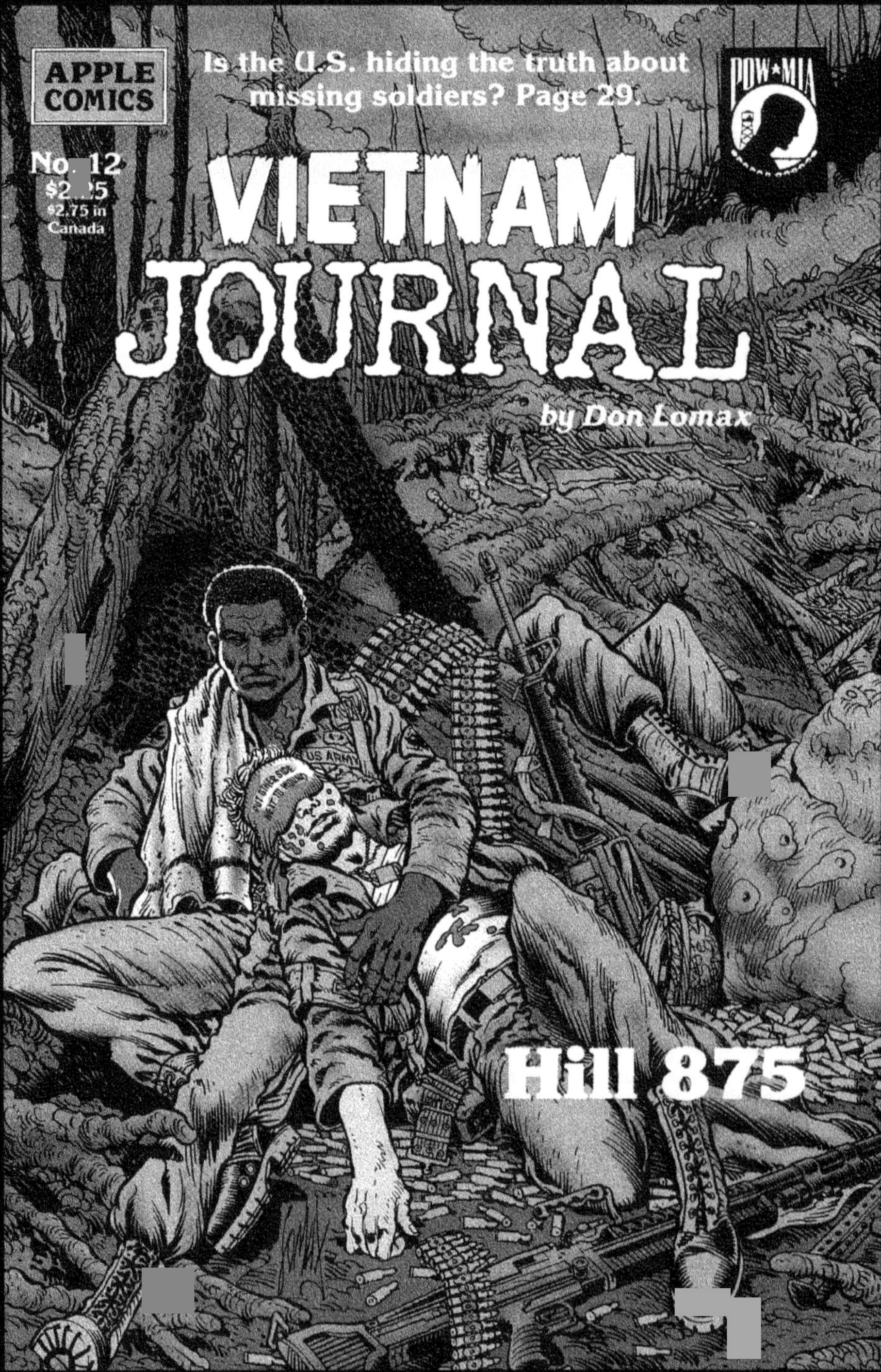
APPLE COMICS
Is the U.S. hiding the truth about missing soldiers? Page 29.
POW★MIA
No. 12
$2.25
$2.75 in Canada
VIETNAM JOURNAL
by Don Lomax
US ARMY
Hill 875

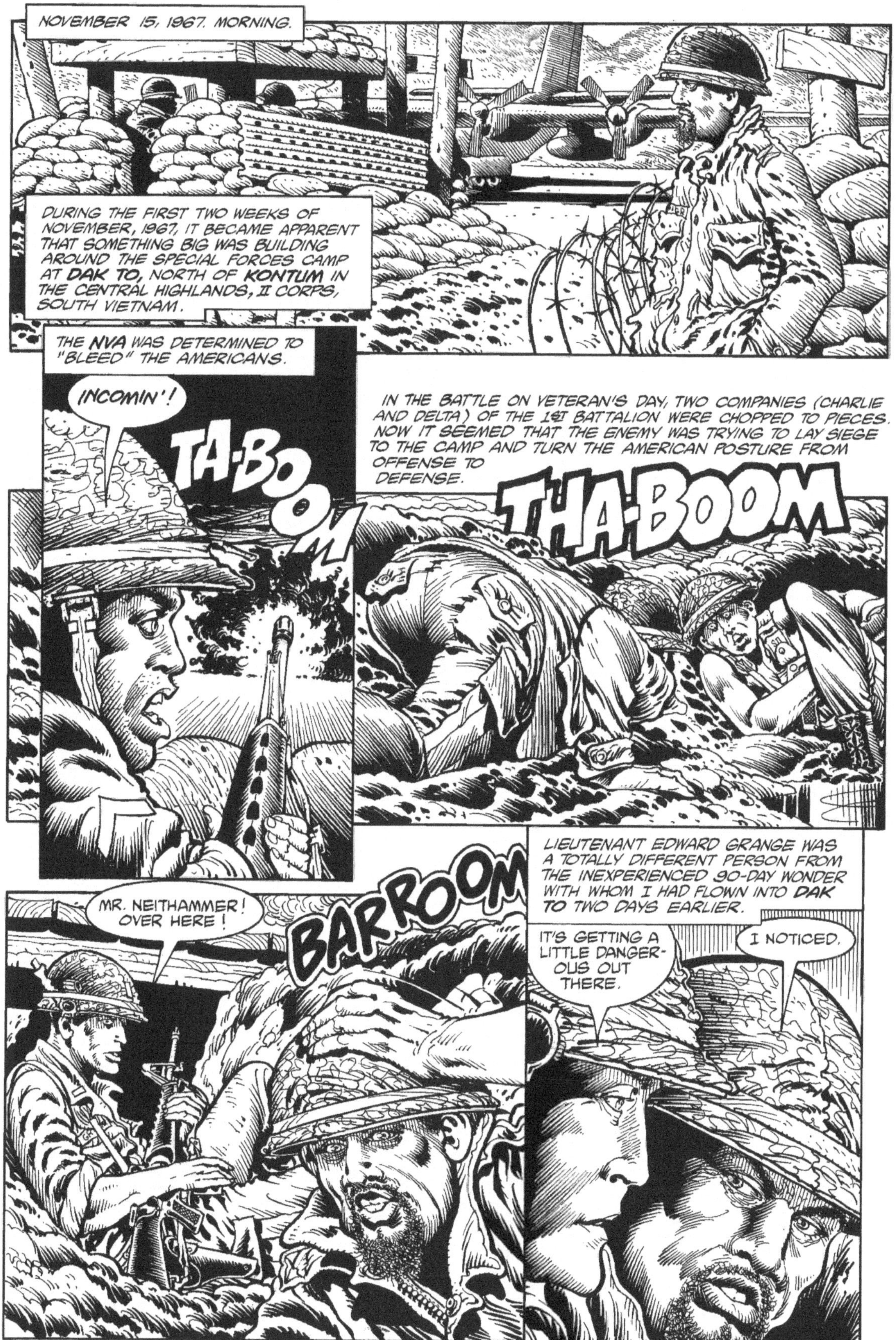
NOVEMBER 15, 1967. MORNING.
DURING THE FIRST TWO WEEKS OF NOVEMBER, 1967, IT BECAME APPARENT THAT SOMETHING BIG WAS BUILDING AROUND THE SPECIAL FORCES CAMP AT DAK TO, NORTH OF KONTUM IN THE CENTRAL HIGHLANDS, II CORPS, SOUTH VIETNAM.
THE NVA WAS DETERMINED TO "BLEED" THE AMERICANS.
INCOMIN'!
TA-BOOM
IN THE BATTLE ON VETERAN'S DAY, TWO COMPANIES (CHARLIE AND DELTA) OF THE 1ST BATTALION WERE CHOPPED TO PIECES. NOW IT SEEMED THAT THE ENEMY WAS TRYING TO LAY SIEGE TO THE CAMP AND TURN THE AMERICAN POSTURE FROM OFFENSE TO DEFENSE.
THA-BOOM
MR. NEITHAMMER! OVER HERE!
BARROOM
LIEUTENANT EDWARD GRANGE WAS A TOTALLY DIFFERENT PERSON FROM THE INEXPERIENCED 90-DAY WONDER WITH WHOM I HAD FLOWN INTO DAK TO TWO DAYS EARLIER.
IT'S GETTING A LITTLE DANGER-OUS OUT THERE.
I NOTICED.

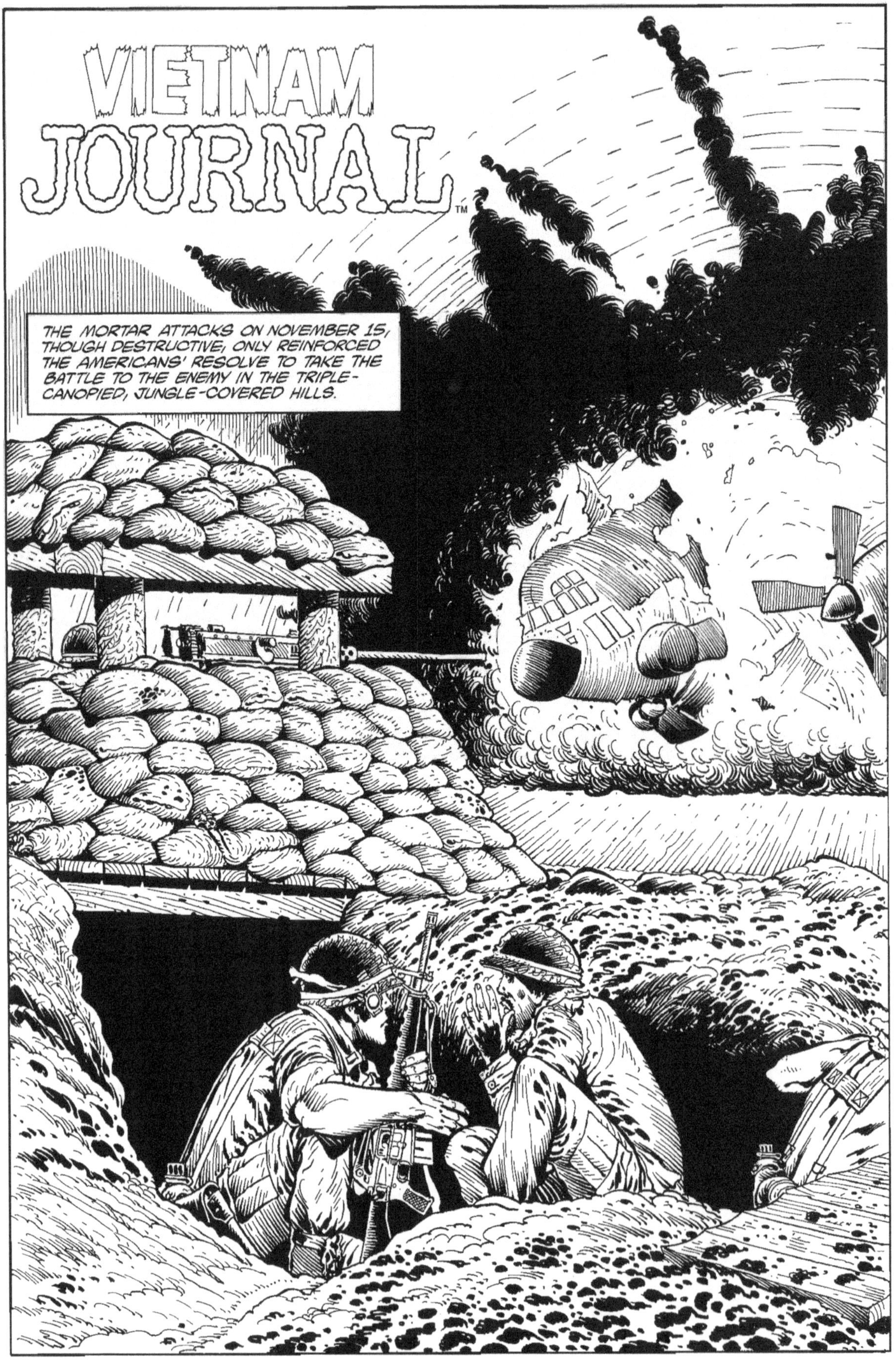
VIETNAM JOURNAL™
THE MORTAR ATTACKS ON NOVEMBER 15, THOUGH DESTRUCTIVE, ONLY REINFORCED THE AMERICANS' RESOLVE TO TAKE THE BATTLE TO THE ENEMY IN THE TRIPLE-CANOPIED, JUNGLE-COVERED HILLS.

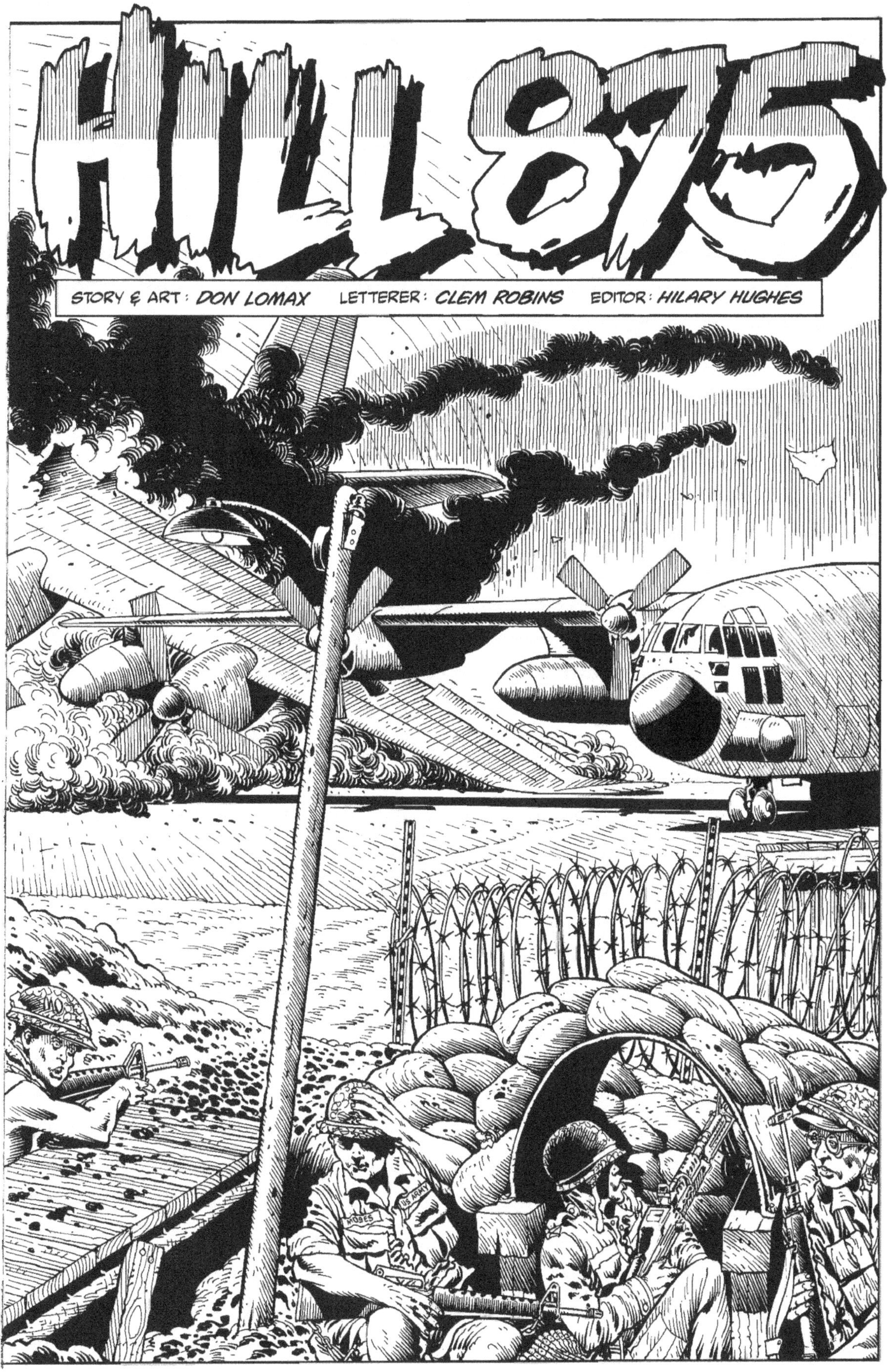
HILL 875
STORY & ART: DON LOMAX LETTERER: CLEM ROBINS EDITOR: HILARY HUGHES

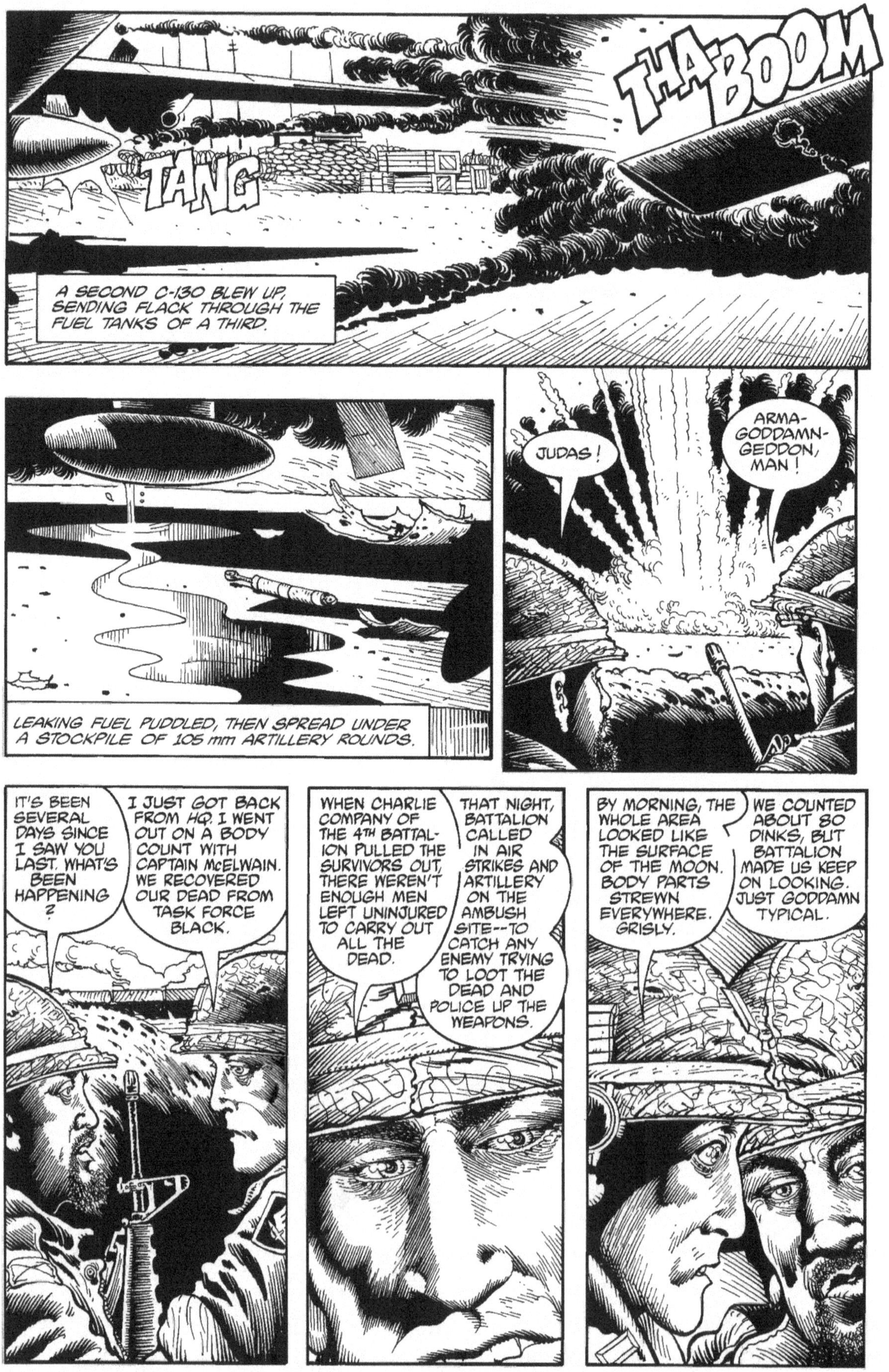
THA-BOOM
TANG
A SECOND C-130 BLEW UP, SENDING FLACK THROUGH THE FUEL TANKS OF A THIRD.
LEAKING FUEL PUDDLED, THEN SPREAD UNDER A STOCKPILE OF 105 mm ARTILLERY ROUNDS.
JUDAS!
ARMA-GODDAMN-GEDDON, MAN!
IT'S BEEN SEVERAL DAYS SINCE I SAW YOU LAST. WHAT'S BEEN HAPPENING?
I JUST GOT BACK FROM HQ. I WENT OUT ON A BODY COUNT WITH CAPTAIN McELWAIN. WE RECOVERED OUR DEAD FROM TASK FORCE BLACK.
WHEN CHARLIE COMPANY OF THE 4TH BATTALION PULLED THE SURVIVORS OUT, THERE WEREN'T ENOUGH MEN LEFT UNINJURED TO CARRY OUT ALL THE DEAD.
THAT NIGHT, BATTALION CALLED IN AIR STRIKES AND ARTILLERY ON THE AMBUSH SITE--TO CATCH ANY ENEMY TRYING TO LOOT THE DEAD AND POLICE UP THE WEAPONS.
BY MORNING, THE WHOLE AREA LOOKED LIKE THE SURFACE OF THE MOON. BODY PARTS STREWN EVERYWHERE. GRISLY.
WE COUNTED ABOUT 80 DINKS, BUT BATTALION MADE US KEEP ON LOOKING. JUST GODDAMN TYPICAL.

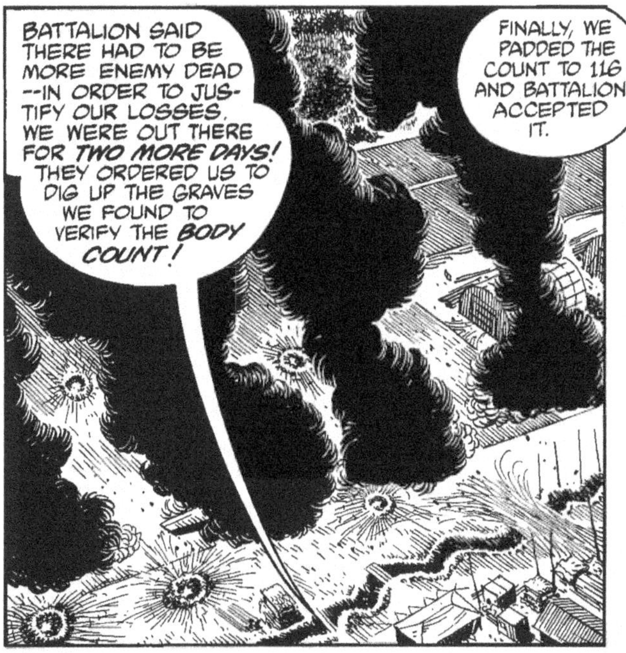
BATTALION SAID THERE HAD TO BE MORE ENEMY DEAD --IN ORDER TO JUSTIFY OUR LOSSES. WE WERE OUT THERE FOR TWO MORE DAYS! THEY ORDERED US TO DIG UP THE GRAVES WE FOUND TO VERIFY THE BODY COUNT!
FINALLY, WE PADDED THE COUNT TO 116 AND BATTALION ACCEPTED IT.

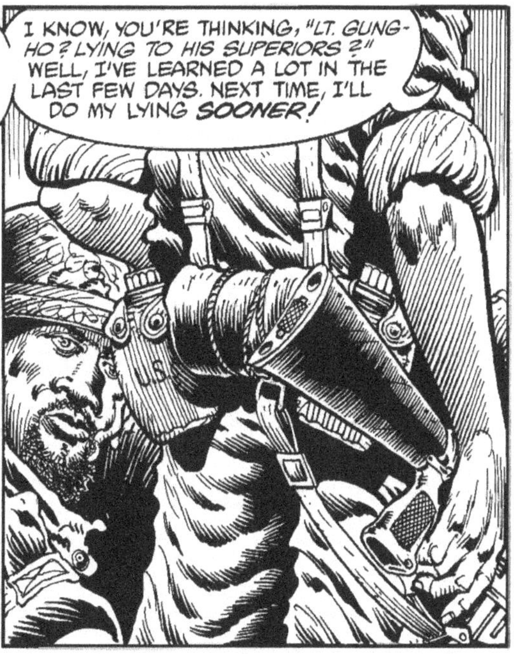
I KNOW, YOU'RE THINKING, "LT. GUNG-HO? LYING TO HIS SUPERIORS?" WELL, I'VE LEARNED A LOT IN THE LAST FEW DAYS. NEXT TIME, I'LL DO MY LYING SOONER!

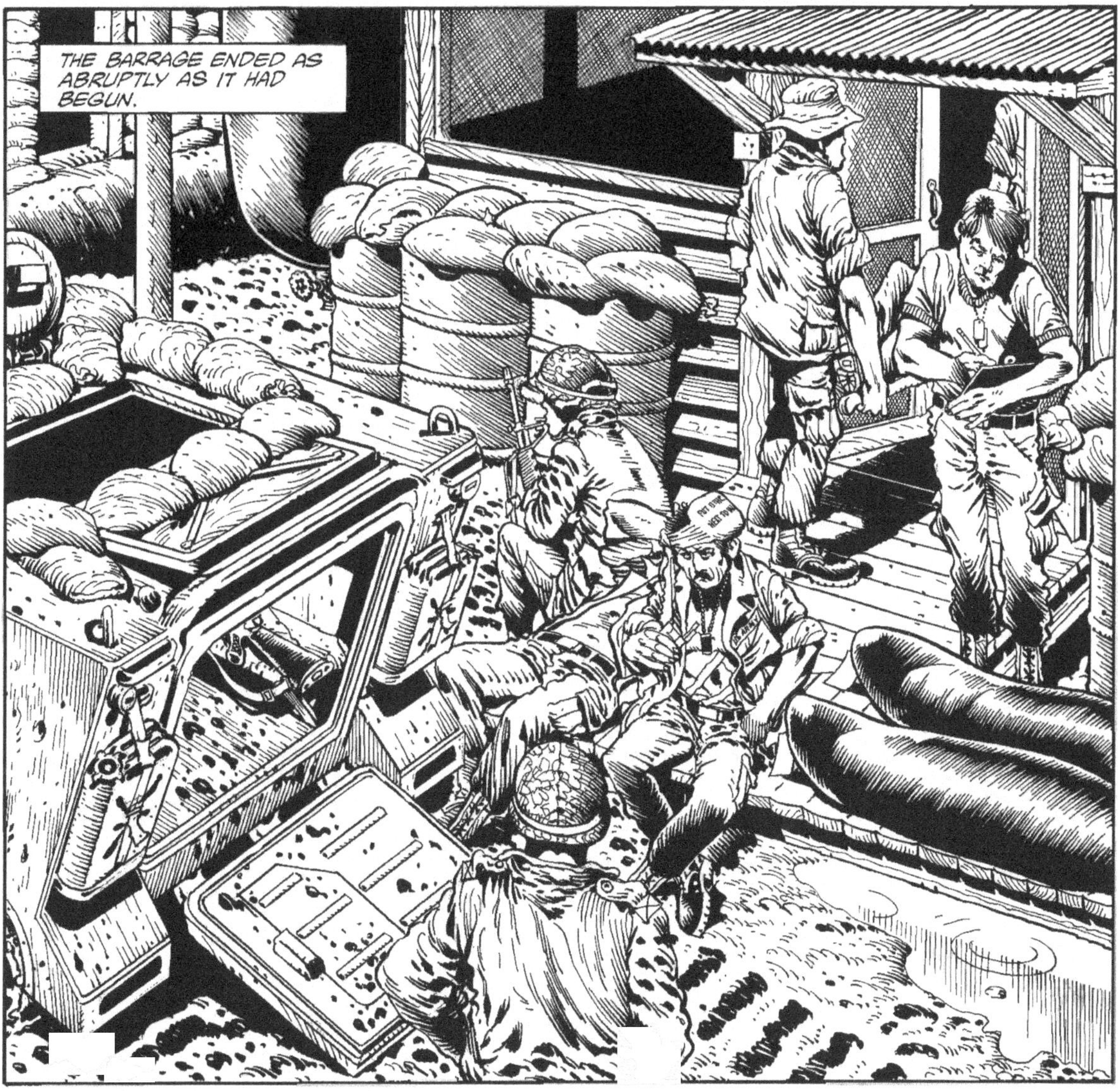
THE BARRAGE ENDED AS ABRUPTLY AS IT HAD BEGUN.

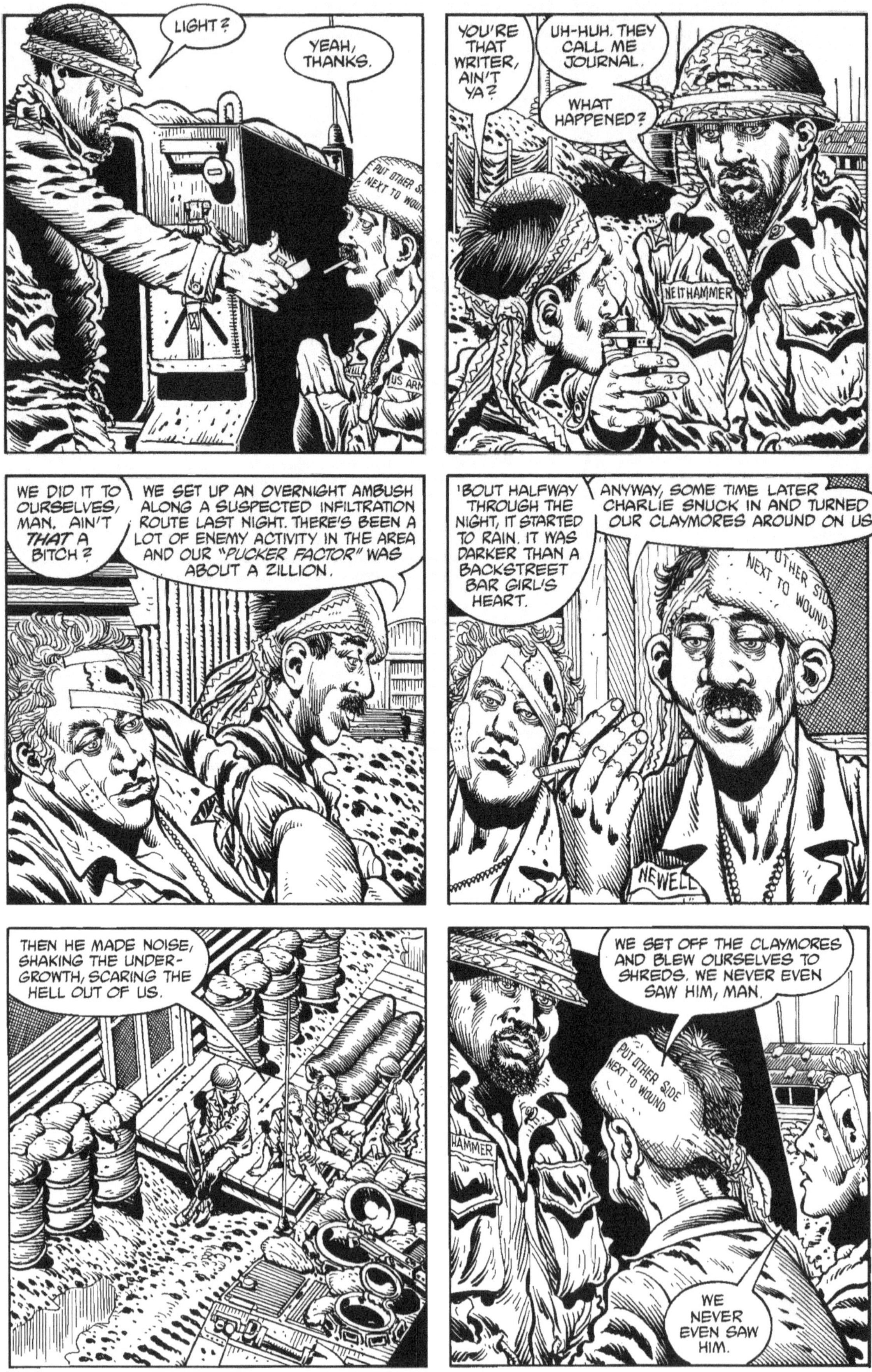
LIGHT?
YEAH, THANKS.
YOU'RE THAT WRITER, AIN'T YA?
UH-HUH. THEY CALL ME JOURNAL.
WHAT HAPPENED?
NEITHAMMER
WE DID IT TO OURSELVES, MAN. AIN'T *THAT* A BITCH?
WE SET UP AN *OVERNIGHT* AMBUSH ALONG A SUSPECTED INFILTRATION ROUTE LAST NIGHT. THERE'S BEEN A LOT OF ENEMY ACTIVITY IN THE AREA AND OUR *"PUCKER FACTOR"* WAS ABOUT A ZILLION.
'BOUT HALFWAY THROUGH THE NIGHT, IT STARTED TO RAIN. IT WAS DARKER THAN A BACKSTREET BAR GIRL'S HEART.
ANYWAY, SOME TIME LATER CHARLIE SNUCK IN AND TURNED OUR CLAYMORES AROUND ON US.
NEWELL
THEN HE MADE NOISE, SHAKING THE UNDER-GROWTH, SCARING THE HELL OUT OF US.
WE SET OFF THE CLAYMORES AND BLEW OURSELVES TO SHREDS. WE NEVER EVEN SAW HIM, MAN.
PUT OTHER SIDE NEXT TO WOUND
WE NEVER EVEN SAW HIM.

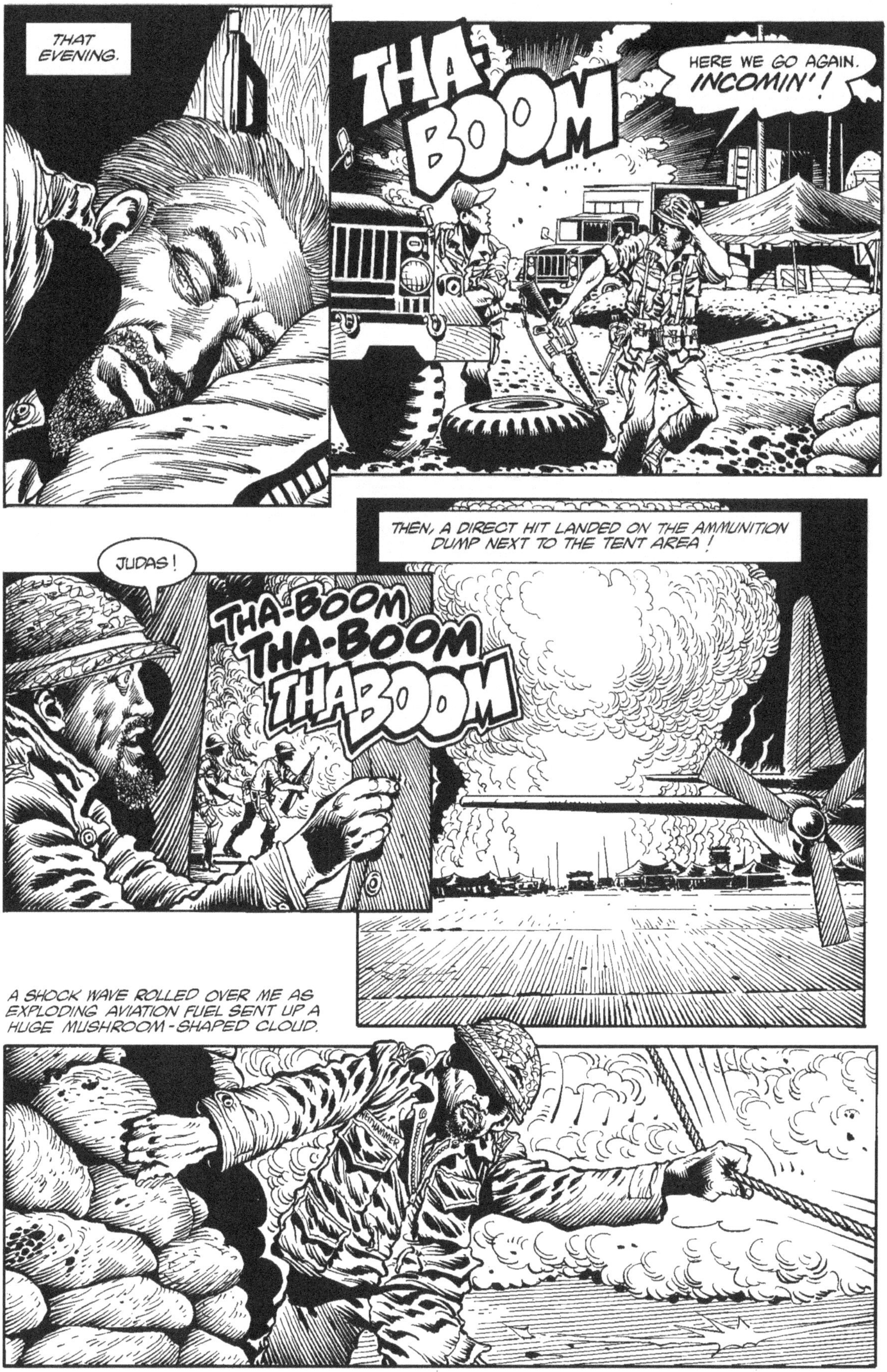
THAT EVENING.
THA-BOOM
HERE WE GO AGAIN. INCOMIN'!
THEN, A DIRECT HIT LANDED ON THE AMMUNITION DUMP NEXT TO THE TENT AREA!
JUDAS!
THA-BOOM THA-BOOM THABOOM
A SHOCK WAVE ROLLED OVER ME AS EXPLODING AVIATION FUEL SENT UP A HUGE MUSHROOM-SHAPED CLOUD.

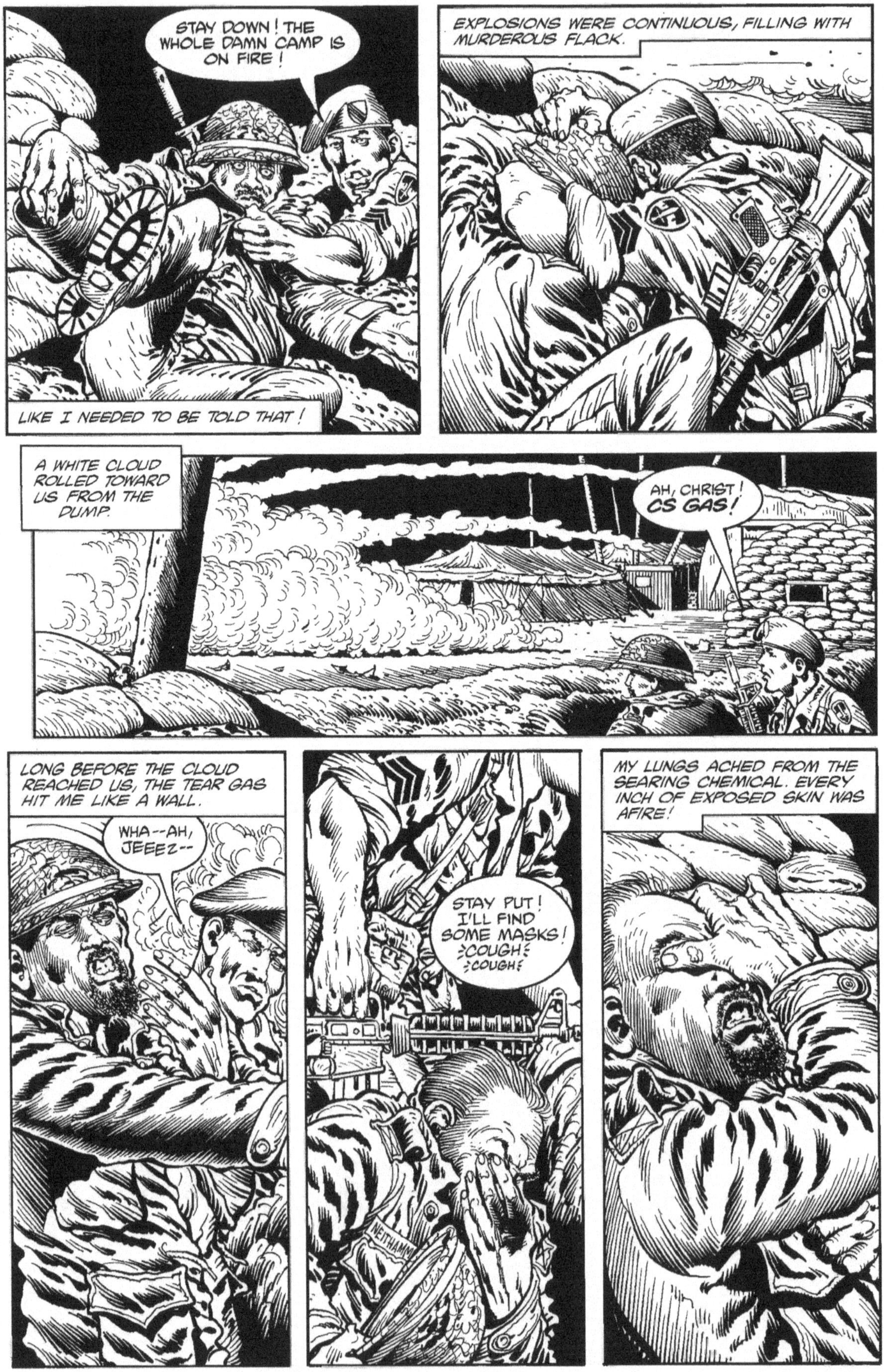
STAY DOWN! THE WHOLE DAMN CAMP IS ON FIRE!
LIKE I NEEDED TO BE TOLD THAT!
EXPLOSIONS WERE CONTINUOUS, FILLING WITH MURDEROUS FLACK.
A WHITE CLOUD ROLLED TOWARD US FROM THE DUMP.
AH, CHRIST! CS GAS!
LONG BEFORE THE CLOUD REACHED US, THE TEAR GAS HIT ME LIKE A WALL.
WHA--AH, JEEEZ--
STAY PUT! I'LL FIND SOME MASKS! COUGH COUGH
MY LUNGS ACHED FROM THE SEARING CHEMICAL. EVERY INCH OF EXPOSED SKIN WAS AFIRE!

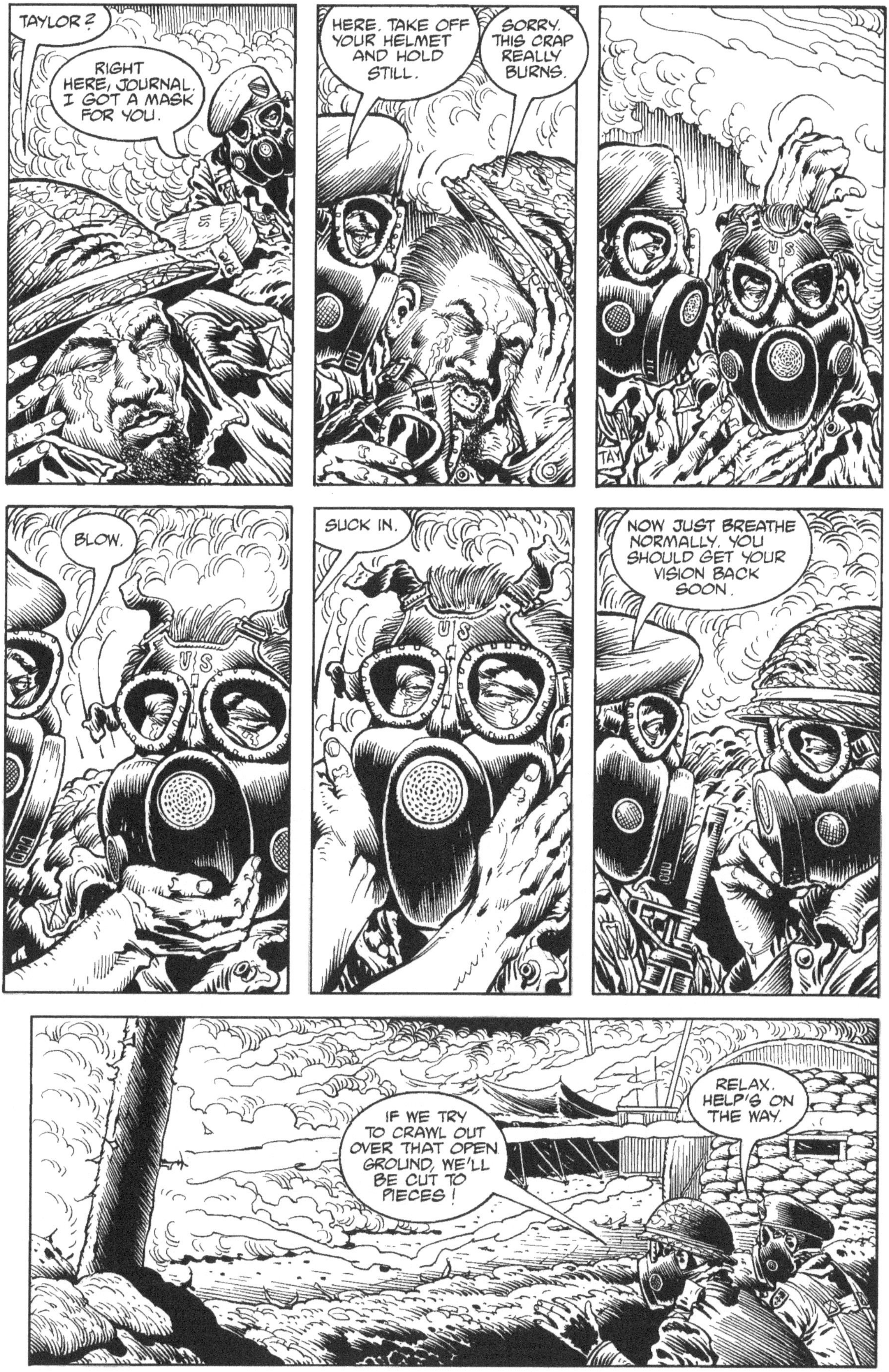
TAYLOR?
RIGHT HERE, JOURNAL. I GOT A MASK FOR YOU.
HERE. TAKE OFF YOUR HELMET AND HOLD STILL.
SORRY. THIS CRAP REALLY BURNS.
BLOW.
SUCK IN.
NOW JUST BREATHE NORMALLY. YOU SHOULD GET YOUR VISION BACK SOON.
IF WE TRY TO CRAWL OUT OVER THAT OPEN GROUND, WE'LL BE CUT TO PIECES!
RELAX. HELP'S ON THE WAY.

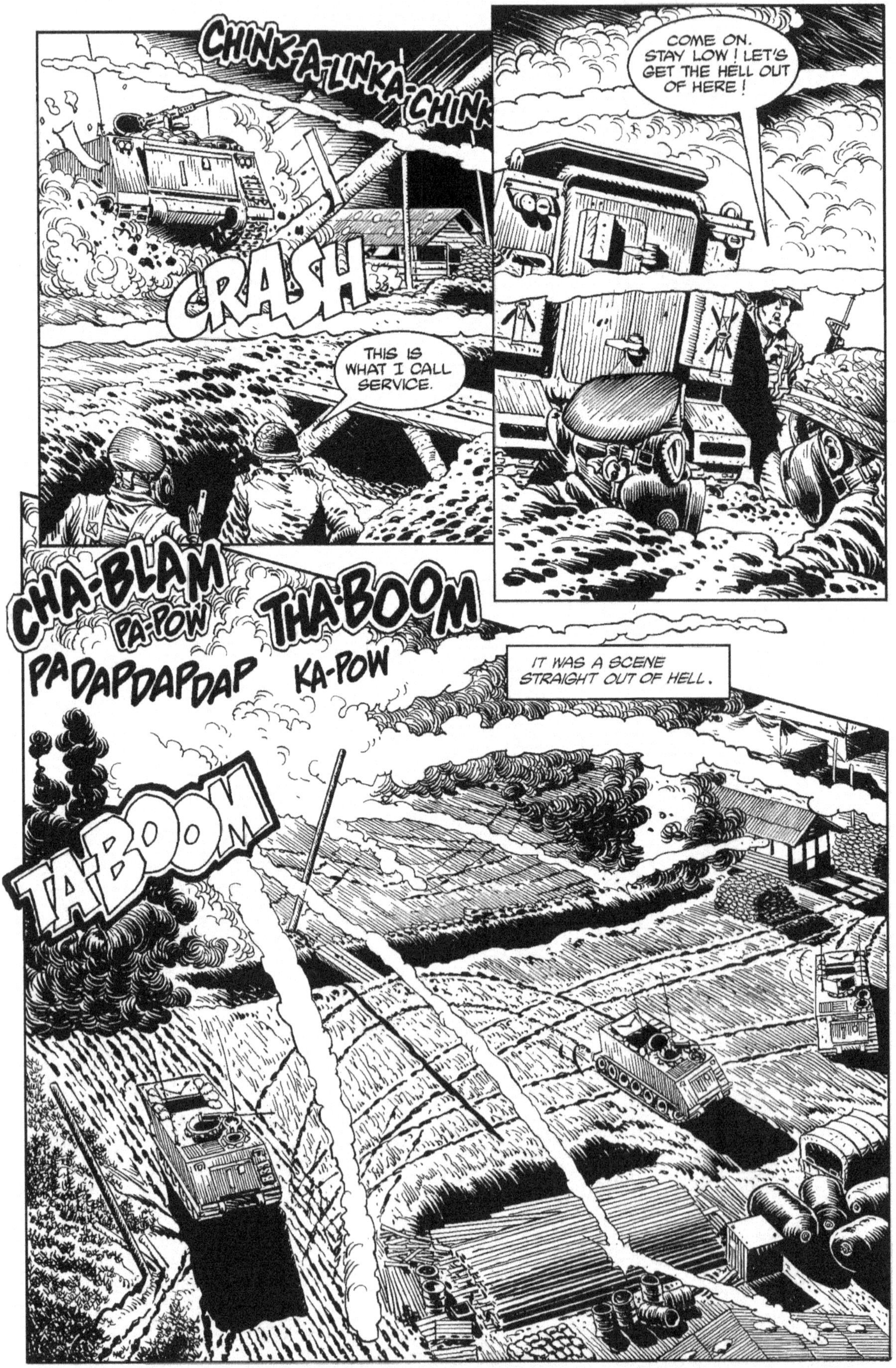
CHINK-A-LINKA-CHINK
CRASH
THIS IS WHAT I CALL SERVICE.
COME ON. STAY LOW! LET'S GET THE HELL OUT OF HERE!
CHA-BLAM
PA-POW
THA-BOOM
PA DAP DAP DAP DAP
KA-POW
IT WAS A SCENE STRAIGHT OUT OF HELL.
TA-BOOM

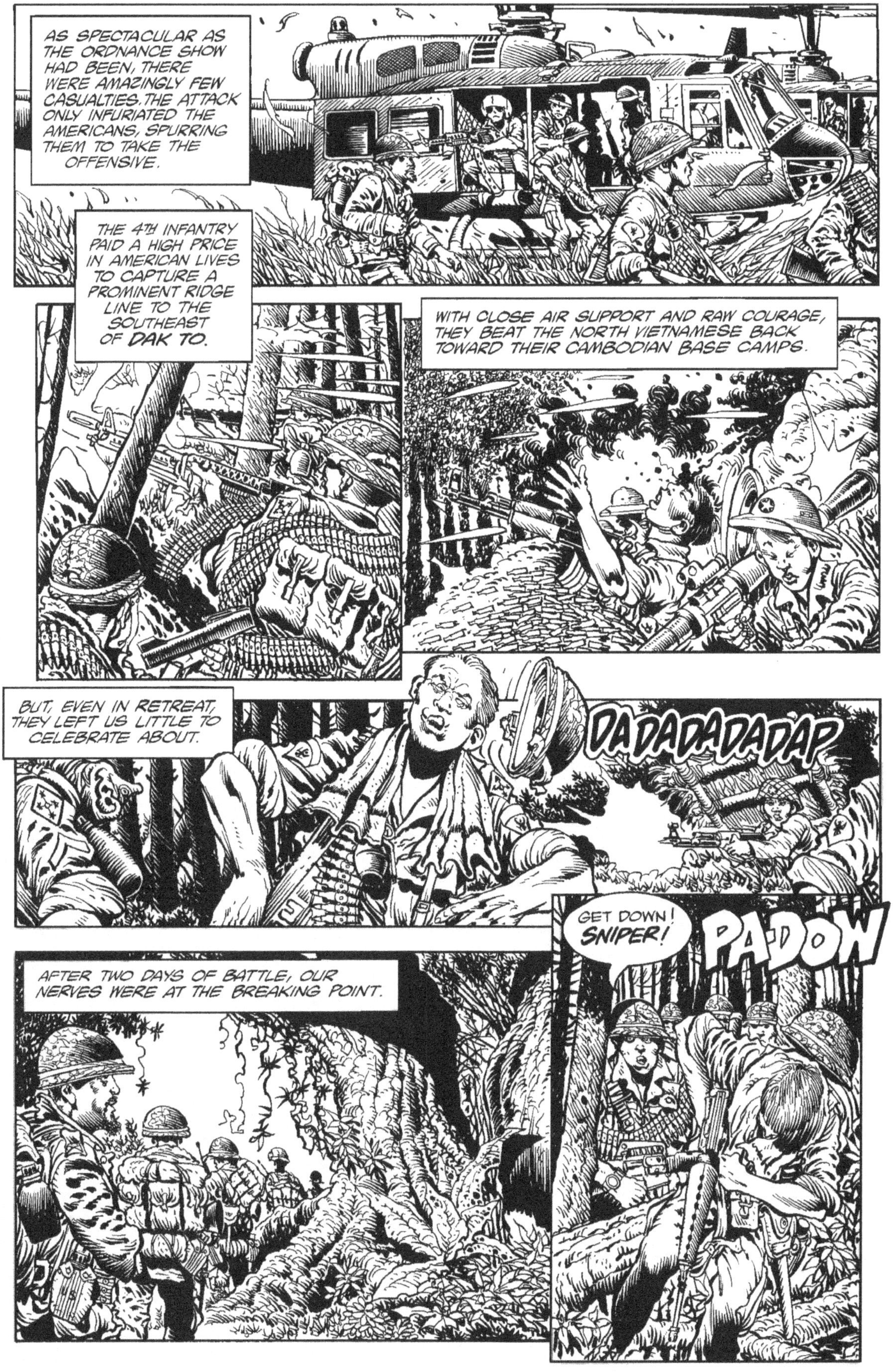

AS SPECTACULAR AS THE ORDNANCE SHOW HAD BEEN, THERE WERE AMAZINGLY FEW CASUALTIES. THE ATTACK ONLY INFURIATED THE AMERICANS, SPURRING THEM TO TAKE THE OFFENSIVE.
THE 4TH INFANTRY PAID A HIGH PRICE IN AMERICAN LIVES TO CAPTURE A PROMINENT RIDGE LINE TO THE SOUTHEAST OF DAK TO.
WITH CLOSE AIR SUPPORT AND RAW COURAGE, THEY BEAT THE NORTH VIETNAMESE BACK TOWARD THEIR CAMBODIAN BASE CAMPS.
BUT, EVEN IN RETREAT, THEY LEFT US LITTLE TO CELEBRATE ABOUT.
DADADADADADAP
AFTER TWO DAYS OF BATTLE, OUR NERVES WERE AT THE BREAKING POINT.
GET DOWN! SNIPER!
PA-DOW

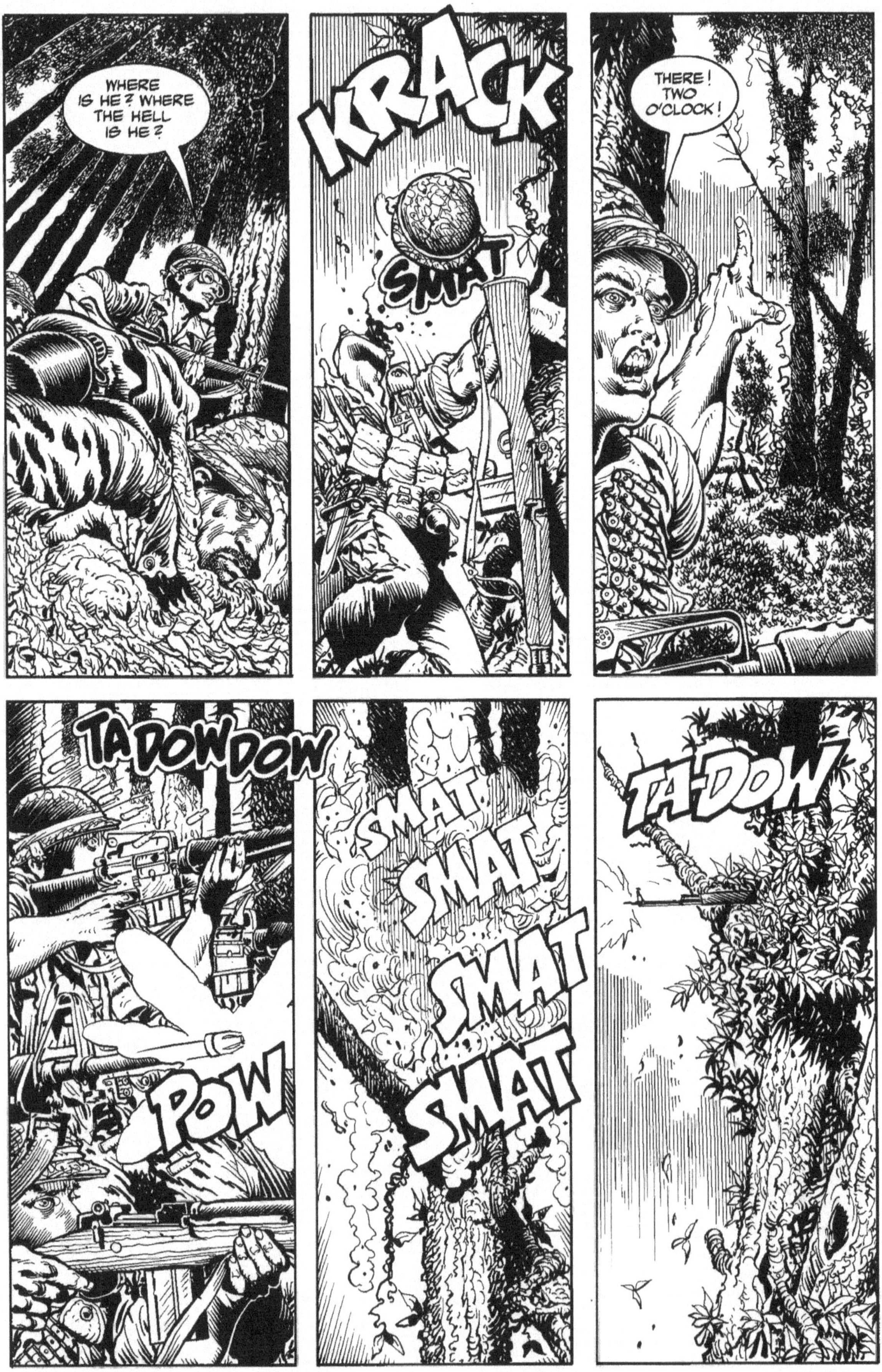
WHERE IS HE? WHERE THE HELL IS HE?
KRACK
SMAT
THERE! TWO O'CLOCK!
TADOWDOW
POW
SMAT
SMAT
SMAT
SMAT
TA-DOW

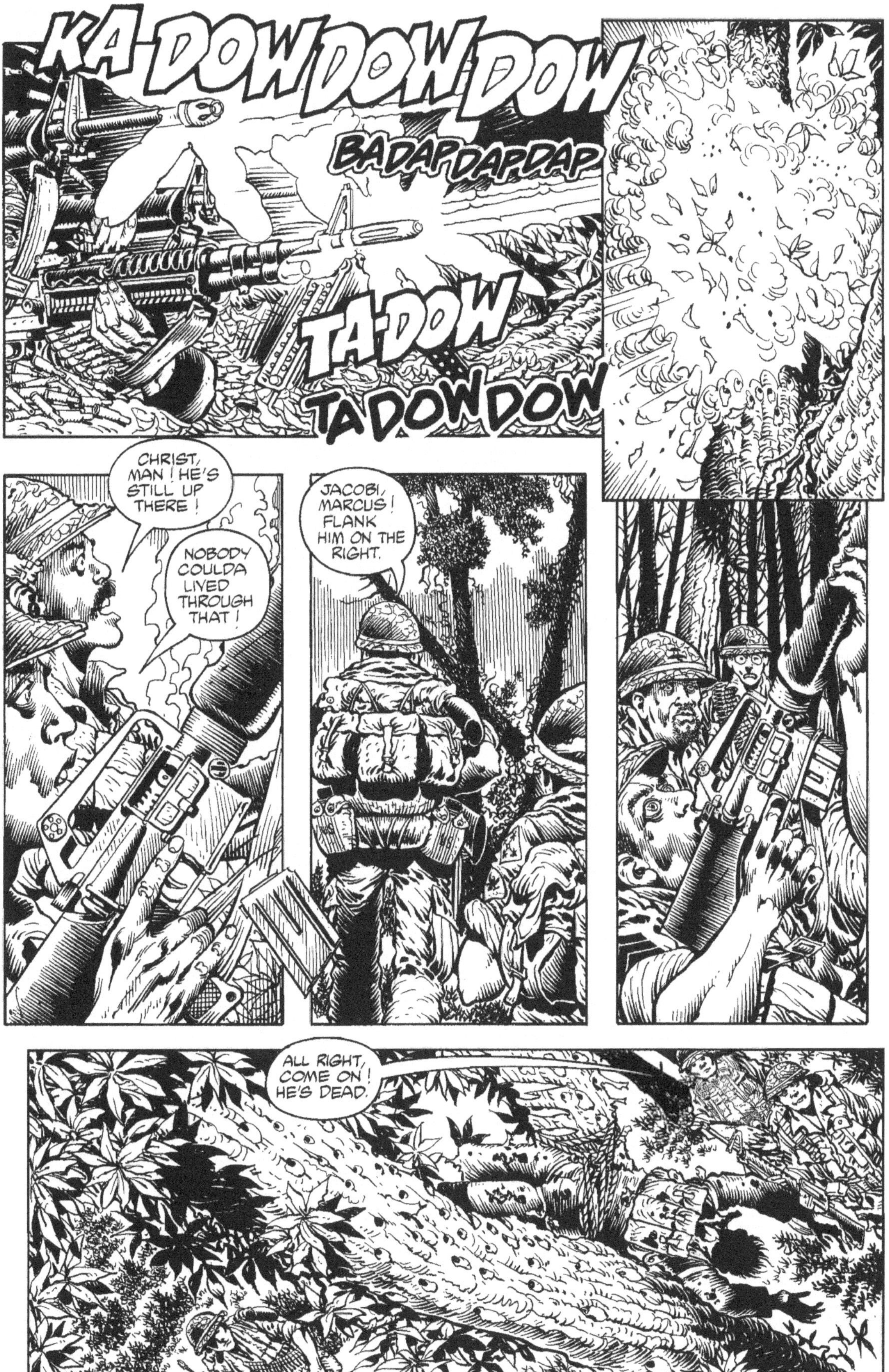
KA-DOW DOW DOW DOW
BADAP DAP DAP
TA-DOW
TA DOW DOW
CHRIST, MAN! HE'S STILL UP THERE!
NOBODY COULDA LIVED THROUGH THAT!
JACOBI, MARCUS! FLANK HIM ON THE RIGHT.
ALL RIGHT, COME ON! HE'S DEAD.

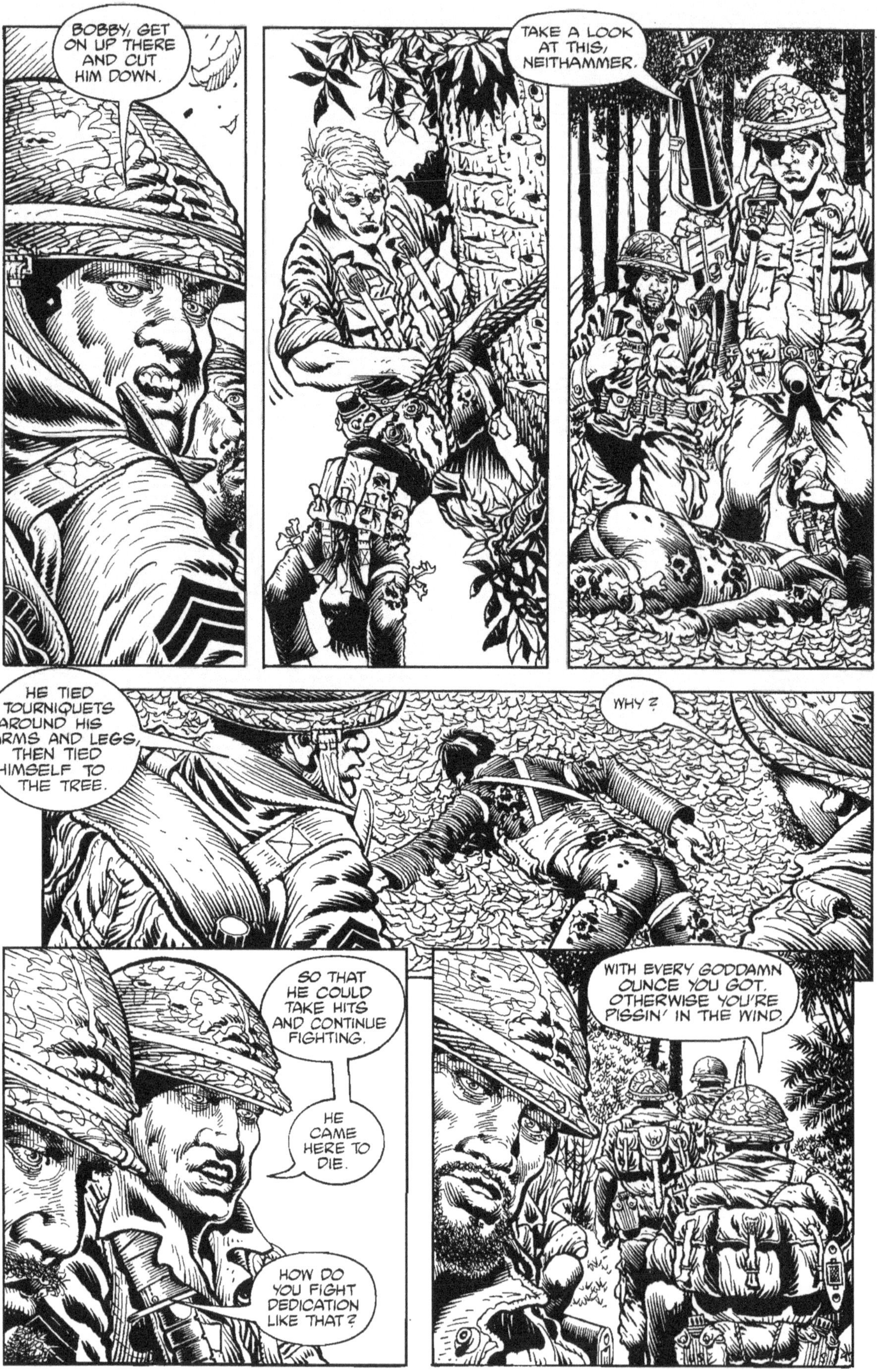
BOBBY, GET ON UP THERE AND CUT HIM DOWN.
TAKE A LOOK AT THIS, NEITHAMMER.
HE TIED TOURNIQUETS AROUND HIS ARMS AND LEGS, THEN TIED HIMSELF TO THE TREE.
WHY?
SO THAT HE COULD TAKE HITS AND CONTINUE FIGHTING.
HE CAME HERE TO DIE.
HOW DO YOU FIGHT DEDICATION LIKE THAT?
WITH EVERY GODDAMN OUNCE YOU GOT. OTHERWISE YOU'RE PISSIN' IN THE WIND.

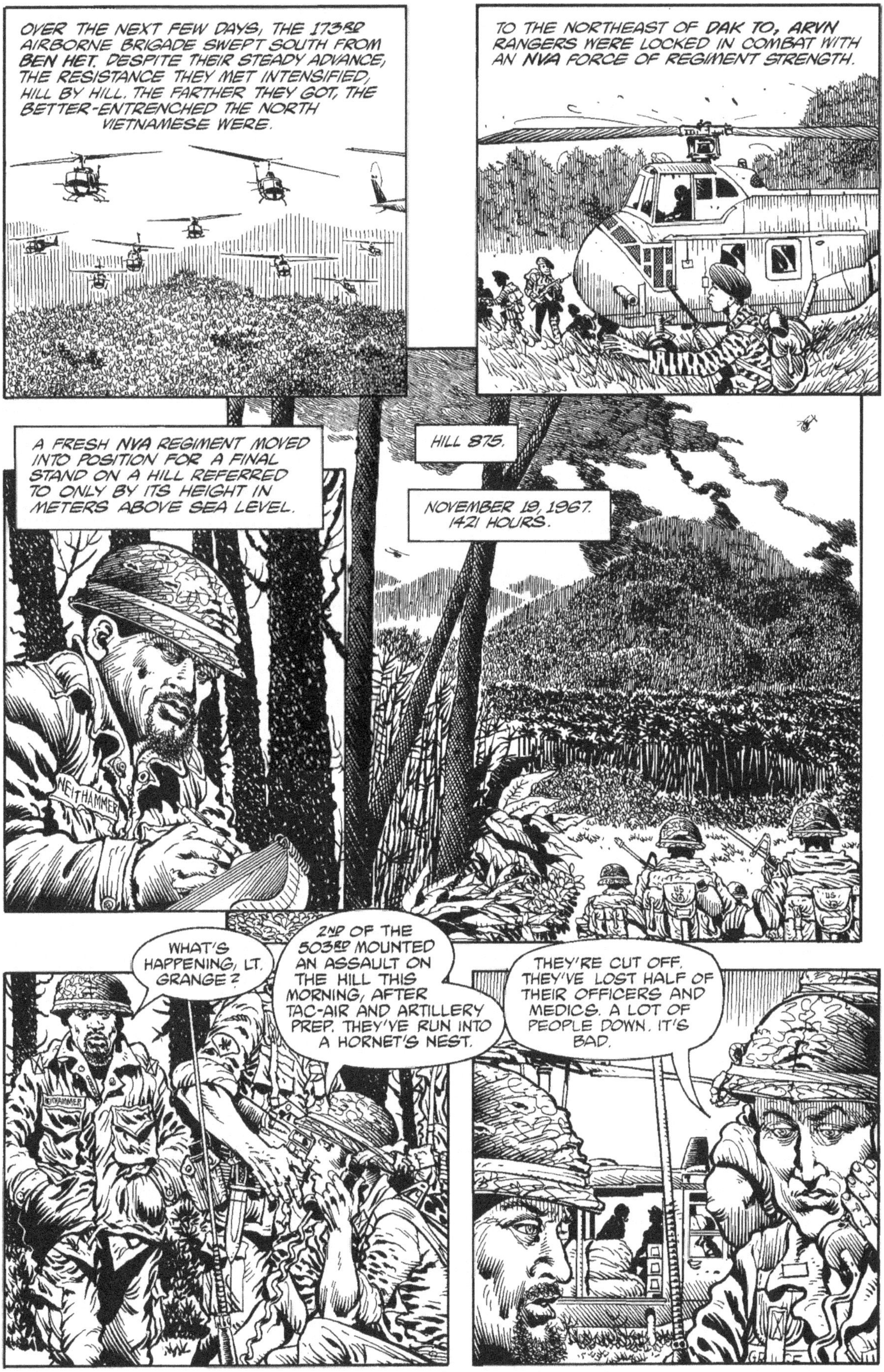

OVER THE NEXT FEW DAYS, THE 173RD AIRBORNE BRIGADE SWEPT SOUTH FROM BEN HET. DESPITE THEIR STEADY ADVANCE, THE RESISTANCE THEY MET INTENSIFIED, HILL BY HILL. THE FARTHER THEY GOT, THE BETTER-ENTRENCHED THE NORTH VIETNAMESE WERE.
TO THE NORTHEAST OF DAK TO, ARVN RANGERS WERE LOCKED IN COMBAT WITH AN NVA FORCE OF REGIMENT STRENGTH.
A FRESH NVA REGIMENT MOVED INTO POSITION FOR A FINAL STAND ON A HILL REFERRED TO ONLY BY ITS HEIGHT IN METERS ABOVE SEA LEVEL.
NEITHAMMER
HILL 875.
NOVEMBER 19, 1967. 1421 HOURS.
US
WHAT'S HAPPENING, LT. GRANGE?
2ND OF THE 503RD MOUNTED AN ASSAULT ON THE HILL THIS MORNING, AFTER TAC-AIR AND ARTILLERY PREP. THEY'VE RUN INTO A HORNET'S NEST.
NEITHAMMER
THEY'RE CUT OFF. THEY'VE LOST HALF OF THEIR OFFICERS AND MEDICS. A LOT OF PEOPLE DOWN. IT'S BAD.

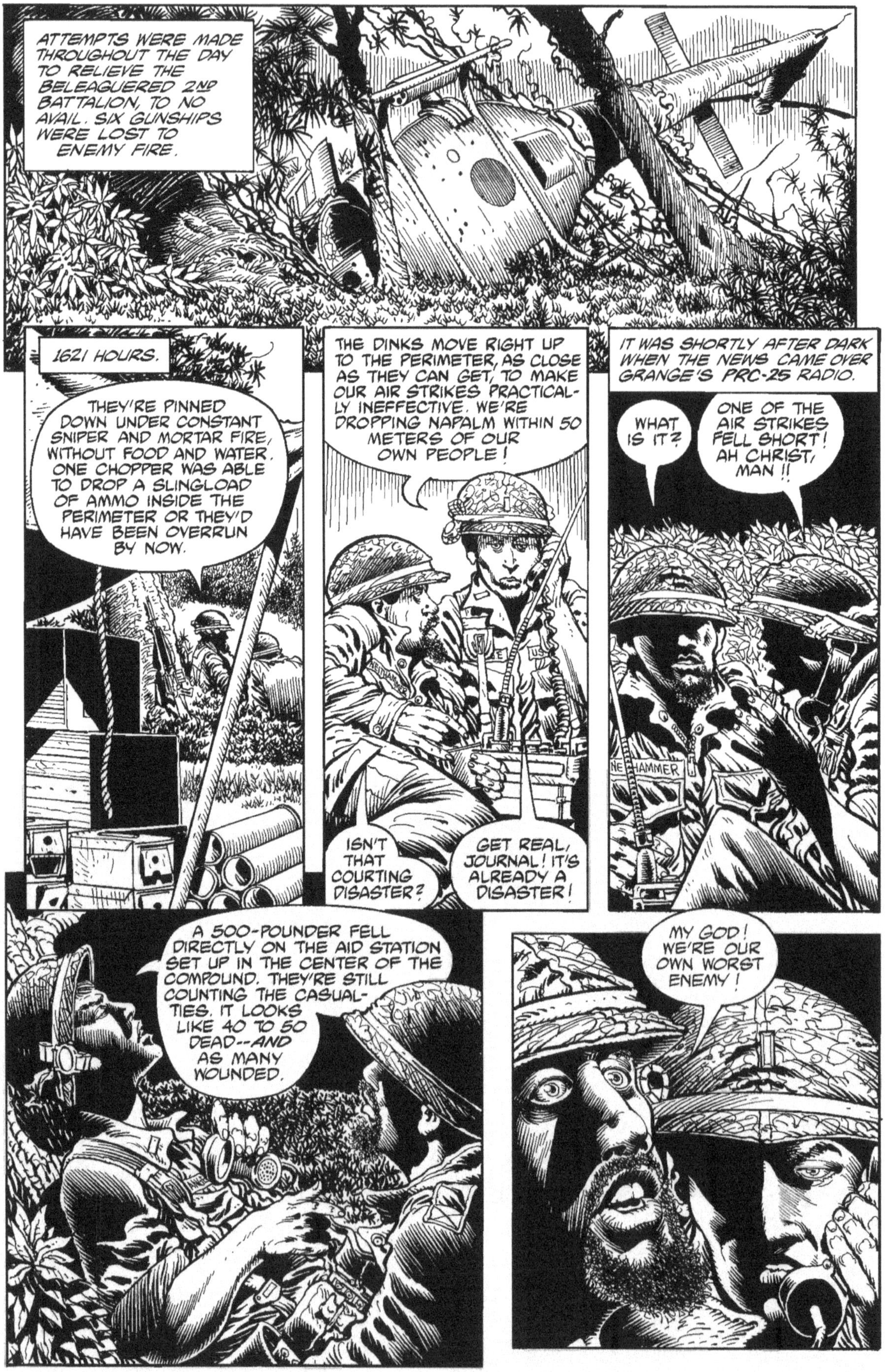

ATTEMPTS WERE MADE THROUGHOUT THE DAY TO RELIEVE THE BELEAGUERED 2ND BATTALION, TO NO AVAIL. SIX GUNSHIPS WERE LOST TO ENEMY FIRE.
1621 HOURS.
THEY'RE PINNED DOWN UNDER CONSTANT SNIPER AND MORTAR FIRE, WITHOUT FOOD AND WATER. ONE CHOPPER WAS ABLE TO DROP A SLINGLOAD OF AMMO INSIDE THE PERIMETER OR THEY'D HAVE BEEN OVERRUN BY NOW.
THE DINKS MOVE RIGHT UP TO THE PERIMETER, AS CLOSE AS THEY CAN GET, TO MAKE OUR AIR STRIKES PRACTICALLY INEFFECTIVE. WE'RE DROPPING NAPALM WITHIN 50 METERS OF OUR OWN PEOPLE!
ISN'T THAT COURTING DISASTER?
GET REAL, JOURNAL! IT'S ALREADY A DISASTER!
IT WAS SHORTLY AFTER DARK WHEN THE NEWS CAME OVER GRANGE'S PRC-25 RADIO.
WHAT IS IT?
ONE OF THE AIR STRIKES FELL SHORT! AH CHRIST, MAN!!
NEHAMMER
A 500-POUNDER FELL DIRECTLY ON THE AID STATION SET UP IN THE CENTER OF THE COMPOUND. THEY'RE STILL COUNTING THE CASUALTIES. IT LOOKS LIKE 40 TO 50 DEAD--AND AS MANY WOUNDED.
MY GOD! WE'RE OUR OWN WORST ENEMY!

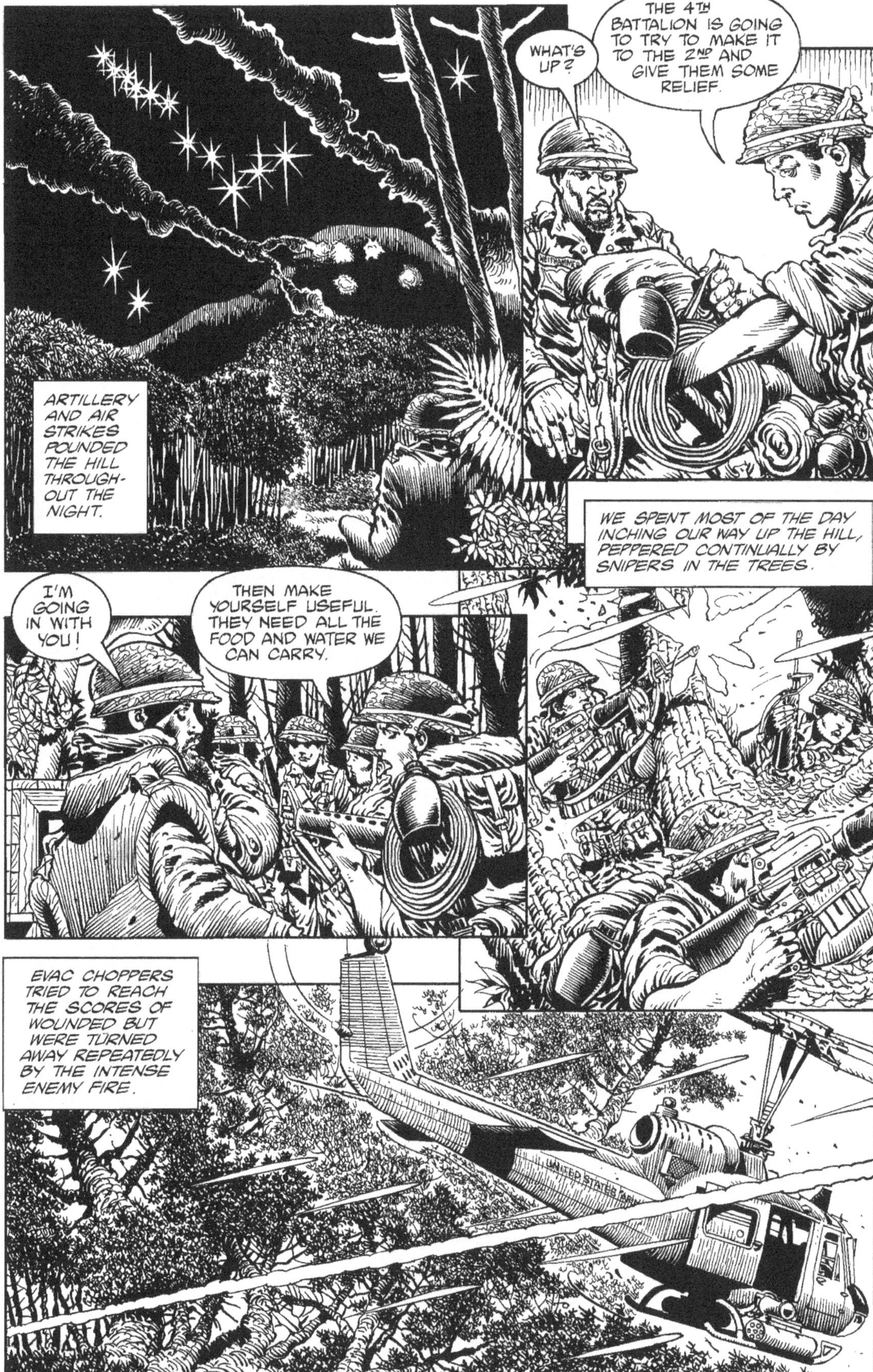
ARTILLERY AND AIR STRIKES POUNDED THE HILL THROUGH-OUT THE NIGHT.
WHAT'S UP?
THE 4TH BATTALION IS GOING TO TRY TO MAKE IT TO THE 2ND AND GIVE THEM SOME RELIEF.
I'M GOING IN WITH YOU!
THEN MAKE YOURSELF USEFUL. THEY NEED ALL THE FOOD AND WATER WE CAN CARRY.
WE SPENT MOST OF THE DAY INCHING OUR WAY UP THE HILL, PEPPERED CONTINUALLY BY SNIPERS IN THE TREES.
EVAC CHOPPERS TRIED TO REACH THE SCORES OF WOUNDED BUT WERE TURNED AWAY REPEATEDLY BY THE INTENSE ENEMY FIRE.

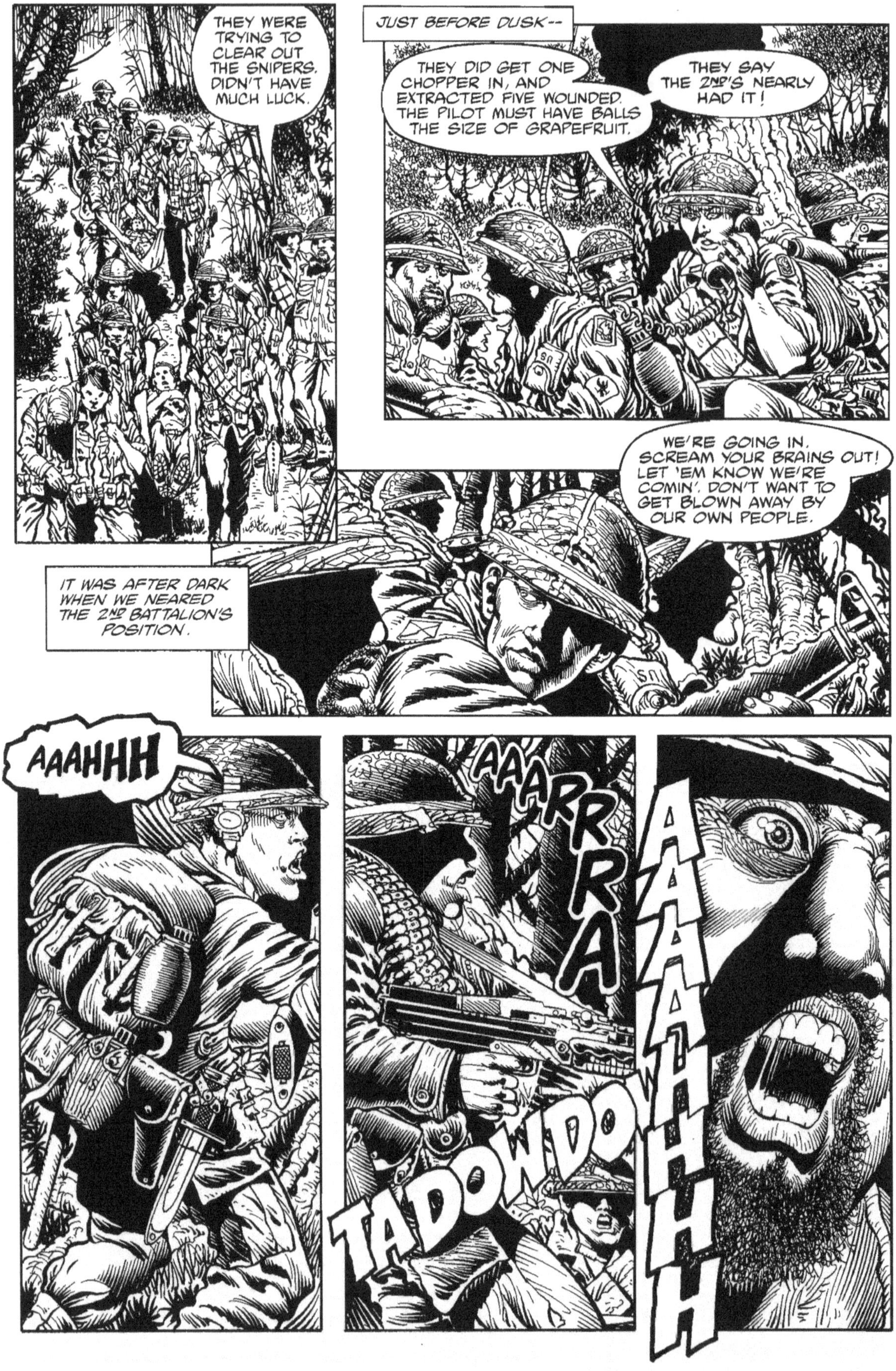
THEY WERE TRYING TO CLEAR OUT THE SNIPERS. DIDN'T HAVE MUCH LUCK.
JUST BEFORE DUSK--
THEY DID GET ONE CHOPPER IN, AND EXTRACTED FIVE WOUNDED. THE PILOT MUST HAVE BALLS THE SIZE OF GRAPEFRUIT.
THEY SAY THE 2ND'S NEARLY HAD IT!
WE'RE GOING IN. SCREAM YOUR BRAINS OUT! LET 'EM KNOW WE'RE COMIN'. DON'T WANT TO GET BLOWN AWAY BY OUR OWN PEOPLE.
IT WAS AFTER DARK WHEN WE NEARED THE 2ND BATTALION'S POSITION.
AAAHHH
AAARRRA
TADOWDOW
AAAAAHHHHHH

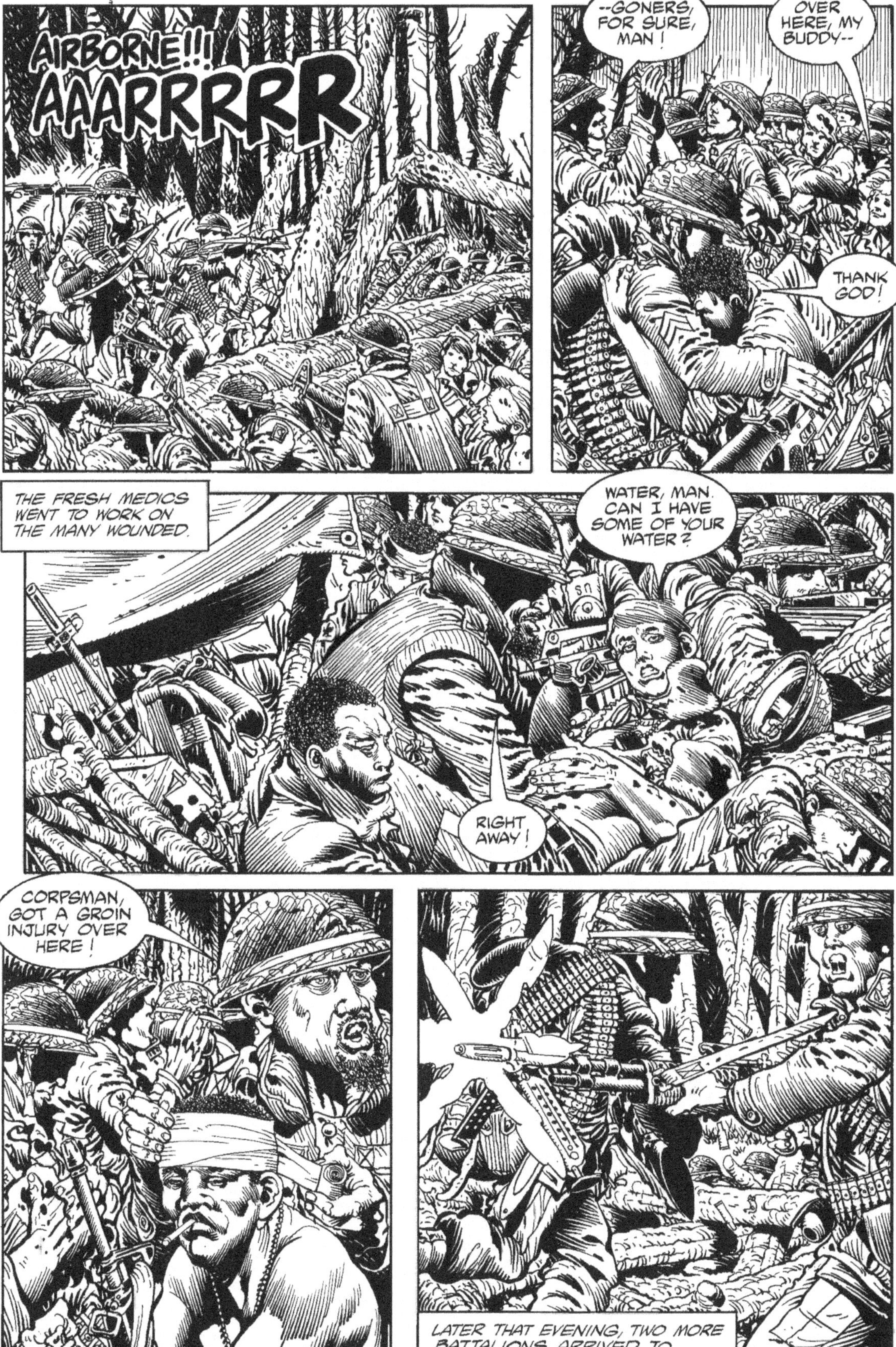
AIRBORNE!!!
AAARRRRR
--GONERS, FOR SURE, MAN!
OVER HERE, MY BUDDY--
THANK GOD!
THE FRESH MEDICS WENT TO WORK ON THE MANY WOUNDED.
WATER, MAN. CAN I HAVE SOME OF YOUR WATER?
RIGHT AWAY!
CORPSMAN, GOT A GROIN INJURY OVER HERE!
LATER THAT EVENING, TWO MORE BATTALIONS ARRIVED TO FORTIFY THE POSITION.

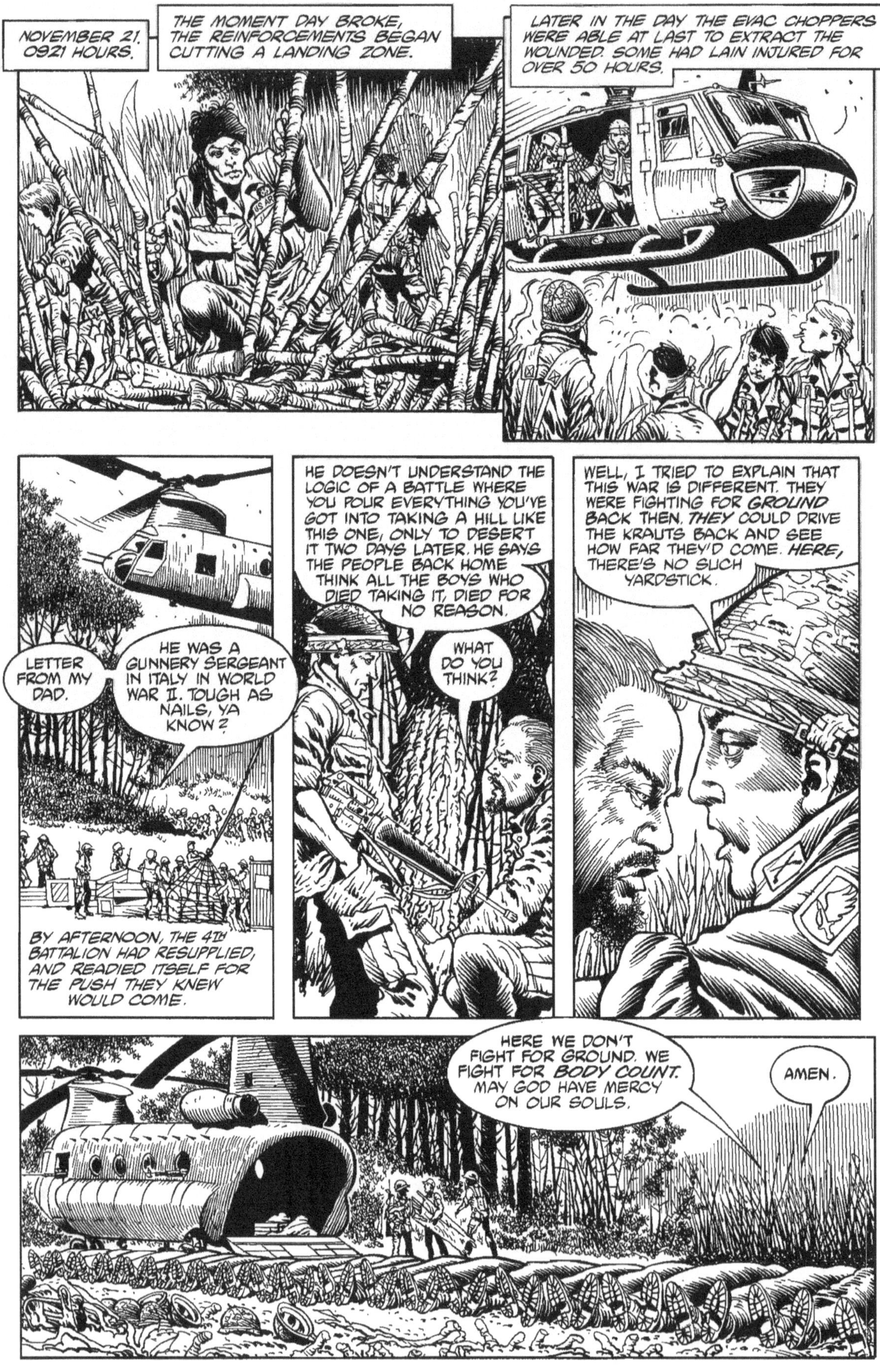
NOVEMBER 21, 0921 HOURS.
THE MOMENT DAY BROKE, THE REINFORCEMENTS BEGAN CUTTING A LANDING ZONE.
LATER IN THE DAY THE EVAC CHOPPERS WERE ABLE AT LAST TO EXTRACT THE WOUNDED. SOME HAD LAIN INJURED FOR OVER 50 HOURS.
LETTER FROM MY DAD.
HE WAS A GUNNERY SERGEANT IN ITALY IN WORLD WAR II. TOUGH AS NAILS, YA KNOW?
BY AFTERNOON, THE 4TH BATTALION HAD RESUPPLIED, AND READIED ITSELF FOR THE PUSH THEY KNEW WOULD COME.
HE DOESN'T UNDERSTAND THE LOGIC OF A BATTLE WHERE YOU POUR EVERYTHING YOU'VE GOT INTO TAKING A HILL LIKE THIS ONE, ONLY TO DESERT IT TWO DAYS LATER. HE SAYS THE PEOPLE BACK HOME THINK ALL THE BOYS WHO DIED TAKING IT, DIED FOR NO REASON.
WHAT DO YOU THINK?
WELL, I TRIED TO EXPLAIN THAT THIS WAR IS DIFFERENT. THEY WERE FIGHTING FOR GROUND BACK THEN. THEY COULD DRIVE THE KRAUTS BACK AND SEE HOW FAR THEY'D COME. HERE, THERE'S NO SUCH YARDSTICK.
HERE WE DON'T FIGHT FOR GROUND. WE FIGHT FOR BODY COUNT. MAY GOD HAVE MERCY ON OUR SOULS.
AMEN.

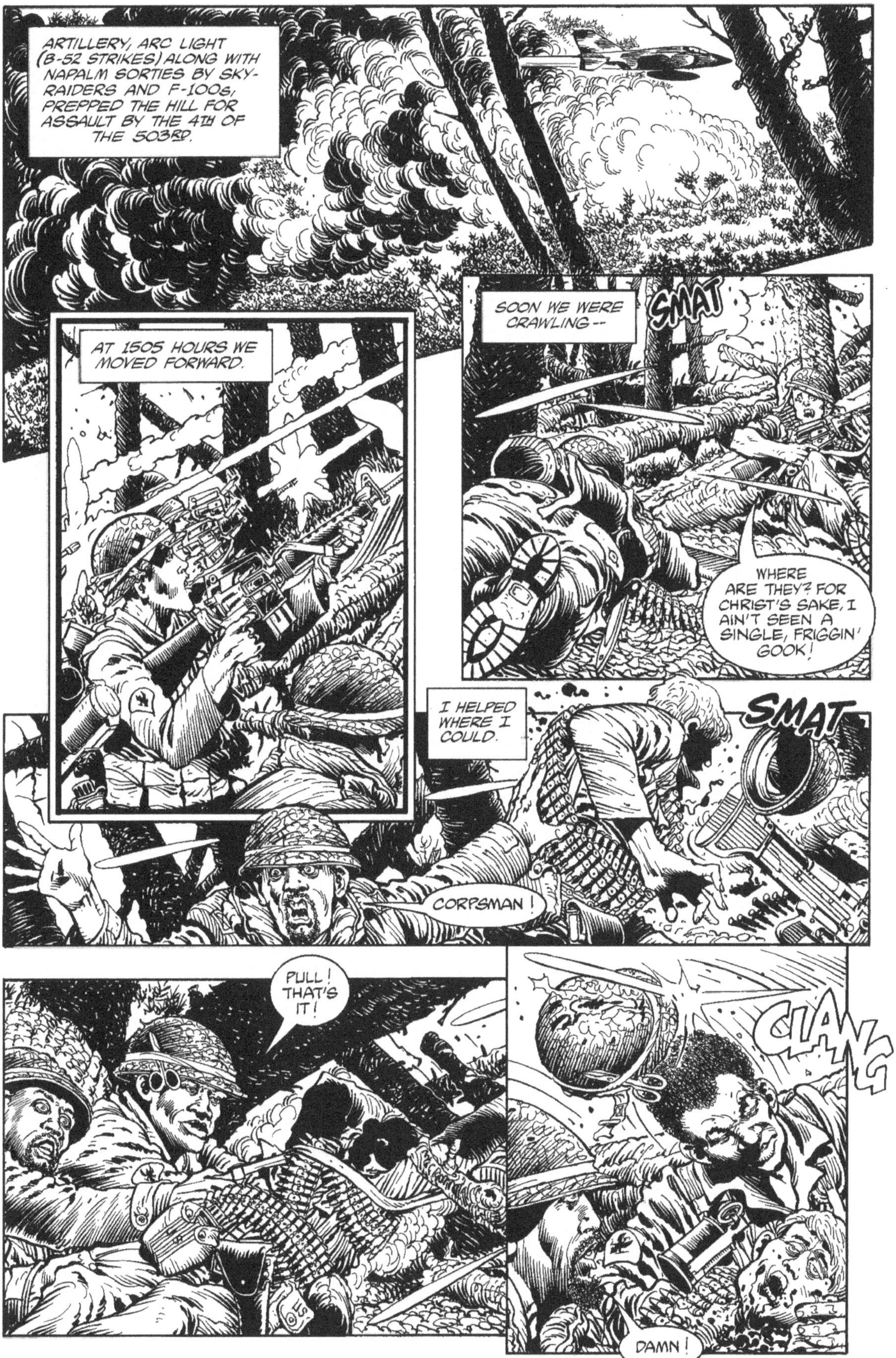

ARTILLERY, ARC LIGHT (B-52 STRIKES) ALONG WITH NAPALM SORTIES BY SKY-RAIDERS AND F-100s, PREPPED THE HILL FOR ASSAULT BY THE 4TH OF THE 503RD.
AT 1505 HOURS WE MOVED FORWARD.
SOON WE WERE CRAWLING --
SMAT
WHERE ARE THEY? FOR CHRIST'S SAKE, I AIN'T SEEN A SINGLE, FRIGGIN' GOOK!
I HELPED WHERE I COULD.
SMAT
CORPSMAN!
PULL! THAT'S IT!
CLANG
DAMN!

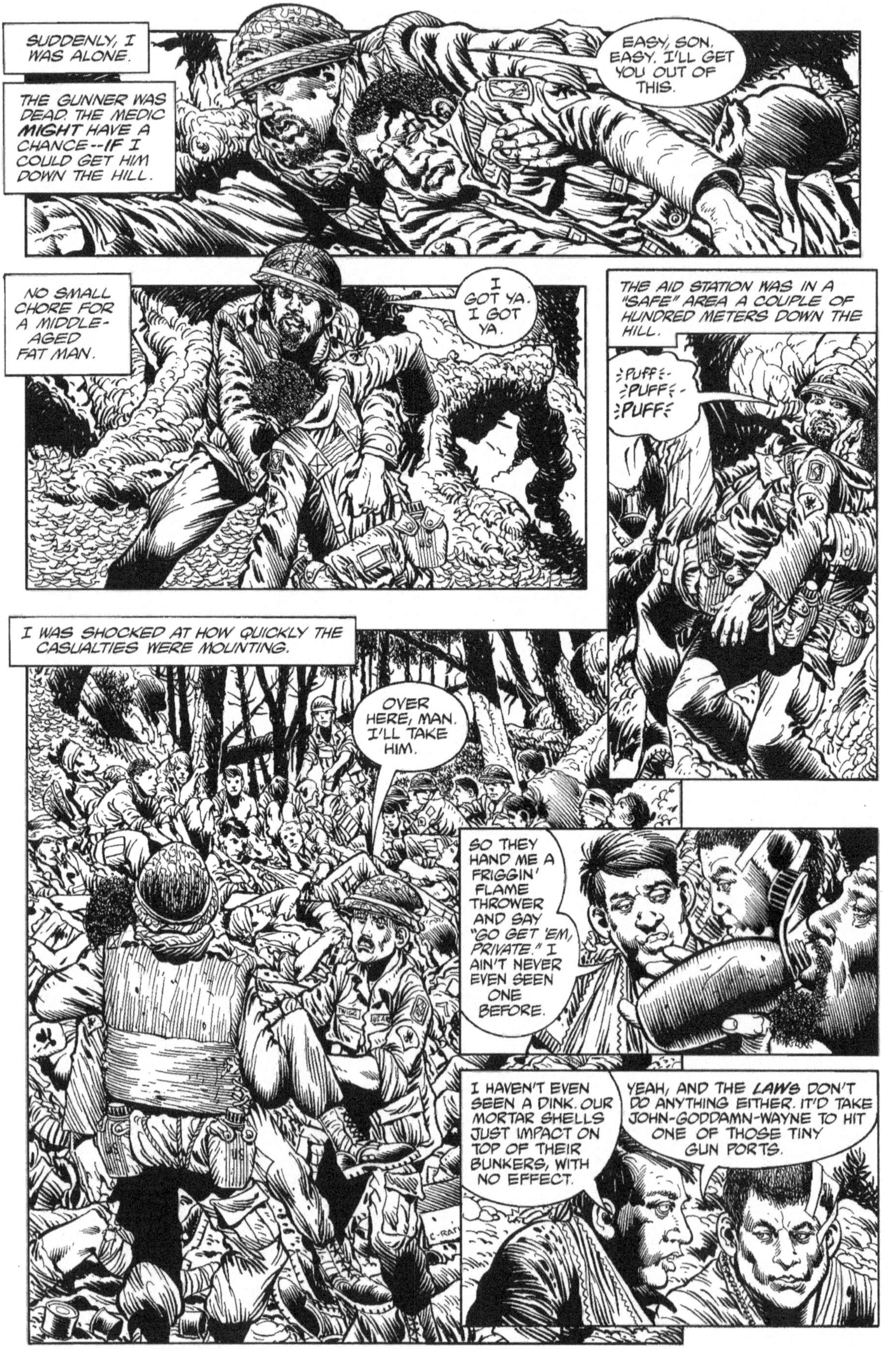
SUDDENLY, I WAS ALONE.
THE GUNNER WAS DEAD. THE MEDIC **MIGHT** HAVE A CHANCE--**IF** I COULD GET HIM DOWN THE HILL.
EASY, SON. EASY. I'LL GET YOU OUT OF THIS.
NO SMALL CHORE FOR A MIDDLE-AGED FAT MAN.
I GOT YA. I GOT YA.
THE AID STATION WAS IN A "SAFE" AREA A COUPLE OF HUNDRED METERS DOWN THE HILL.
PUFF - PUFF - PUFF
I WAS SHOCKED AT HOW QUICKLY THE CASUALTIES WERE MOUNTING.
OVER HERE, MAN. I'LL TAKE HIM.
SO THEY HAND ME A FRIGGIN' FLAME THROWER AND SAY "GO GET 'EM, PRIVATE." I AIN'T NEVER EVEN SEEN ONE BEFORE.
I HAVEN'T EVEN SEEN A DINK. OUR MORTAR SHELLS JUST IMPACT ON TOP OF THEIR BUNKERS, WITH NO EFFECT.
YEAH, AND THE ***LAWS*** DON'T DO ANYTHING EITHER. IT'D TAKE JOHN-GODDAMN-WAYNE TO HIT ONE OF THOSE TINY GUN PORTS.

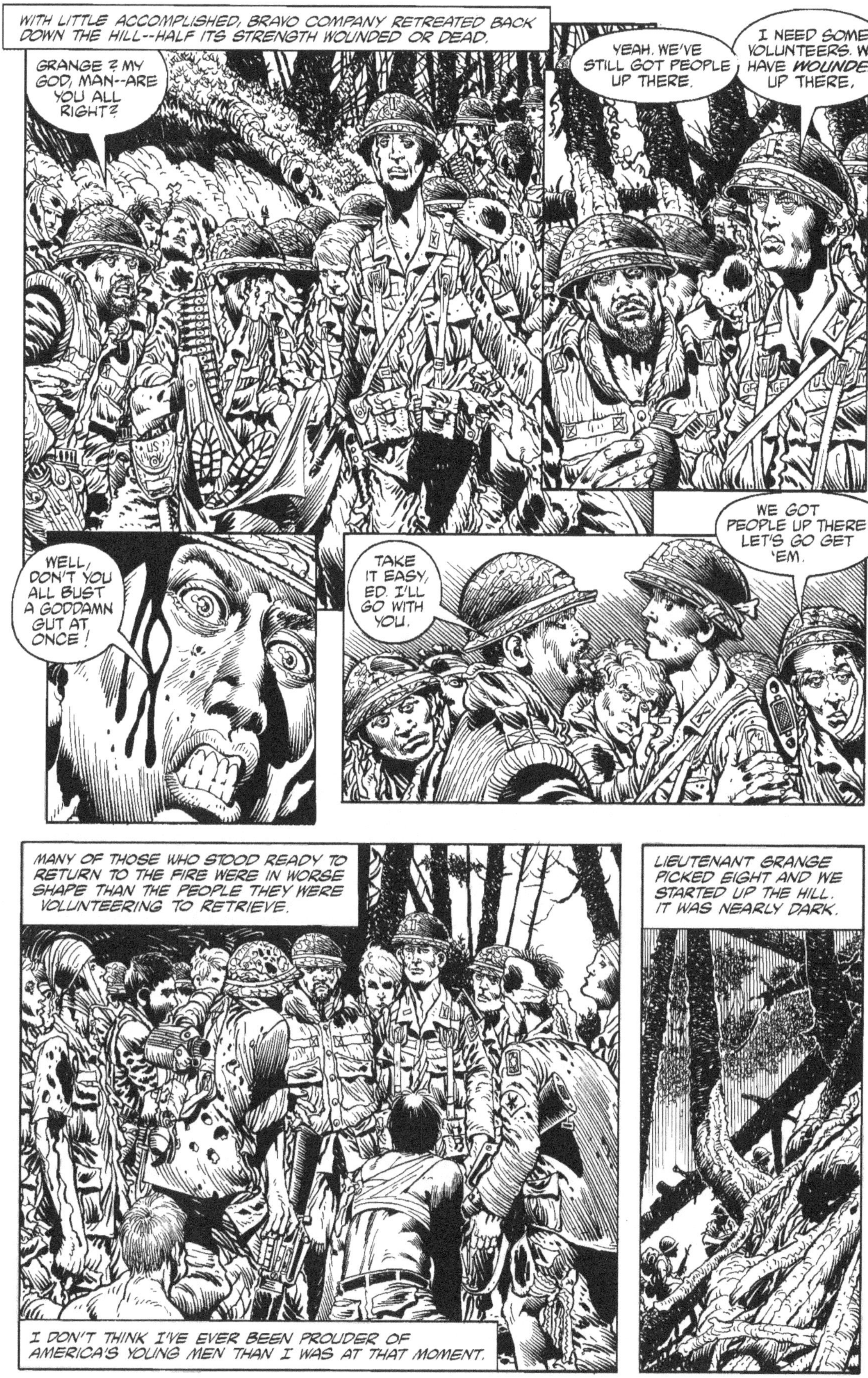
WITH LITTLE ACCOMPLISHED, BRAVO COMPANY RETREATED BACK DOWN THE HILL--HALF ITS STRENGTH WOUNDED OR DEAD.
GRANGE? MY GOD, MAN--ARE YOU ALL RIGHT?
YEAH. WE'VE STILL GOT PEOPLE UP THERE.
I NEED SOME VOLUNTEERS. WE HAVE WOUNDED UP THERE.
WELL, DON'T YOU ALL BUST A GODDAMN GUT AT ONCE!
TAKE IT EASY, ED. I'LL GO WITH YOU.
WE GOT PEOPLE UP THERE? LET'S GO GET 'EM.
MANY OF THOSE WHO STOOD READY TO RETURN TO THE FIRE WERE IN WORSE SHAPE THAN THE PEOPLE THEY WERE VOLUNTEERING TO RETRIEVE.
I DON'T THINK I'VE EVER BEEN PROUDER OF AMERICA'S YOUNG MEN THAN I WAS AT THAT MOMENT.
LIEUTENANT GRANGE PICKED EIGHT AND WE STARTED UP THE HILL. IT WAS NEARLY DARK.

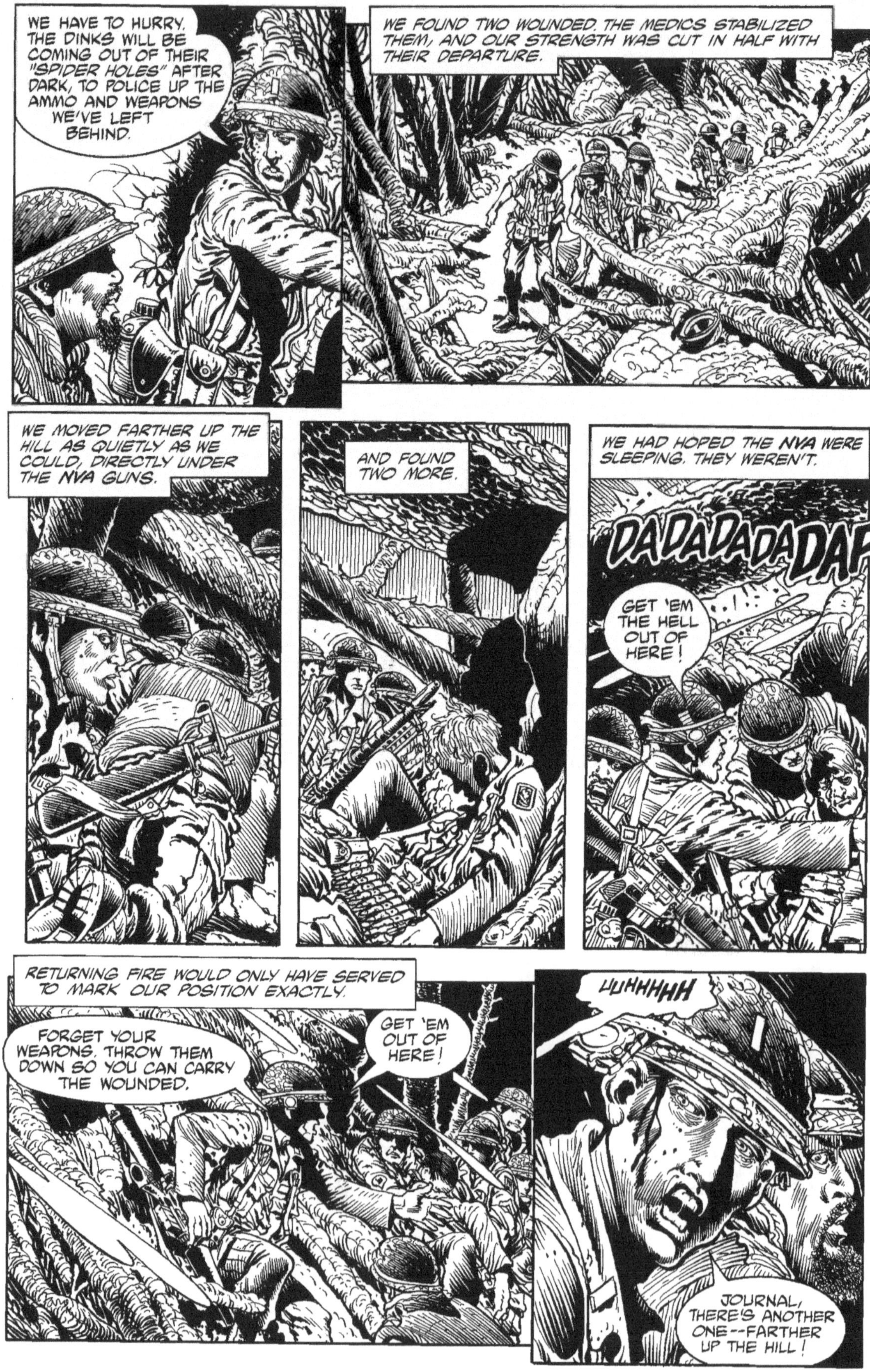
WE HAVE TO HURRY. THE DINKS WILL BE COMING OUT OF THEIR "SPIDER HOLES" AFTER DARK, TO POLICE UP THE AMMO AND WEAPONS WE'VE LEFT BEHIND.
WE FOUND TWO WOUNDED. THE MEDICS STABILIZED THEM, AND OUR STRENGTH WAS CUT IN HALF WITH THEIR DEPARTURE.
WE MOVED FARTHER UP THE HILL AS QUIETLY AS WE COULD, DIRECTLY UNDER THE NVA GUNS.
AND FOUND TWO MORE.
WE HAD HOPED THE NVA WERE SLEEPING. THEY WEREN'T.
DADADADADAP
GET 'EM THE HELL OUT OF HERE!
RETURNING FIRE WOULD ONLY HAVE SERVED TO MARK OUR POSITION EXACTLY.
FORGET YOUR WEAPONS. THROW THEM DOWN SO YOU CAN CARRY THE WOUNDED.
GET 'EM OUT OF HERE!
UUHHHHH
JOURNAL, THERE'S ANOTHER ONE--FARTHER UP THE HILL!

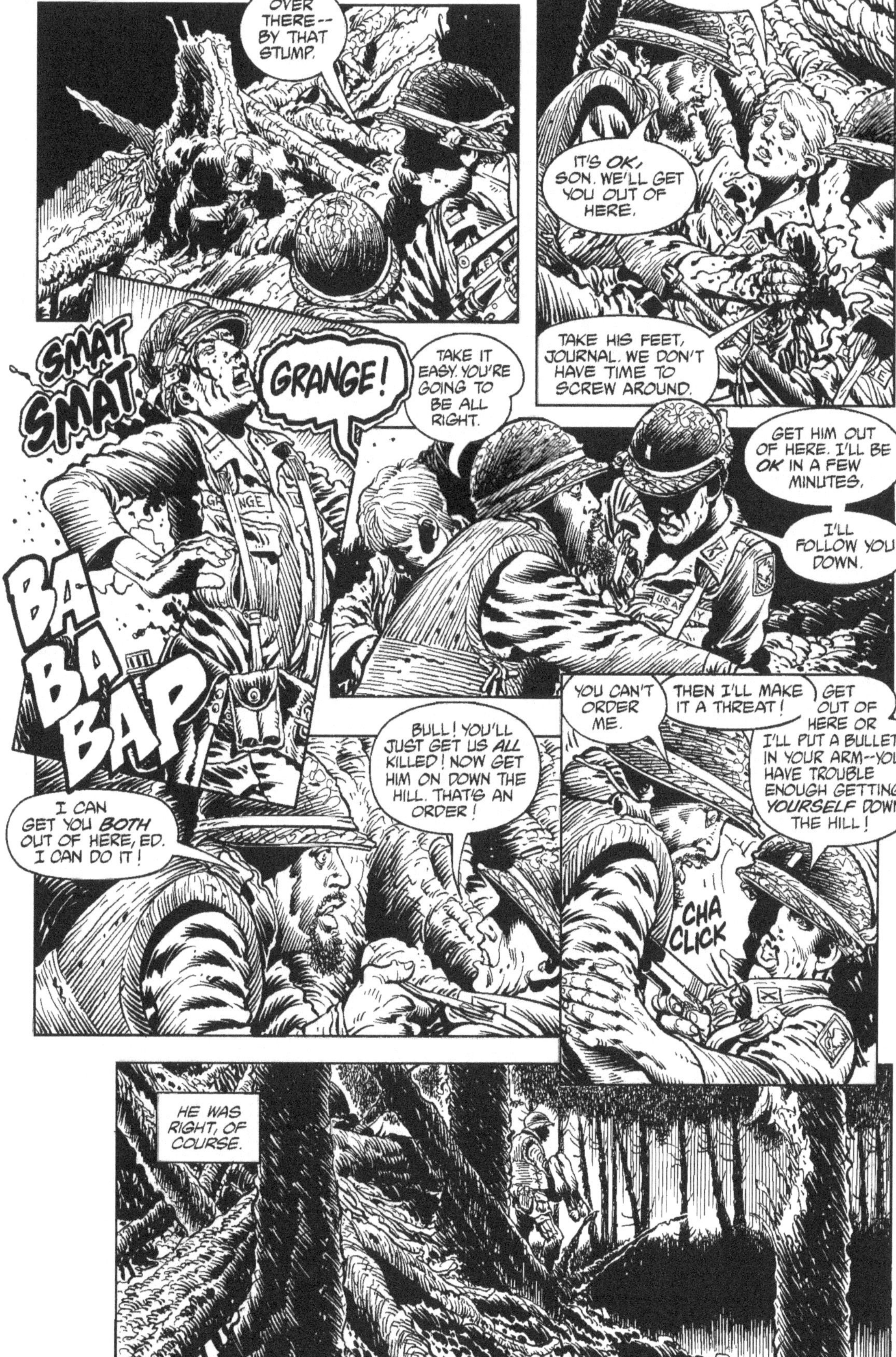
OVER THERE-- BY THAT STUMP.
THANK GOD!
IT'S OK, SON. WE'LL GET YOU OUT OF HERE.
TAKE HIS FEET, JOURNAL. WE DON'T HAVE TIME TO SCREW AROUND.
SMAT SMAT
GRANGE!
BA BA BAP
TAKE IT EASY. YOU'RE GOING TO BE ALL RIGHT.
GET HIM OUT OF HERE. I'LL BE OK IN A FEW MINUTES.
I'LL FOLLOW YOU DOWN.
I CAN GET YOU BOTH OUT OF HERE, ED. I CAN DO IT!
BULL! YOU'LL JUST GET US ALL KILLED! NOW GET HIM ON DOWN THE HILL. THAT'S AN ORDER!
YOU CAN'T ORDER ME.
THEN I'LL MAKE IT A THREAT!
GET OUT OF HERE OR I'LL PUT A BULLET IN YOUR ARM--YOU'LL HAVE TROUBLE ENOUGH GETTING YOURSELF DOWN THE HILL!
CHA CLICK
HE WAS RIGHT, OF COURSE.

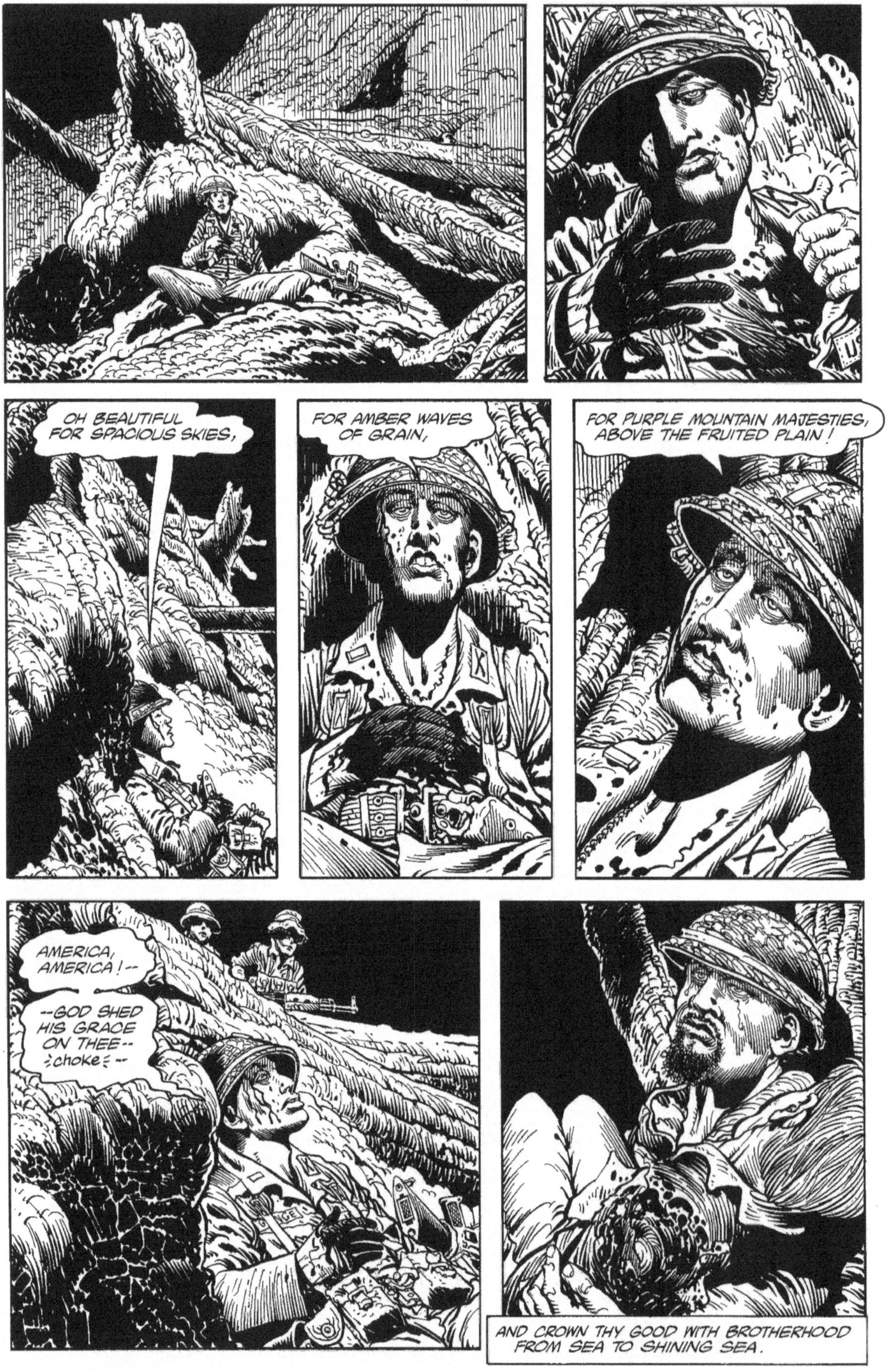
OH BEAUTIFUL FOR SPACIOUS SKIES,
FOR AMBER WAVES OF GRAIN,
FOR PURPLE MOUNTAIN MAJESTIES, ABOVE THE FRUITED PLAIN!
AMERICA, AMERICA!--
--GOD SHED HIS GRACE ON THEE-- choke --
AND CROWN THY GOOD WITH BROTHERHOOD FROM SEA TO SHINING SEA.

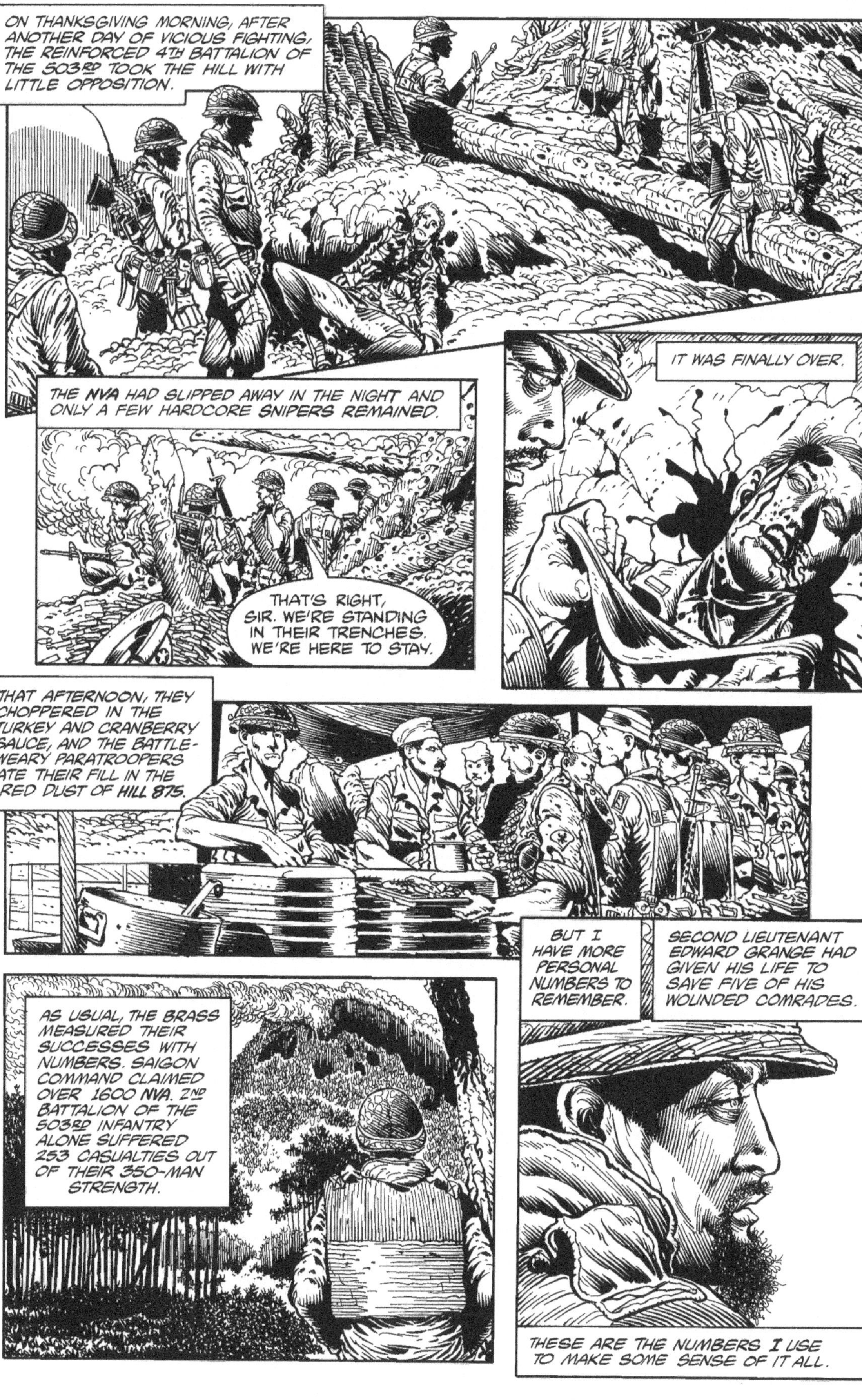
ON THANKSGIVING MORNING, AFTER ANOTHER DAY OF VICIOUS FIGHTING, THE REINFORCED 4TH BATTALION OF THE 503RD TOOK THE HILL WITH LITTLE OPPOSITION.
THE NVA HAD SLIPPED AWAY IN THE NIGHT AND ONLY A FEW HARDCORE SNIPERS REMAINED.
THAT'S RIGHT, SIR. WE'RE STANDING IN THEIR TRENCHES. WE'RE HERE TO STAY.
IT WAS FINALLY OVER.
THAT AFTERNOON, THEY CHOPPERED IN THE TURKEY AND CRANBERRY SAUCE, AND THE BATTLE-WEARY PARATROOPERS ATE THEIR FILL IN THE RED DUST OF HILL 875.
AS USUAL, THE BRASS MEASURED THEIR SUCCESSES WITH NUMBERS. SAIGON COMMAND CLAIMED OVER 1600 NVA. 2ND BATTALION OF THE 503RD INFANTRY ALONE SUFFERED 253 CASUALTIES OUT OF THEIR 350-MAN STRENGTH.
BUT I HAVE MORE PERSONAL NUMBERS TO REMEMBER.
SECOND LIEUTENANT EDWARD GRANGE HAD GIVEN HIS LIFE TO SAVE FIVE OF HIS WOUNDED COMRADES.
THESE ARE THE NUMBERS I USE TO MAKE SOME SENSE OF IT ALL.

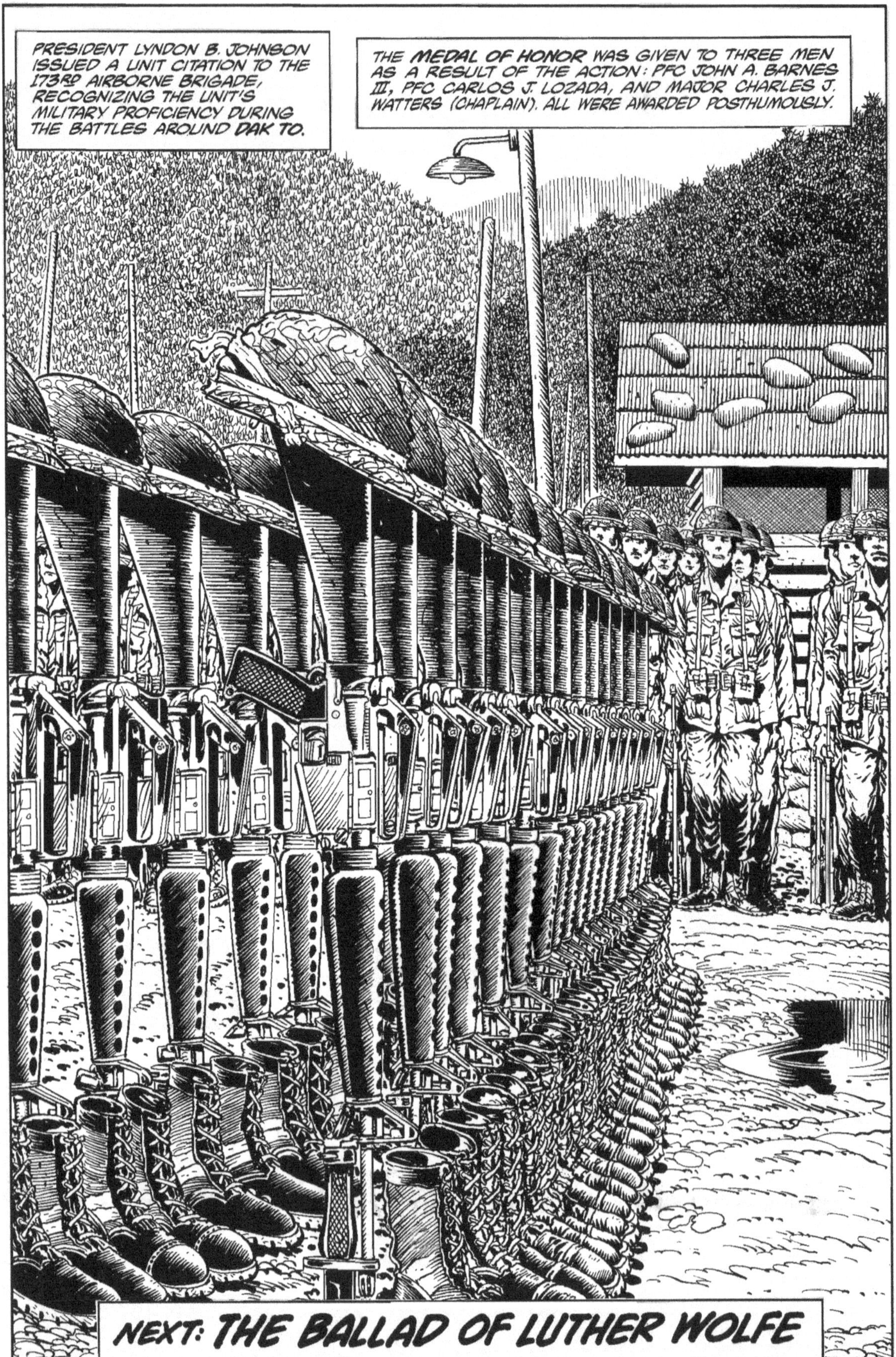
PRESIDENT LYNDON B. JOHNSON ISSUED A UNIT CITATION TO THE 173RD AIRBORNE BRIGADE, RECOGNIZING THE UNIT'S MILITARY PROFICIENCY DURING THE BATTLES AROUND DAK TO.
THE MEDAL OF HONOR WAS GIVEN TO THREE MEN AS A RESULT OF THE ACTION: PFC JOHN A. BARNES III, PFC CARLOS J. LOZADA, AND MAJOR CHARLES J. WATTERS (CHAPLAIN). ALL WERE AWARDED POSTHUMOUSLY.
NEXT: THE BALLAD OF LUTHER WOLFE

DUST - OFF

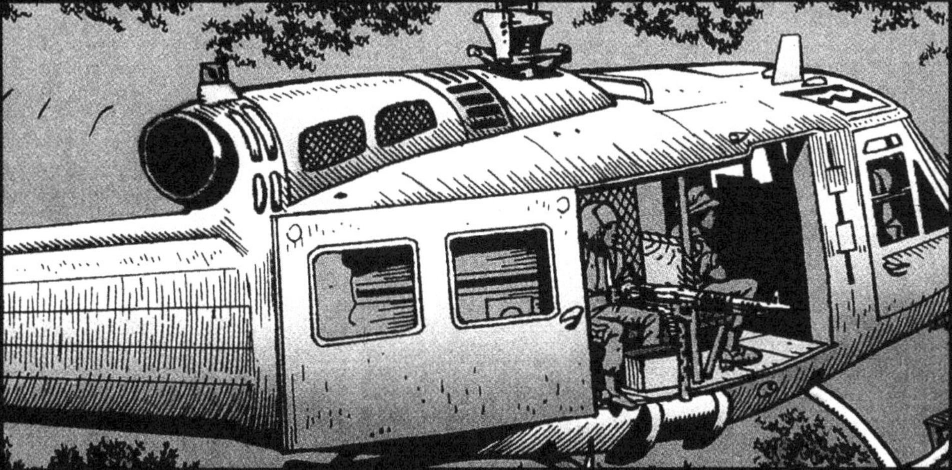

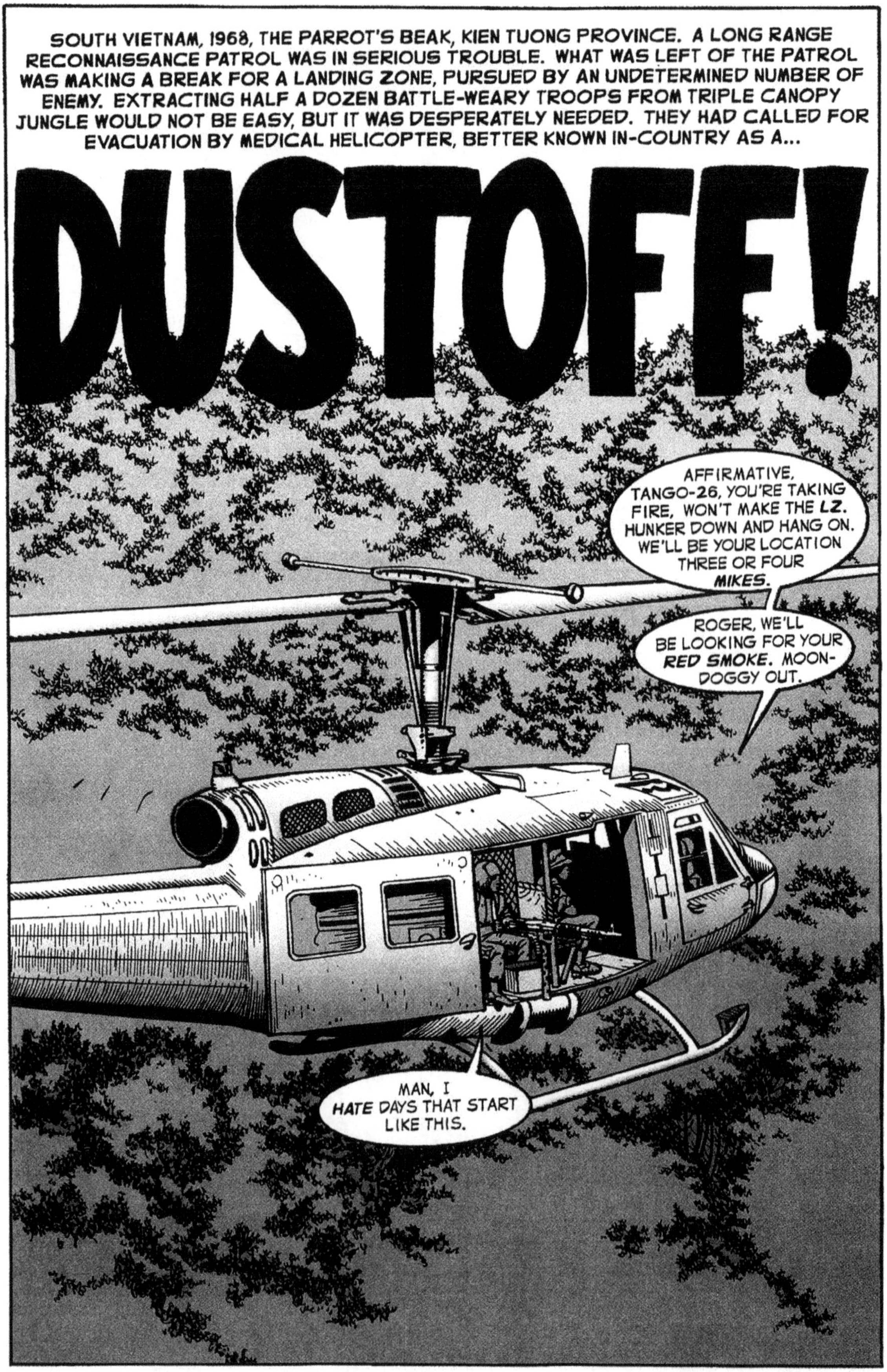
SOUTH VIETNAM, 1968, THE PARROT'S BEAK, KIEN TUONG PROVINCE. A LONG RANGE RECONNAISSANCE PATROL WAS IN SERIOUS TROUBLE. WHAT WAS LEFT OF THE PATROL WAS MAKING A BREAK FOR A LANDING ZONE, PURSUED BY AN UNDETERMINED NUMBER OF ENEMY. EXTRACTING HALF A DOZEN BATTLE-WEARY TROOPS FROM TRIPLE CANOPY JUNGLE WOULD NOT BE EASY, BUT IT WAS DESPERATELY NEEDED. THEY HAD CALLED FOR EVACUATION BY MEDICAL HELICOPTER, BETTER KNOWN IN-COUNTRY AS A...
DUSTOFF!
AFFIRMATIVE, TANGO-26, YOU'RE TAKING FIRE, WON'T MAKE THE LZ. HUNKER DOWN AND HANG ON. WE'LL BE YOUR LOCATION THREE OR FOUR MIKES.
ROGER, WE'LL BE LOOKING FOR YOUR RED SMOKE. MOON-DOGGY OUT.
MAN, I HATE DAYS THAT START LIKE THIS.

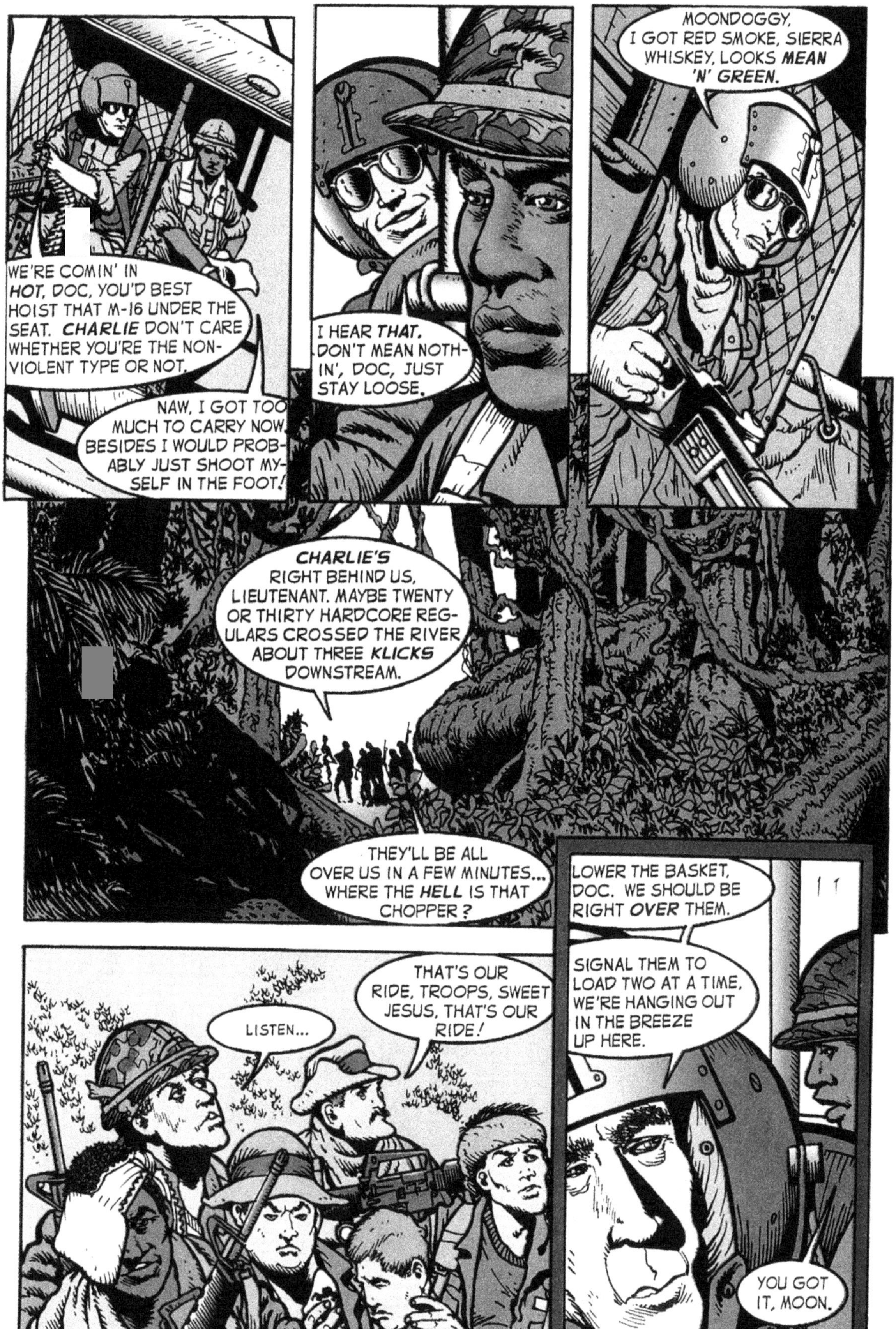
WE'RE COMIN' IN HOT, DOC, YOU'D BEST HOIST THAT M-16 UNDER THE SEAT. CHARLIE DON'T CARE WHETHER YOU'RE THE NON-VIOLENT TYPE OR NOT.
NAW, I GOT TOO MUCH TO CARRY NOW. BESIDES I WOULD PROBABLY JUST SHOOT MYSELF IN THE FOOT!
I HEAR THAT. DON'T MEAN NOTHIN', DOC, JUST STAY LOOSE.
MOONDOGGY, I GOT RED SMOKE, SIERRA WHISKEY, LOOKS MEAN 'N' GREEN.
CHARLIE'S RIGHT BEHIND US, LIEUTENANT. MAYBE TWENTY OR THIRTY HARDCORE REGULARS CROSSED THE RIVER ABOUT THREE KLICKS DOWNSTREAM.
THEY'LL BE ALL OVER US IN A FEW MINUTES... WHERE THE HELL IS THAT CHOPPER?
LISTEN...
THAT'S OUR RIDE, TROOPS, SWEET JESUS, THAT'S OUR RIDE!
LOWER THE BASKET, DOC. WE SHOULD BE RIGHT OVER THEM.
SIGNAL THEM TO LOAD TWO AT A TIME, WE'RE HANGING OUT IN THE BREEZE UP HERE.
YOU GOT IT, MOON.

LOAD *BOONE* AND *COWBOY*, THEY'RE THE WORST. AND MOVE IT! THAT CHOPPER IS LIKE A GIANT BILLBOARD POINTING OUT OUR LOCATION!

THIS WAS ALWAYS THE TENSE TIME. THE BIG GREEN HUEY MAY AS WELL HAVE HAD A TARGET PAINTED ON THE SIDE.

STEADY! TWO COMIN' UP!

COME ON, COME ON, *COME ON...*

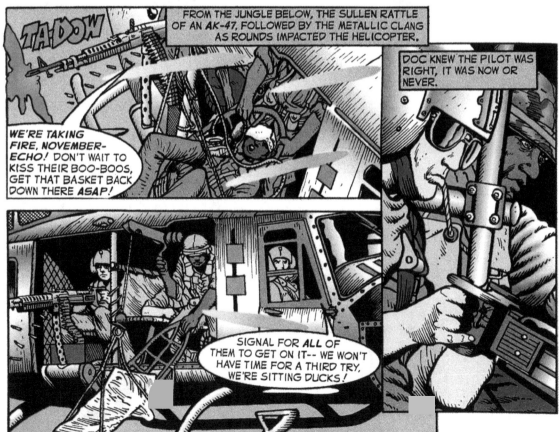

FROM THE JUNGLE BELOW, THE SULLEN RATTLE OF AN *AK-47,* FOLLOWED BY THE METALLIC CLANG AS ROUNDS IMPACTED THE HELICOPTER.

TA-DOW

WE'RE TAKING FIRE, NOVEMBER-ECHO! DON'T WAIT TO KISS THEIR BOO-BOOS, GET THAT BASKET BACK DOWN THERE *ASAP!*

DOC KNEW THE PILOT WAS RIGHT, IT WAS NOW OR NEVER.

SIGNAL FOR *ALL* OF THEM TO GET ON IT-- WE WON'T HAVE TIME FOR A THIRD TRY, WE'RE SITTING DUCKS!

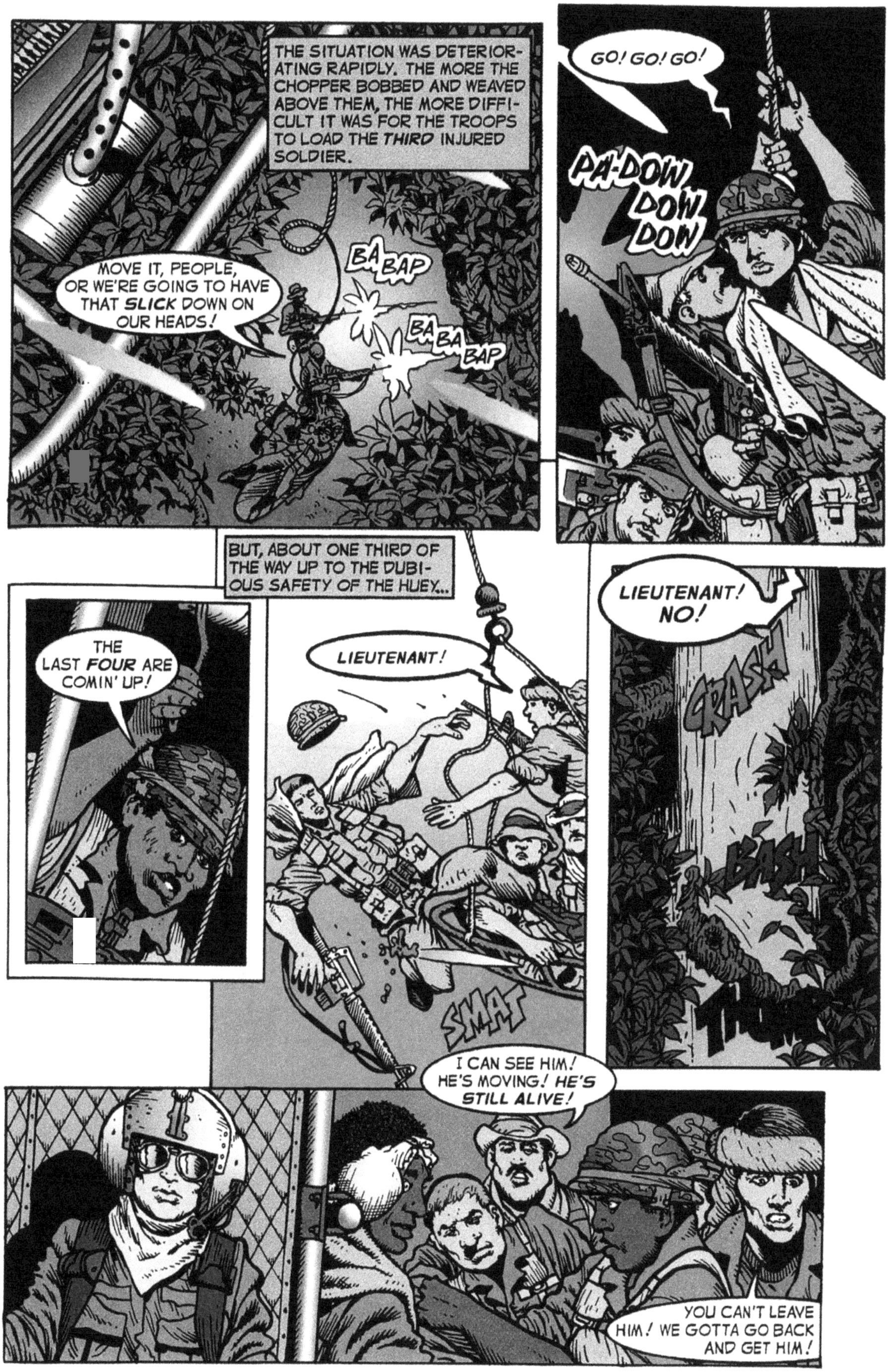
THE SITUATION WAS DETERIORATING RAPIDLY. THE MORE THE CHOPPER BOBBED AND WEAVED ABOVE THEM, THE MORE DIFFICULT IT WAS FOR THE TROOPS TO LOAD THE *THIRD* INJURED SOLDIER.
MOVE IT, PEOPLE, OR WE'RE GOING TO HAVE THAT *SLICK* DOWN ON OUR HEADS!
BA BAP
BA BA BAP
GO! GO! GO!
PA-DOW DOW DOW
BUT, ABOUT ONE THIRD OF THE WAY UP TO THE DUBIOUS SAFETY OF THE HUEY...
THE LAST *FOUR* ARE COMIN' UP!
LIEUTENANT!
SMAT
LIEUTENANT! NO!
CRASH
BASH
I CAN SEE HIM! HE'S MOVING! *HE'S STILL ALIVE!*
YOU CAN'T LEAVE HIM! WE GOTTA GO BACK AND GET HIM!

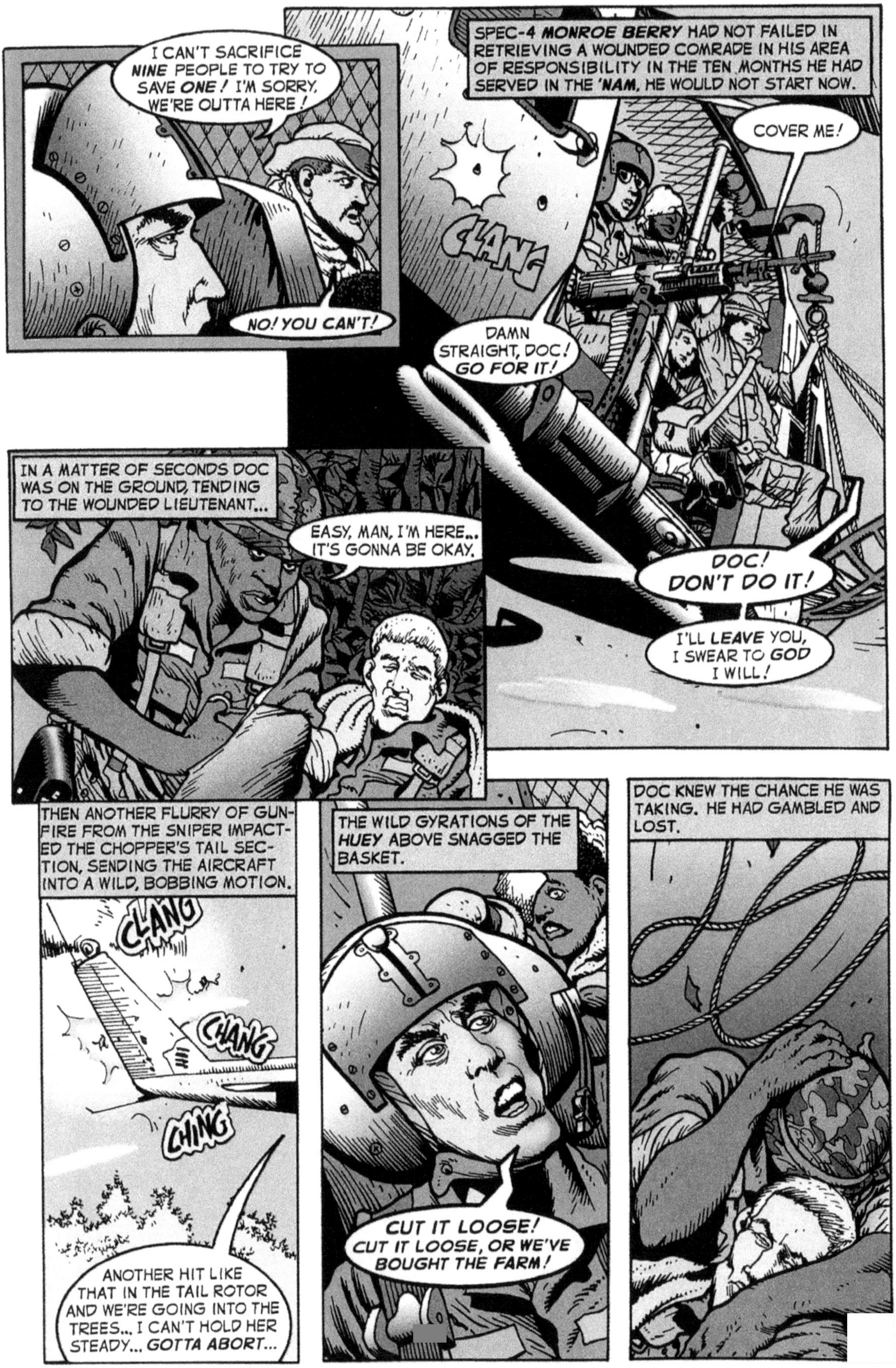
I CAN'T SACRIFICE NINE PEOPLE TO TRY TO SAVE ONE! I'M SORRY, WE'RE OUTTA HERE!
NO! YOU CAN'T!
SPEC-4 MONROE BERRY HAD NOT FAILED IN RETRIEVING A WOUNDED COMRADE IN HIS AREA OF RESPONSIBILITY IN THE TEN MONTHS HE HAD SERVED IN THE 'NAM. HE WOULD NOT START NOW.
CLANG
COVER ME!
DAMN STRAIGHT, DOC! GO FOR IT!
DOC! DON'T DO IT!
I'LL LEAVE YOU, I SWEAR TO GOD I WILL!
IN A MATTER OF SECONDS DOC WAS ON THE GROUND, TENDING TO THE WOUNDED LIEUTENANT...
EASY, MAN, I'M HERE... IT'S GONNA BE OKAY.
THEN ANOTHER FLURRY OF GUNFIRE FROM THE SNIPER IMPACTED THE CHOPPER'S TAIL SECTION, SENDING THE AIRCRAFT INTO A WILD, BOBBING MOTION.
CLANG
CHANG
CHING
ANOTHER HIT LIKE THAT IN THE TAIL ROTOR AND WE'RE GOING INTO THE TREES... I CAN'T HOLD HER STEADY... GOTTA ABORT...
THE WILD GYRATIONS OF THE HUEY ABOVE SNAGGED THE BASKET.
CUT IT LOOSE! CUT IT LOOSE, OR WE'VE BOUGHT THE FARM!
DOC KNEW THE CHANCE HE WAS TAKING. HE HAD GAMBLED AND LOST.

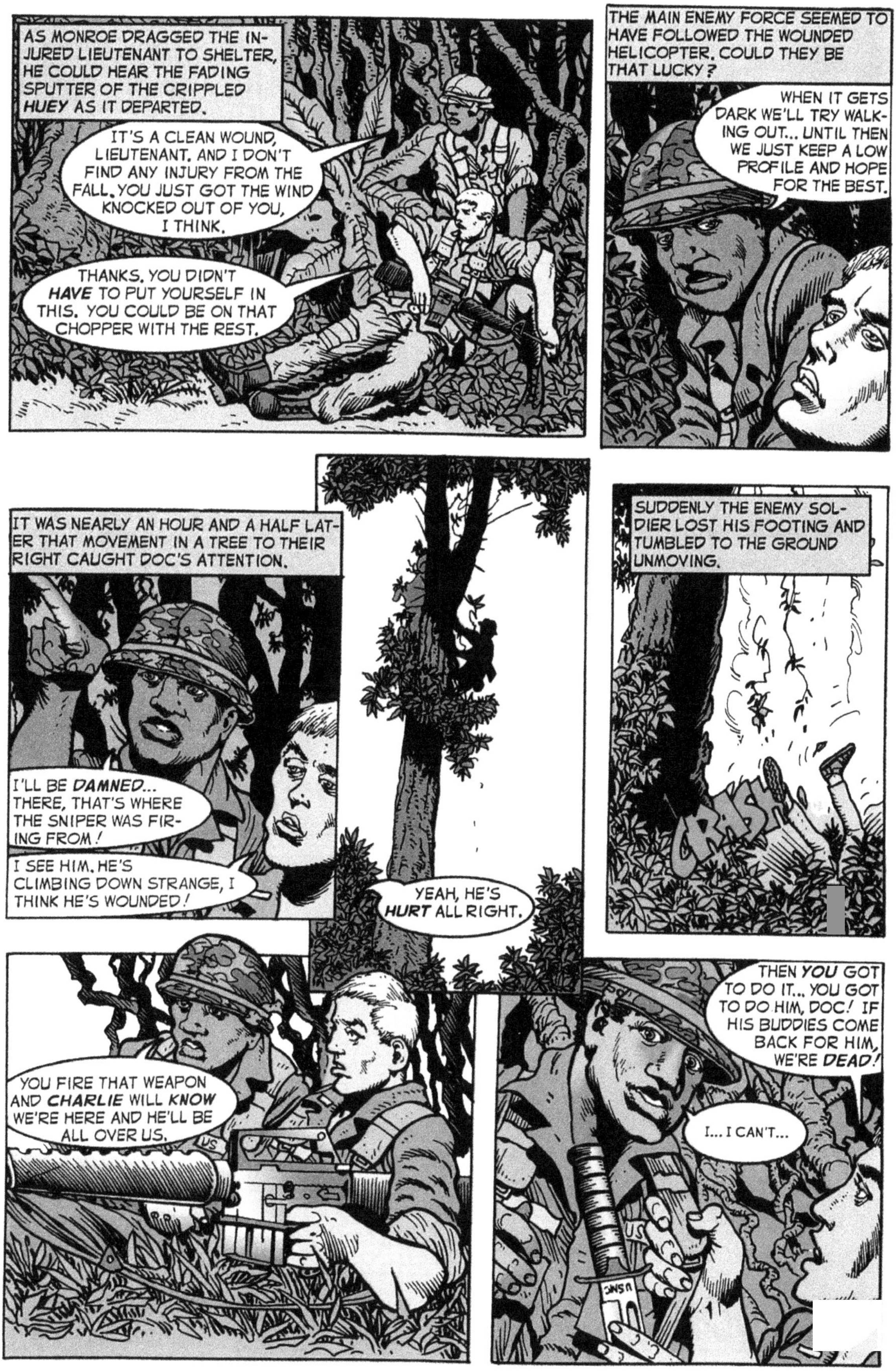
AS MONROE DRAGGED THE INJURED LIEUTENANT TO SHELTER, HE COULD HEAR THE FADING SPUTTER OF THE CRIPPLED HUEY AS IT DEPARTED.
IT'S A CLEAN WOUND, LIEUTENANT. AND I DON'T FIND ANY INJURY FROM THE FALL. YOU JUST GOT THE WIND KNOCKED OUT OF YOU, I THINK.
THANKS. YOU DIDN'T HAVE TO PUT YOURSELF IN THIS. YOU COULD BE ON THAT CHOPPER WITH THE REST.
THE MAIN ENEMY FORCE SEEMED TO HAVE FOLLOWED THE WOUNDED HELICOPTER. COULD THEY BE THAT LUCKY?
WHEN IT GETS DARK WE'LL TRY WALKING OUT... UNTIL THEN WE JUST KEEP A LOW PROFILE AND HOPE FOR THE BEST.
IT WAS NEARLY AN HOUR AND A HALF LATER THAT MOVEMENT IN A TREE TO THEIR RIGHT CAUGHT DOC'S ATTENTION.
I'LL BE DAMNED... THERE, THAT'S WHERE THE SNIPER WAS FIRING FROM!
I SEE HIM. HE'S CLIMBING DOWN STRANGE, I THINK HE'S WOUNDED!
YEAH, HE'S HURT ALL RIGHT.
SUDDENLY THE ENEMY SOLDIER LOST HIS FOOTING AND TUMBLED TO THE GROUND UNMOVING.
CRASH
YOU FIRE THAT WEAPON AND CHARLIE WILL KNOW WE'RE HERE AND HE'LL BE ALL OVER US.
THEN YOU GOT TO DO IT... YOU GOT TO DO HIM, DOC! IF HIS BUDDIES COME BACK FOR HIM, WE'RE DEAD!
I... I CAN'T...

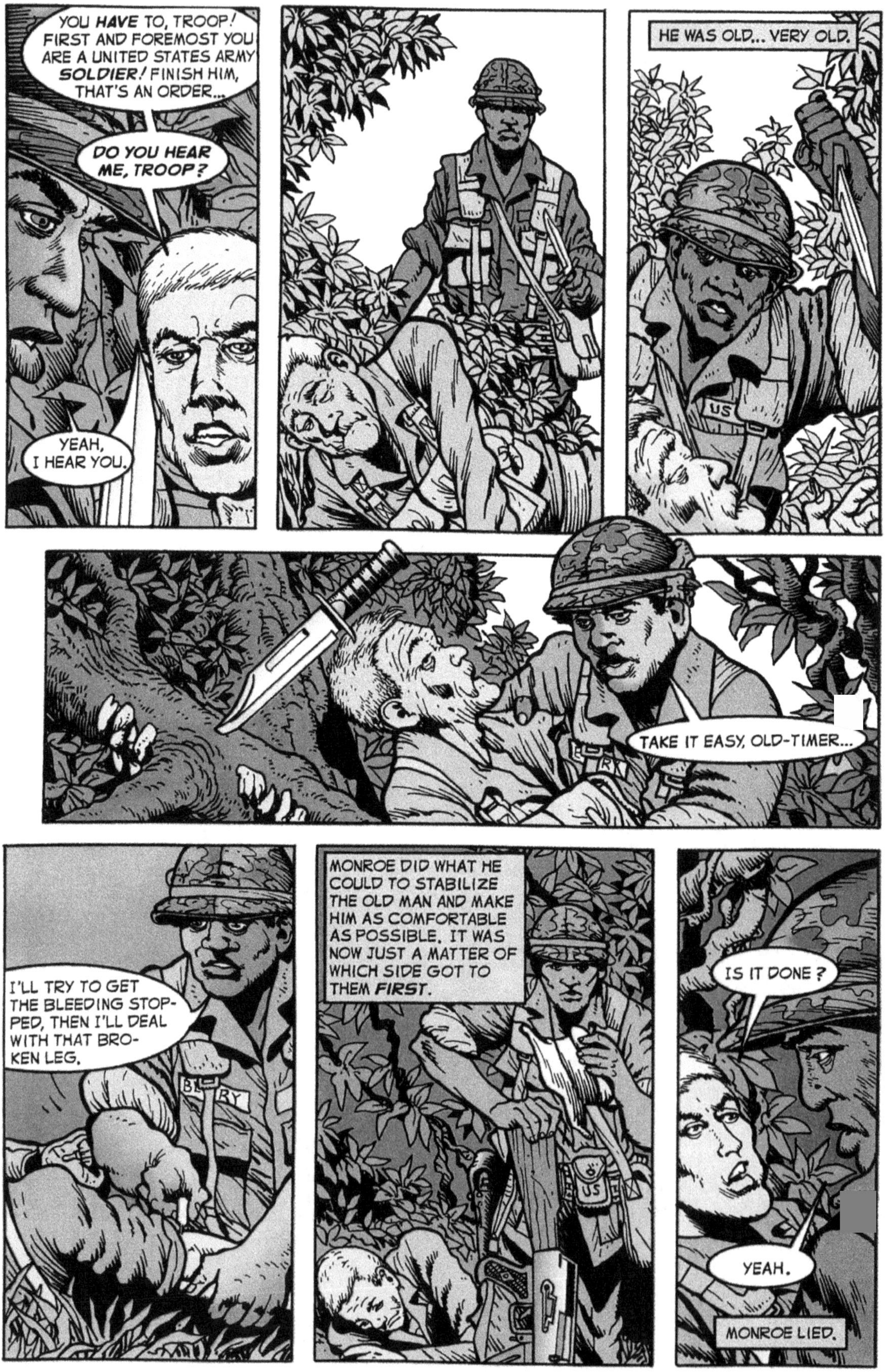
YOU HAVE TO, TROOP! FIRST AND FOREMOST YOU ARE A UNITED STATES ARMY SOLDIER! FINISH HIM, THAT'S AN ORDER...
DO YOU HEAR ME, TROOP?
YEAH, I HEAR YOU.
HE WAS OLD... VERY OLD.
TAKE IT EASY, OLD-TIMER...
I'LL TRY TO GET THE BLEEDING STOPPED, THEN I'LL DEAL WITH THAT BROKEN LEG.
MONROE DID WHAT HE COULD TO STABILIZE THE OLD MAN AND MAKE HIM AS COMFORTABLE AS POSSIBLE. IT WAS NOW JUST A MATTER OF WHICH SIDE GOT TO THEM FIRST.
IS IT DONE?
YEAH.
MONROE LIED.

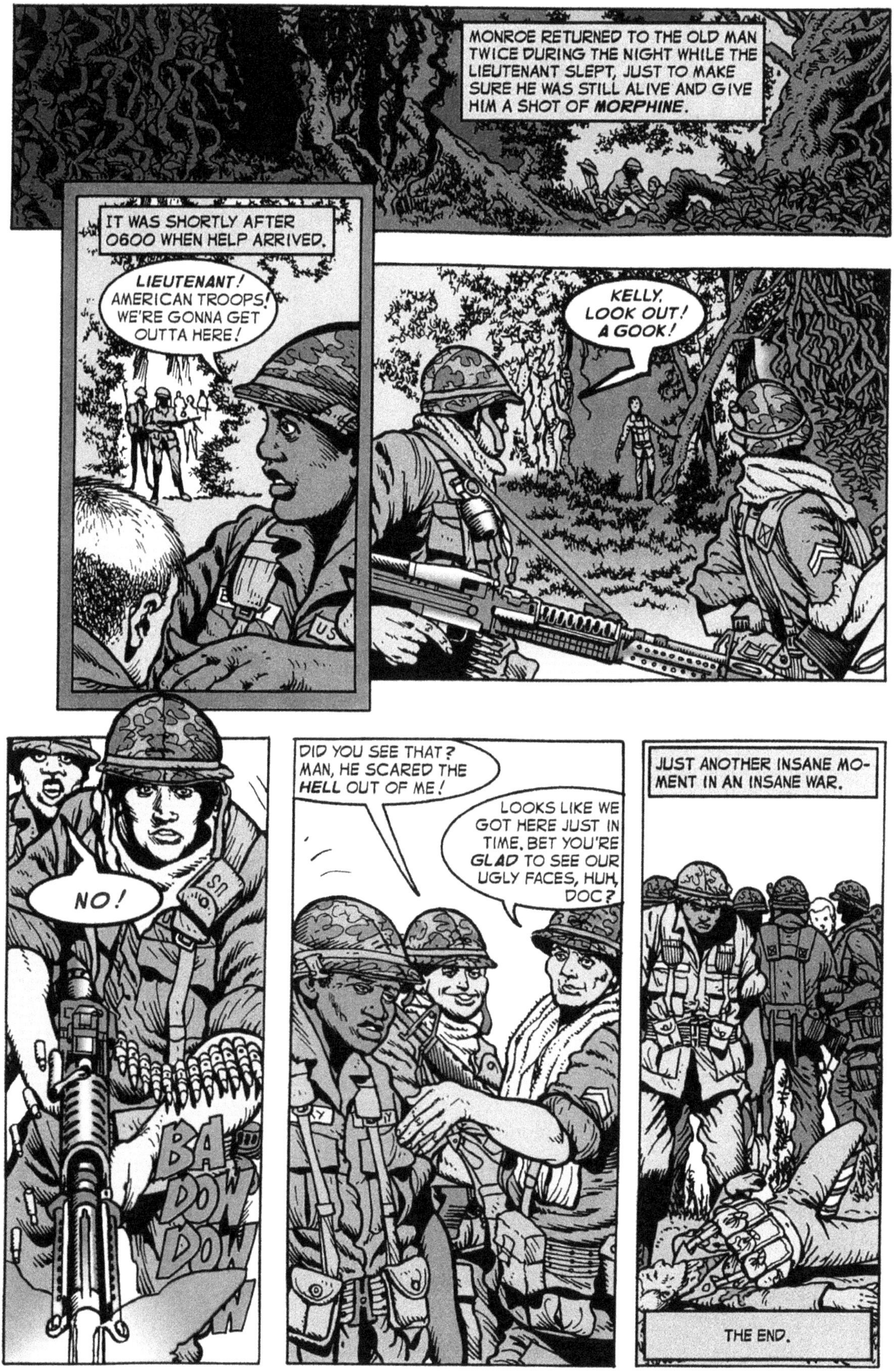

MONROE RETURNED TO THE OLD MAN TWICE DURING THE NIGHT WHILE THE LIEUTENANT SLEPT, JUST TO MAKE SURE HE WAS STILL ALIVE AND GIVE HIM A SHOT OF MORPHINE.
IT WAS SHORTLY AFTER 0600 WHEN HELP ARRIVED.
LIEUTENANT! AMERICAN TROOPS! WE'RE GONNA GET OUTTA HERE!
KELLY, LOOK OUT! A GOOK!
NO!
BA DOW DOW
DID YOU SEE THAT? MAN, HE SCARED THE HELL OUT OF ME!
LOOKS LIKE WE GOT HERE JUST IN TIME. BET YOU'RE GLAD TO SEE OUR UGLY FACES, HUH, DOC?
JUST ANOTHER INSANE MOMENT IN AN INSANE WAR.
THE END.

DON LOMAX

A look at the creator of Vietnam Journal

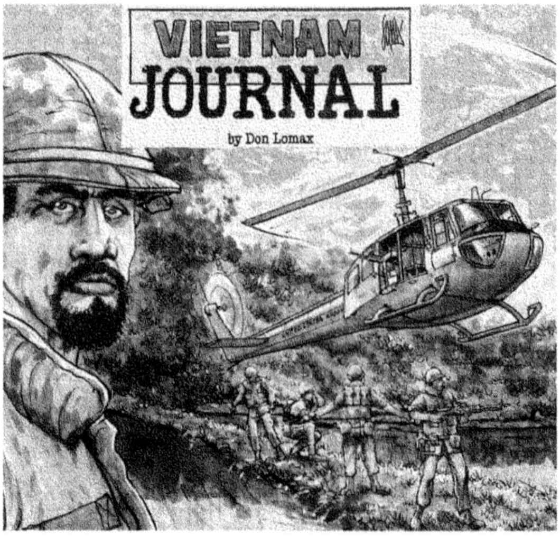
VIETNAM
JOURNAL
by Don Lomax

Don Lomax has established himself with Vietnam Journal, his project of two decades which continues today. The series is a rarity in comics in that it appeals not only to comic fans but also to those outside the traditional realm of comics.

But Don is by no means a one trick pony. For nearly 40 years he has had comics and cartoons appearing in a score of national magazines on a regular basis including Easyrider, CARtoons, Heavy Metal, Overdrive, Police and Security News, American Towman, and many others. His work in the adult magazine realm is legendary with story illustrations, comics, and cartoons appearing in virtually every "slick", "girly magazine" imaginable. But he also worked for most of the major comic book imprints including Pacific, Marvel, First, Americomics, Fantagraphics, Eros and others. He said he enjoyed working on American Flagg written by Alan Moore and inking Tom Sutton's pencils on Sleepwalker from Marvel. A multi-talented creator, Don also did some work on Munden's Bar which was a regular feature in First

Lomax based Vietnam Journal on his experiences on his tour of duty in Vietnam in the mid 1960's. He utilizes a war correspondent, to chronicle the combat experiences of the soldiers. Each issue spotlights a soldier or event with the narrative flowing to create story arcs.

The School Library Journal provides an insightful summary of the series. "Sent to Vietnam to report on the conflict, Scott "Journal" Neithammer expects to do no more than produce another sterilized war report. However, he soon realizes that, "the real story was in the bush with the slime, the stink, the constant fear and frustration." Each episode is a mix of the absurd and horrific as Journal befriends an ever-changing cast of doomed soldiers. As he confronts the death, illogic, and contradiction around him, he becomes as conflicted as the war itself, finally losing his journalistic objectivity in a fit of frustrated rage. The black-and-white artwork is powerful, and Journal's world is a rumpled fusion of realism and caricature. "

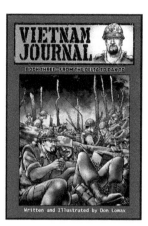

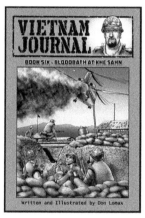

ALSO AVAILABLE FROM CALIBER COMICS

QUALITY GRAPHIC NOVELS TO ENTERTAIN

THE SEARCHERS
VOLUME ONE
THE SHAPE OF THINGS TO COME

THE SEARCHERS: VOLUME 1
The Shape of Things to Come

Before League of Extraordinary Gentlemen there was The Searchers. At the dawn of the 20th century the greatest literary adventurers from the likes of Wells, Verne, Doyle, Burroughs, and Haggard were created. All thought to be the work of pure fiction. However, a century later, the real-life descendants of those famous adventurers are recruited by the legendary Professor Challenger in order to save mankind's future. Collected for the first time.

"Searchers is the comic book I have on the wall with a sign reading - 'Love books? Never read a comic? Try this one! ....money back guarantee...'" - Dark Star Books.

WAR OF THE WORLDS: INFESTATION

Based on the H.G. Wells classic! The "Martian Invasion" has begun again and now mankind must fight for its very humanity. It happened slowly at first but by the third year, it seemed that the war was almost over... the war was almost lost.

"Writer Randy Zimmerman has a fine grasp of drama, and spins the various strands of the story into a coherent whole... imaginative and very gritty."
- war-of-the-worlds.co.uk

SEQUEL TO THE H.G. WELLS SCIENCE FICTION CLASSIC
THE WAR OF THE WORLDS
INFESTATION
ZIMMERMAN • HORUS

HELSING
LEGACY BORN
GARY REED JOHN LOWE

HELSING: LEGACY BORN

From writer Gary Reed (Deadworld) and artists John Lowe (Captain America), Bruce McCorkindale (Godzilla). She was born into a legacy she wanted no part of and pushed into a battle recessed deep in the shadows of the night. Samantha Helsing is torn between two worlds...two allegiances...two families. The legacy of the Van Helsing family and their crusade against the "night creatures" comes to modern day with the most unlikely of all warriors.

"Congratulations on this masterpiece..."
- Paul Dale Roberts, Compuserve Reviews

"All in all, another great package from Caliber."
- Paul Haywood, Comics Forum

HEROES AND HORRORS

Heroes and Horrors anthology provides nine rarely seen or never-before-published heroic and horrifying comic stories from the mind of veteran comic writer Steven Philip Jones.

Featured are entertaining stories with art by Octavio Cariello (The Action Bible), S. Clarke Hawbaker (Nomad), Christopher Jones (Young Justice), Dan Jurgens (Death of Superman), and many more! Foreword by Phil Hester.

"Incredibly creative...Steve's stories are masterworks of what new comics should be: absorbing and exciting and read again and again." - Clive Cussler, international bestselling author.

HEROES and HORRORS
BY STEVEN PHILIP JONES & FRIENDS

DAYS WRATH
WAYNE VANSANT

DAYS OF WRATH

Award winning comic writer & artist Wayne Vansant brings his gripping World War II saga of war in the Pacific to Guadalcanal and the Battle of Bloody Ridge. This is the powerful story of the long, vicious battle for Guadalcanal that occurred in 1942-43. When the U.S. Navy orders its outnumbered and outgunned ships to run from the Japanese fleet, they abandon American troops on a bloody, battered island in the South Pacific.

"Heavy on authenticity, compellingly written and beautifully drawn."
- Comics Buyers Guide

BECK and CAUL INVESTIGATIONS:
Where the Nightmares Walk

- Collects the entire Beck & Caul series for the FIRST TIME!

There is a place where evil lives. Where all of mankind's nightmares are a reality. It is the Underside. From this realm of myth and shadow was born Jonas Beck who teams up with a young woman, Mercedes Guillane and their paths meld into one...to battle evil in all its guises. Set in the voodoo influenced city of New Orleans, Beck and Caul are paranormal detectives who scrounge the streets of this dark, mystical city in order to combat and protect people from supernatural attacks and events.

BECK & CAUL INVESTIGATIONS
WHERE THE
NIGHTMARES WALK

COUNTER-PARTS

From best selling author Stefan Petrucha (MARVEL's Deadpool, Captain America). Think people can be disingenuous? Of course and in the future they try on new personas like hats. But when Hieronymus Jones overdoses on TPGs (temporary personality grafts), his original personality is destroyed. Now an experimental cure gives him not 1, but 6 new personalities. Each inhabiting a different part of his body. There's: Bogey, the hard-boiled right arm; Kik-li, the Kung-Fu master right leg; Jake, the self-involved torso; Buckley, the too-smart head; Don, the romantic left arm and; Tootsie, the femme fatale left leg! Together, they fight corruption & crime as one strange superhero team. Strap yourself in for one wild ride!

VELDA: GIRL DETECTIVE - VOL. 2

A unique take on the more lurid of the 1950s crime comics as if it actually existed as a Golden Age comic. More than a homage to noir films and hard-boiled detective writing of the 50s it includes in issues features such as a Velda paper doll kit & complete '52 Velda pinup calendar. Also added are vintage ads to amuse readers and shorts such as "Hawkshaw Hawk, Bird Detective" and "Neolithica: Girl of the Pleistocene" ."Velda is the kind of detective I like."- Richard S. Prather (writer, Shell Scott novels). "A pulp classic! If you like your action gritty, yet full of surprises, then you'll love Velda..." - Rick Overton (writer, Dennis Miller Show). "The Velda Comic is spectacular.." - Bob Burns.

The COMPLETE
Volume 2
VELDA
Girl Detective
STORIES FROM REAL DETECTIVE FILES

CALIBER®
COMICS
www.calibercomics.com

CPSIA information can be obtained
at www.ICGtesting.com
Printed in the USA
LVHW111515110122
708310LV00008B/754